D0787837

Victorian

Domesticity

Victorian Domesticity

Families in the Life and Art

of

Louisa May Alcott

•

CHARLES STRICKLAND

FOREWORD BY ROBERT COLES

The University of Alabama Press

Library of Congress Cataloging in Publication Data

Strickland, Charles, 1930–
  Victorian domesticity.

  Bibliography: p.
  Includes index.
  1. Alcott, Louisa May, 1832–1888.   2. Authors,
American—19th century—Biography.   3. Family—United
States—History—19th century.   4. Family in literature.
5. Feminism and literature.   I. Title.
PS1018.S77   1985   813'.4   [B]   84-8654
ISBN 0-8173-0237-9

To the women in my life—

MY MOTHER, IRENE BARTON STRICKLAND
MY WIFE, EYCKE STRICKLAND
MY DAUGHTER, KIRSTEN STRICKLAND

Contents

Foreword

This book is at once historical and literary in its approach to matters our age tends to regard as psychological and political: the questions of how women live (and ought live) their lives, of how families manage, given the strains upon them from the outside world (never mind those we choose to call "inter-personal") and not least, that most vexing question of how we ought bring up our children. It is important that we stop and ask ourselves why social scientists and physicians have so significantly replaced novelists and moral philosophers and the clergy as our mentors, so to speak, on these subjects, and this book provides a valuable occasion for such a consideration.

The author is himself a historian, with no small gifts as a literary critic and social observer. He has been interested in the "history of childhood," as it were—the ways boys and girls were regarded and treated in different places and times in the past. He has wanted to know, really, what moral values and ideals inspired parents, in previous generations, to behave in the particular ways they did toward their sons and daughters. His "methodology," as we put it, has been that of the persistent and resourceful social historian—an examination of *texts*: letters and records and diaries and not least, the stories and essays and poems of one or another era, which tell not only about the writer's purposes, but those of his or her readers.

Especially in earlier decades of this century, or in the nineteenth century, when radio and television were not the universal presences they are now, the pervasive power of a given storyteller, such as Louisa May Alcott, or Charles Dickens, was enormous. Dickens knew well his impact upon the English homes of the middle years of the nineteenth century—the hunger so many of his readers had for not only entertainment, but advice, a perspective on what is important, on what ought be ignored as unimportant, and not least, on what deserves to be shunned altogether. Certainly, Louisa May Alcott was similarly engaged with her readers: Americans trying to settle not a new country, but rather, the interior domain—how to think about oneself, one's husband and wife, one's children, one's responsibilities in this all too brief spell of time we call a life. She was, put differently, a teacher and preacher of sorts, eager to harness her fiction to the education as well as the pleasurable diversion of her fellow citizens.

Without question, Professor Strickland has brought to life this once much-celebrated New England writer, and so doing, reminded us of our nation's social past. He is, himself, a clear and strong writer. He leads us directly and thoughtfully through the life of an inspired yet also troubled family—and as we get to know the Alcotts, we come closer not only to their struggles, aspirations, disappointments, but our own, too. When such an outcome takes place, one is in the presence of the transforming power of art—in this instance, the literary and prophetic voice of the Alcotts, offered us by a sensitive and knowing mediator.

In a country less given to faddish celebration of fake or overwrought claims to originality, a book such as this would be eagerly sought and thankfully read by the many thousands of us who all too readily seek to buy volume after volume on "women's liberation," on "child care," on "psychology of the family"—those dreary contemporary genres whose prominence surely will interest some future historian of Professor Strickland's kind. After all, what this study offers us, really, is the terribly important reminder that there are some tensions which are utterly human, are embedded in the very nature of the human creature, hence change only in this respect, or that one—in their form but not in their essence as a continuous aspect of existence. So Louisa May Alcott knew—the contradictions and inconsistencies which will be with us after every cocksure authority and expert has handed down every solution and unqualified formulation or generalization or recommendation. So the author tells us—a wise historian choosing a marvelously instructive subject matter and working with it tactfully and thoughtfully, to the great benefit of those of us lucky enough to come upon the result, this book.

Acknowledgments

The author owes thanks to the following who have made valuable suggestions at various stages in the completion of this study: Nancy Anderson, Erik Erikson, Kai Erikson, the late James Jordan, G. Alexander Moore, Robert Wheeler, Richard Ward, and, especially, Charles Burgess. Thanks also to the U.S. Office of Education and Emory University for grants; to Patsy Stockbridge of Emory's history department, whose patience and efficiency saw the manuscript through several typed versions; and to Susanne Rolland for careful checking of sources.

Gratitude should also be expressed to Mrs. F. Wolsey Pratt and the Harvard College Library for permission to quote at length from the Alcott Family Manuscripts deposited by Mrs. Pratt in Harvard's Houghton Library. Finally, the author wishes to acknowledge the work of Eycke Strickland, who not only transformed Alcott's child diaries into a legible typescript, but who also shared her hard-won insights into the nature of family life.

Preface

"I do think that families are the most beautiful things in all the world!" exclaims Jo March at the conclusion of *Little Women*. This remark, and others like it in this popular children's book, has served to fix an aura of sentimentality around the novel as well as around the reputation of its author, thus assuring later and more skeptical generations that both Louisa May Alcott and her work are irrelevant to an understanding of family life in Victorian America. Of late, however, historians are beginning to uncover another dimension of Alcott's life and art, one that suggests that the author was not as sentimental as we had thought. For one thing, a close examination of Alcott's personal life reveals that she was at times more pessimistic than her heroine Jo about families, having remarked on one occasion that she knew little about marriages, "except observing that very few were happy ones." One might conclude, then, that Alcott did not believe everything she put into her fiction, but the story is a bit more complex even than that. A closer examination of her work, the work for the adult reader as well as the children's literature, reveals that her writing is more than a simpleminded celebration of togetherness. While it is true that Alcott was deeply influenced by popular currents of sentimentality, it is also true that her own experience exposed her to the confusions and contradictions generated when sentiment confronted the reality of life in nineteenth-century America. That confrontation and the way it affected Alcott's vision of family life are the subjects of this book.

Because sentiment so deeply affected both Alcott's childhood and her later work, it forms the subject of Chapter 1, which outlines the ways that sentimentality colored the perception of nineteenth-century

Americans about such emotionally laden issues as courtship, marriage, the relationship between the sexes, the relationship between the generations and, finally, the relationship between the nuclear family unit and the community outside it. This "sentimental revolution" provided the heritage with which Alcott was forced to come to terms, both as a woman and as a writer. Chapter 2 traces Alcott's earliest childhood experiences, showing the ways her parents attempted to live up to the sentimental ideal of family life, but revealing also the tensions that developed between Louisa and her father when he discovered that she did not conform to his sentimental ideal of childhood, and when he discovered that he himself was not cut out to be a careful provider. Chapter 3 continues the story into Louisa's adolescence, detailing the way she carried the double burden of being both poor and female as she struggled to find her identity as a writer.

The fruits of this early experience form the substance of the following six chapters. Chapter 4 provides an introduction to the body of Alcott's writing, pointing out the three audiences for whom she wrote and the way she shaped her view of young womanhood in response to each audience. The chapter draws the perhaps surprising conclusion that her juvenile fiction provided the most complex portrait of the three and the most radical departure from sentimental convention. Chapter 5 explores the impact of feminism on Alcott's life and traces the relationship of feminist ideology to the family in Alcott's fiction. Chapters 6 and 7 deal with the varieties of family life that appear in Alcott's stories, ranging from "old fashioned" families to families of fashion, to sentimental families, and, finally, to Alcott's effort to project a novel ideal of family life that was neither fashionable nor sentimental, and that instead celebrated the possibilities of companionate marriage, a genuine sharing of privileges and responsibilities between husbands and wives. If Alcott transcended sentimental convention in her portrayal of relations between the sexes, she remained loyal to the sentimental emphasis on the importance of child nurture, which is the subject of Chapter 8. Chapter 9, in many ways the most significant for those interested in questions of family life and public policy, deals with the relationships that Alcott perceived between the family and the world around it and concludes that sentimental convention clouded Alcott's understanding of the problems faced by poor families in Victorian America. Able to transcend sentimental convention in portraying relations between the sexes and between the generations, Alcott was ultimately unable to transcend in her imagination the barriers which nineteenth-century America placed between social classes. The Epilogue attempts an assessment of the legacy of the Victorian family ideal, contrasting it with major trends in American family life during the period since 1945.

Victorian
Domesticity

Alcott's Heritage:

The Sentimental Revolution

Louisa May Alcott's life and art provide an avenue along which to approach that most difficult task faced by historians, which is to assess the quality of an era even as they attempt to describe and explain it. When the era in question is the Victorian, the task is doubly hard because our Victorian ancestors have not been treated kindly by later and more skeptical generations. At some point in the twentieth century, as historian Henry May has observed, Americans passed through a cultural revolution that made the Victorian era "a completely vanished world."[1] It has been difficult for modern American intellectuals and writers to comprehend, let alone admire, the Victorians or their ways. To modern sensibilities they seem straitlaced, intolerant, narrow, sexually repressed and, worst of all, hypocritical. Robert Falk has pointed out: "Few periods of American thought, taste, and literary expression have been subjected to such a parade of disparaging epithets and historical idols. In its social character, its art and architecture, its manners, morals and literature, the period has been portrayed in many a colorful and perjorative term. Common to them all is the concept of decline."[2] To this broadly based cultural revolt has been added in recent times the specific dissatisfactions expressed by feminists, who have singled out Victorian values and Victorian family life as among the more formidable obstacles to the achievement of sexual equality.[3]

There is, as we shall see, some justification for the twentieth century's dissatisfaction with Victorian culture, but it is important not to allow this dissatisfaction to cloud our comprehension. It will require an extraordinary effort of research and imagination not only to understand the world in which Victorians lived, but, more importantly, to understand how they perceived it and how they felt about it. Fortunately, that effort is underway. Insofar as family life is concerned, a consensus seems to be emerging among historians that profound changes were occurring during Alcott's lifetime (1832–1888) in relations between husbands and wives, in relations between parents and children, and in relations between the home and the marketplace.[4] Carl Degler has called attention to the increasing importance of affection and mutual respect between marriage partners, the increasing influence of women within the home (even as they seemed to lose influence outside it), the growing emphasis on the role of the woman in child-care and in home maintenance, the decline in rates of fertility, and the consequent decline in the average size of the household.[5] Focusing on a single community—Oneida County, New York—Mary Ryan has found a similar transformation in middle-class domestic arrangements from 1800 to 1865, marked by less emphasis on patriarchal authority within the household and more emphasis on affection, by the growing influence of women within the home, and by sharper sex-role segregation. Ryan also suggests that the early nineteenth century produced a greater emphasis on sexual restraint, temperate habits, maternal socialization, and extended education.[6] Most of these observations apply, of course, only to the urban, white middle class, and research on the family life of rural Americans, black Americans, immigrants, and the working class is only beginning to emerge.[7] Nevertheless, we seem justified in assuming that these changes in domestic arrangements among the urban middle class represented the wave of the future and eventually described the norms against which all American families were to be judged during the Victorian era.

Alcott's experience is certainly relevant to this ongoing inquiry, for if we are to understand more than the hard surfaces of family life in the nineteenth century we must probe beneath statistical charts and tables. In particular, we will benefit from the experience of an insider, someone whose life was shaped by these domestic changes and who, moreover, left a monumental body of fiction exploring its meaning. Having been a child, having been a woman, having felt in her life the lash of poverty, and having decided opinions about men, Alcott provides a unique perspective on nineteenth-century family life and in particular about that cultural expression of it we have labeled Victorian domesticity. There is, however, still another sense in which Alcott's life and art are important to us. As a writer, and an extremely influential one at that, she served to perpetuate the values of Victorian domesticity to subsequent generations. Rare is the American girl who did not read one or more of Alcott's books during the highly impressionable preadolescent or adolescent years. Alcott's fiction thus has served to shape the attitudes of subsequent generations of women toward the sensitive issues of women's roles and family life. Her influence may in fact serve to explain, in part at least, the strange persistence of Victorian values among Americans, despite the nearly unanimous declaration of intellectuals that those values are no longer relevant to life in the twentieth century.

The key to understanding the values of Victorian domesticity in general and Alcott's rendering of them in particular, is to grasp an intellectual and literary movement that gave birth to those values and that shaped her early life. This movement, which has sometimes been called the sentimental revolution, brought about during the early years of the nineteenth century a transformation in the opinions of the American social elite on such sensitive matters as courtship, marriage, religion, education, and child-rearing.[8] As we shall see, Alcott broke free of sentimental conventions in certain critical ways, especially in her view of women and children, but sentimentality remained a profound influence on her attitudes toward courtship and marriage, on the proper rearing of children, and on such political and economic questions as the relationship between the nuclear family and the community. What we here are calling Victorian domesticity was a product of a confrontation between the ideals of sentimentality and the reality experienced by nineteenth-century Americans.

Even before Louisa's birth, the sentimental revolution was well underway as a host of women took up the pen, usually under the pressure of necessity, to turn out novels, articles, and books of advice.[9] They were joined by clergymen who found in popular publication a new pulpit from which to make known their views on family matters. Together, the clergymen and the women were able to reach a wide audience, thanks to innovations in the print media after 1830 that made possible the publication of cheap books, newspapers, and periodicals for mass consumption. Much of it took the form of fiction. Between 1830 and 1850 more than a thousand works of fiction by American-born authors were published in the United States. That was more than five times as many as in the preceding sixty years. Most of this fiction was by women and for women and most was concerned with domestic themes—courtship, marriage, religion, home management, child-rearing, and education. [10] Whether fiction or not, the flood of literature was profoundly didactic, for it was widely understood by the authors that even novels were supposed to teach, and that every episode should be followed by a moral lesson.

The transformation in values that the women and clergymen created was a revolution in the sense that this body of popular literature called for a new way of looking at courtship, marriage, and family life, and it pointed to new sets of relations between husbands and wives, between parents and children, and even between the family circle and the marketplace. It has been called a "sentimental" revolution because of the emphasis the popular literature placed on sentiment, not merely in the sense that it attempted to set readers awash in a flood of tears, but in the more profound sense that the authors declared allegiance to sentiment, or feeling, as the preferred guide in perceiving reality and acting on it. Specifically condemned was the old reliance on prudential reasoning about human affairs, and exalted instead were the reasons of the heart which would henceforth govern relations between the sexes and between the generations.

While offering a new way of looking at domestic matters, however, the sentimental revolution was also conservative in the sense that it advocated new forms of family life to promote what were essentially traditional institutions. More specifically, the sentimentalists were anxious about the secular and egalitarian tendencies of the Jacksonian era. The decades preceding the Civil War were marked by a ferment of reform, aimed at winning converts to the cause of the abolition of slavery and the abolition of war (two contradictory crusades as events proved), at promoting equal rights for women, reform of prisons, reform of the treatment of the insane, temperance, religious re-

4

vivalism, vegetarianism, public education, and the founding of utopian communities.[11] There was not, Ralph Waldo Emerson reported
in 1840, "a kingdom, town, statute, rite, calling, man or woman,
but is threatened by the new spirit."[12] The toleration—if not the
enthusiasm—which antebellum Americans displayed toward social
reform was astounding and not to be matched by an American generation before or since, with the possible exception of the cultural revolt
of the 1960s. The sentimental writers themselves enlisted in many of
these causes, most notably religious revivals, temperance, and the
cause of abolition (if they happened to live above the Mason-Dixon
line). But at the same time they worried that the currents of reform
might go too far. They feared that in moving so quickly toward an
unknown future, Americans were leaving behind the solid virtues of
an earlier, simpler society. If the Jacksonian era was opening up vistas
of human progress, it also provoked worry about law and order in a
nation that seemed ungoverned and ungovernable. Many Americans
worried in particular about the materialistic and secular tendencies of
the age, and about what they perceived to be the declining authority
of the church.[13] Likewise the future of the family was a matter of
great concern, for, in a sense, the sentimentalists were carving out a
new and more ambitious role for this most basic of human institutions. It was to serve as a moral counterweight to a restless, materialistic, individualistic, and egalitarian society. The family was, in
fact, to serve many of the functions formerly reserved for the church.
Religion, which had been disestablished in the public sphere during
the upheavals of the eighteenth century, would now be reestablished
in the private sphere of the family and placed in the keeping of
women. For this reason, more than any other, most sentimentalists
opposed the movement for women's rights, for they perceived it as a
threat to the very institution upon which they counted for moral
redemption.[14]

The irony of the sentimental view should not be ignored. The
sentimentalists often talked as if they were attempting to restore
domestic life as it had been in a more traditional, simpler society,
when in fact they were calling for a new kind of domesticity, one
which envisioned novel ways of looking at courtship and marriage, at
the roles of husbands and wives and at the relations of parents and

children. In the course of advocating these changes, the writers reinforced a series of cults, all interrelated and all dealing with aspects of marriage and family life. The cult of romantic love dealt with the formation of families, and specifically with the rituals of courtship and marriage. The cult of domesticity was a way of marking boundaries between the nuclear family and the world outside it. Finally, the interrelated cults of motherhood and childhood specified the central purpose of family life and the place women were to occupy within it. Together these sentimental cults provided the cultural context within which Alcott came of age and the literary heritage with which she had to come to terms in working out her own views of family life.

The Cult of Romantic Love: Up On the Pedestal

The cult of romantic love inculcated in readers a set of lessons concerning the preferred relationships between sexes: No sexual intercourse without love, no love without marriage, and no marriage without love.[15] Although stated here as rules, the cult of romantic love centered around a new image of woman emerging in the eighteenth century and given currency by a new form of literature, the novel.[16] The venerable notion of woman as Eve the Temptress gave way to the notion of woman as the Persecuted Maiden, who was the victim of seduction rather than its perpetrator. It was a theme particularly popular in Protestant lands, perhaps, as Leslie Fiedler has suggested, because Protestants sought to invest in ordinary women the virtues reserved in Catholic tradition for the Virgin Mary:

> She is the Persecuted Maiden, a projection of male guilt before the female treated as a mere sexual object; and she flees through two hundred years of fiction, hounded by father and lover, brother and fiancé: the heroine of all her sex, who applaud her example but are powerless to help her in her hour of need. She is feeling without passion, and her love climax is tears. She is a Protestant Virgin, proper to a society that destroyed the splendid images of the Mother of God, but she is also the product of an anti-metaphysical Sentimentalism, which found it easier to believe that the human could achieve divinity than that the divine could descend into the human.[17]

The literary source of this image may be traced most directly to the British writer Samuel Richardson, whose *Clarissa* startled Europe with a new image of women and also with a new literary form, the novel. The heroine of *Clarissa* is a beautiful and intelligent daughter of a bourgeois family who is hated by a jealous brother and bullied by a greedy father. They drive her into the arms of a handsome, lustful nobleman, Lovelace, who has sex on his mind more than marriage. Clarissa loves the bounder, but will not submit to his advances without marriage, resisting all his efforts at seduction. Becoming desperate, Lovelace drugs and rapes her, but, since his pride requires willing consent, he is dissatisfied with his conquest. Reluctantly, he proposes marriage as the only way to win her over, but, although she still loves him, Clarissa recognizes that he is motivated by lust more than love and she refuses his proposal, dying a lonely but virtuous death.

Richardson's story spawned a multitude of novels dealing with the theme of the Persecuted Maiden, and in America none was more popular than Mrs. Susanna Rowson's *Charlotte Temple*, which went through 160 editions after its publication in America in 1794.[18] Again we find a virtuous young woman pursued by a scoundrel, who promises her marriage. She runs away with him, but he abandons her in favor of a lady who can bring more money to a marriage. Cast off, without friends or money, Charlotte bears a child in poverty and finally dies in the arms of her father. The story was calculated not only to evoke tears, but also to serve as a cautionary tale to young women to surrender their virginity only with a man they love and only after the compact has been sealed with marriage.

One of the difficulties that pure maidens encounter in attempting to adhere to these rules is provided by the Avaricious Parent, who pressures the daughter to marry for money or prestige. Again, Richardson's *Clarissa* provides the *locus classicus* when the heroine's father attempts to persuade his daughter to marry a repulsive man simply because he owns a large estate. The theme of the Avaricious Parent was taken up with enthusiasm by American authors, including the anonymous person who penned *Fidelity Rewarded*. In this novel a father advises his daughter that "a large estate is all that you ought to look after . . . why need you care about his morals, as long as he has money enough?" Also suffering parental persecution was the heroine of *Constantius and Pulchera,* who tells her lover: "Ambition! Cruel ambition is the cause of our misfortune. No man was ever better pleased with another than my father was with you until Monsieur le Monte, only son and heir to a rich nobleman in France, waited on him, and offered to make me his wife. . . . The temptation was too great for him to withstand." John Davis told the readers of *Ferdinand and Elizabeth* that his novel was intended to "admonish parents and guardians to consult the hearts as well as the interests of their children in the sacred bond of marriage."[19]

While depicting the Persecuted Maiden as the victim of all manner of assaults on her purity and her integrity, the sentimental novelists would not provide her with the escape hatch of leading a single life. Most sentimental authors made it clear that marriage was the only possible destiny for a woman. Both male and female authors drew the most unflattering portraits of the spinster, making her the object of contempt and ridicule. Death was the only alternative to marriage and, in fact, suicide was a favorite theme of sentimental authors, an act much in keeping with the delicate, sensitive natures of women.[20]

THE CULT OF DOMESTICITY:
"THERE'S NO PLACE LIKE HOME"

Once the sentimental heroine undertook the seemingly inevitable step of marriage, she entered a world dramatically isolated from the society around it, and there she was expected to stay. The central cult in this sentimental vision was the cult of domesticity. Never before had the household been made the object of such adoration as the sentimental writers heaped upon it.[21] It was as if all the Utopian impulses of the Jacksonian period were here directed into the private sphere of the nuclear family. It was, in the view of moralists, a "sacred institution," and indeed, it appears that the home was now more important than the church in the preservation of religious values.[22] In the process of sanctifying the home, the sentimentalists widened into a yawning chasm the boundary between the nuclear family and the world around it. To use the words of a then-popular song, there was "no place like home." The home was to be the repository for what we could today call the "expressive" values of love, warmth, and intimacy, in stark contrast to the cold competitiveness of the marketplace, a sentiment leading to a melodramatic confrontation between "home, sweet home" and the "cold, cruel world."[23] The novelists portrayed the home as a fortress besieged by all manner of evils. The city posed an especial threat, populated as it was by seducers, saloons, gambler's dens, and a fashionable society which promoted vanity and wasted resources.[24] This sentimentalization of the home was, in fact, a severe if subtle indictment of nineteenth-century American society, but it led to no revolutionary plans for action. The rallying cry was for retreat from society rather than the reform of it, and the home was to provide refuge for the harried husband.[25]

The sentimental insistence on the radical separation of the public and the private spheres reflected, it should be observed, an emerging economic reality. The colonial family had been the center of economic production, with the consequence that there was a rich commerce between the household and the marketplace, and distinctions between the home and the world outside it were vague at best.[26] For millions of American families in the nineteenth century, especially in rural areas, this pattern persisted, but the sentimentalists were addressing themselves to an emerging class of urban Americans for whom the older pattern was no longer relevant. The sentimental vision of the family as a place apart was grounded in a new economic reality, namely that economic production was leaving the household for the office or the factory. There were, however, other implications of the interplay between the sentimental vision and economic realities, and they had to do with relations between the sexes. The sentimentalists had inherited from European literary tradition the image of the woman on a moral pedestal, but this inheritance gained added meaning with the increased separation of the public and private spheres of life. If, as the sentimentalists insisted, woman's place was in the home, and if the home was a world radically apart from the marketplace, then it followed that woman's role and identity would be radically different from that of man. The departure of economic production from the household, elaborated and reinforced by the sentimental revolution, led nineteenth-century urban Americans to assume that women and men would lead radically different lives: he to venture outside the refuge of the family to do battle with the barbarians in the marketplace, she to remain within the haven of the home. The "doctrine of the two spheres," as it came to be known, and the increased sex-role differentiation that it implied were, however, merely a prelude to the sentimental insistence that the "masculine" and the "feminine" temperaments were as unlike as night and day.[27]

Secluded within the refuge of the home, the woman did not necessarily find domestic bliss, according to the sentimentalists. Marriage did little to alter the essential warfare that marked the relationship between the sexes. The man was as lustful and untrustworthy as ever, while the woman lost none of her virtue though she might surrender her virginity. The theme of martyrdom persisted, but the image of the Persecuted Maiden was replaced by that of the Long-Suffering Wife. A woman must be prepared to suffer, and to suffer in silence, for it was not her place to challenge the authority of her husband, imperfect though he might be. Her only release from suffering and subordination came through death, for the sentimentalist also condemned separation and divorce.[28]

It is evident that sentimentalists had little or no sympathy with the slogans of nineteenth-century feminism. The cause of women's rights received no votes among most sentimental novelists, who held up passivity as an ideal and who regarded any imitation of masculine traits as a surrender of the woman's claim to superior moral virtue. The antifeminist attitude of the novelists was echoed among the writers of didactic essays, who with a few exceptions condemned feminism.[29]

THE CULT OF MOTHERHOOD

Although the sentimental heroine might find little satisfaction in her role as wife, sentimentalists did not deprive her of purpose or power altogether. Expected to confine herself to the home, she could work a subtle influence there, both as cultural arbiter and as mother. For these tasks women are endowed by nature with superior moral character and intuitive insight. For one thing, wives are less interested than their husbands in sexual passion, which their premarital

10

battles to preserve their virginity amply proved. For another, women are endowed by a greater capacity for tenderness and a greater sensitivity to others. These qualifications prepare women, as Catharine Beecher put it, to take the lead "in matters pertaining to the education of their children, in selection and support of a clergyman, in all benevolent enterprises, and in all questions relating to morals and manners."[30] She might even manage to reform her wayward husband, although sentimentalists did not hold out much hope in that direction.

The woman's principal task after marriage was not as wife, however, but as mother, and here she would find the satisfaction and could exercise the power denied her in other aspects of life. The key to a woman's identity lay in the proper discharge of her responsibilities for the nurture and education of the young child.[31] In keeping with the cult of domesticity, she was advised not to share this sacred responsibility with others. It was assumed, as a matter of course, that the father would be incompetent, uninterested, or absent, but the sentimentalists also discouraged mothers from seeking aid in other directions. They united in praising breast feeding and in condemning the practice of wet nursing, which had been a widespread custom among the affluent in colonial America.[32] Mothers were specifically warned that babies would imbibe the servant's moral character along with her milk. "What mother would not be dismayed by the thought of having her family grow up into the sentiments of her nurse, and come forward into life as being in the succession to her character!" the Reverend Horace Bushnell exclaimed.[33] As the infant grew older, servants would find other ways to corrupt its health and morals by teaching it lower-class habits of speech, granting unwise indulgence to the child's whims and foisting harmful drugs upon it.[34] If the sentimental authors are to be believed, the use of alcohol and even opium to quiet fretful children was widespread in Jacksonian America.[35] Mothers were also advised to monitor carefully influences emanating from outside the home, including the neighboring children with whom the child played and the books the child read.[36] In short, mothers were enjoined to erect around their children a screen behind which the subtle process of mother nurture could do its work.

11

Assignment of nurture exclusively to women was, it should be noted, related to a simultaneous transformation in concepts of child-rearing.[37] Prior to the sentimental revolution, parents were advised to rely on the child's awe of authority or fear of punishment as the principal sanction for discipline. Increasingly, with the emphasis on the mother's role in child-rearing, the sentimental books of advice advocated gentler methods, advising that a bond of affection between parent and child would provide the leverage for obedience. Corporal punishment was discouraged. "Will-breaking," the standard advice of moralists in the colonial period, was disappearing along with Calvinist notions of the depravity of children. By the middle of the nineteenth century parents were being advised to combine firmness with love, to reason with children and, if the children misbehaved, to punish them by withdrawal of approval and affection. "How entire and perfect is this dominion over the unformed character of your infant," the writer Lydia Sigourney told mothers in 1838. "Write what you will upon the printless tablet, with your wand of love." Here was advice that perfectly captured and combined the theories of John Locke with the sentimental insistence on the preeminence of affection.[38]

THE CULT OF CHILDHOOD

Reinforcing the sentimental plea for "gentle" methods was the image of the child, who was portrayed as both saintly and vulnerable.[39] American authors enjoyed considerable help from Charles Dickens in projecting this image, for this most popular of nineteenth-century novelists placed children at the center of his fiction. He marched before his American readers a succession of morally pure yet doomed young heroes and heroines who were exploited, betrayed, and in many instances destroyed by vicious adults. American writers also took up the image of the saintly child and made it a central theme in their fiction.[40] Nathaniel Hawthorne blazed the trail with his "Gentle Boy," but more popular authors also exploited the widespread fascination of Jacksonian Americans with the young. T. S. Arthur's *Angel of the Household* advised parents: "Into every household angels may enter. They come in through the gate of infancy, and bring with them celestial influences. Are there angels in your household? If so, cherish the heavenly visitants."[41] It was Arthur also who wedded the image of the saintly child to the cause of temperance in his most celebrated work, *Ten Nights in a Bar Room*, which was concerned not so much with the plight of the alcoholic male as with the martyrdom he inflicted on his child. Arthur created in little Mary Morgan a child martyr for the cause of temperance. Dealt a fatal blow by a beer mug meant for her father, Mary dies slowly—for sixty pages in fact. Her father suffers the pangs of remorse and is converted to temperance by Mary's deathbed.[42]

Even more popular than Arthur's work among American readers was Susan Warner's *The Wide, Wide World*, which placed a saintly child at the center of the plot and joined this image to other elements in the sentimental revolution.[43] Although Ellen Montgomery strikes the modern eye as something of a pious prig, it was her piety that endeared her to nineteenth-century readers. She is the kind of little girl who spends hours on her knees in prayer, who delights in the gift of a Bible that she can carry around with her, and earns the enmity of her playmates by refusing to participate in an apparently innocent game of twenty questions, because it is Sunday. Says Ellen: "I think Sunday was meant to be spent in growing better and learning good things; and I don't think such plays would help one at all to do that; and I have a kind of *feeling* that I ought not to do it."[44] As might be expected, Ellen suffers a good deal for her pious principles, but the greatest cross she has to bear is the separation from her "mamma" and, ultimately, the mother's death. The separation, ostensibly for the sake of the mother's health, is ordered by Ellen's father, who is portrayed, of course, as something of an insensitive clod. Mother and daughter have no choice but to obey. As Ellen's mother tells her: "Though we *must* sorrow, we must not rebel."[45] All in all, the tale provides ample occasion for tears, and it appears that the author made it a rule not to allow a page to go by without Ellen weeping or at least threatening to do so.

UNCLE TOM'S CABIN:
THE APOGEE OF THE SENTIMENTAL REVOLUTION

Two years after the publication of *Wide, Wide World* there appeared another sentimental book which exceeded even Susan Warner's work in popularity and which became the best-selling American novel of the nineteenth century.[46] In creating *Uncle Tom's Cabin*, Harriet Beecher Stowe produced not merely a popular work of sentiment, but also one whose characters are remembered long after the pious Ellen Montgomery was forgotten. Mrs. Stowe employed all of the themes of the sentimental revolution on behalf of the cause of abolition, and yet transcended all of them. Her book proved to be, as Leslie Fiedler has pointed out, "the greatest of all novels of sentimental protest."[47]

Here once again one finds Persecuted Maidens, villainous men, self-sacrificing mothers, saintly children, and enough death and dying to keep readers weeping and turning the pages. Here also one finds the sentimental condemnation of prudential caution, exemplified by those who would condone slavery for the sake of politics or profit, and the exaltation of feeling as an unerring guide to truth. Characteristically, it is the man who is prudential, the woman who follows her feelings. When Mary Bird confronts her husband, Senator Bird, over the issue of the Fugitive Slave Law, he responds: "But, Mary, just listen to me. Your feelings are all quite right, dear, and interesting, and I love you for them; but, then, dear, we mustn't suffer our feelings to run away with our judgment; you must consider it's not a matter of private feeling—there are great public interests involved,—there is such a state of public agitation rising, that we must put aside our private feelings." To which Mary answers in her characteristically feminine disregard for prudential reason: "I hate reasoning, John,—especially reasoning on such subjects. There's a way you political folks have of coming round and round a plain right thing."[48]

Mrs. Stowe's masterpiece also bears the mark of the sentimental revolution in its insistence on Christian piety, a point which has proved a stumbling block for later generations of secular readers, many of whom find it difficult to accept the idea that though Uncle Tom dies the victim of Simon Legree's brutal rage, he has yet achieved a spiritual triumph. Nevertheless, Mrs. Stowe believed the religious theme essential to the integrity of the story. Writing years later, she remarked with conviction that her novel "shows that, under circumstances of utter desolation and despair, the religion of Christ can enable the poorest and most ignorant human being, not merely to submit, but to trimuph, that the soul of the lowest and weakest, by its aid, can become strong in superhuman virtue, and rise above every threat and terror and danger in a sublime assurance of an ever-present love and an immortal life."[49] It should be noted that the triumph of the meek, here applied to black slaves, echoed the sentimental insistence that women, too, achieve spiritual transcendence through the very fact of their exclusion from worldly power.

Although the grand theme of the novel is the evil of the slavery system, *Uncle Tom's Cabin* is a thoroughly domestic novel, which succeeds in condemning slavery by showing the reader its impact on families—both black and white, slave and free. What could portray more starkly the contrast between free culture and slave culture than the comparison between a Quaker home in Indiana and Simon Legree's deteriorating slave plantation? First the Quaker home:

> A quiet scene now rises before us. A large, roomy, neatly-painted kitchen, its yellow floor glossy and smooth, and without a particle of dust; a neat, well-blacked cooking-stove; rows of shining tin, suggestive of unmentionable good things to the appetite; glossy green wood chairs, old and firm; a small flag-bottomed rocking-chair, with a patchwork cushion in it, neatly contrived out of small pieces of different colored woolen goods, and a larger sized one, motherly and old, whose wide arms breathed hospitable invitation, seconded by the solicitation of its feather cushions—a real comfortable, persuasive old chair. (p. 135)

The Quaker home has both a kitchen and a mother, but Legree's house—one could not call it a home—has neither:

> The sitting room of Legree's establishment was a large, long room, with a wide ample fireplace. It had once been hung with a showy and expensive paper, which now hung mouldering, torn and discolored, from the damp walls. The place had that peculiar sickening, unwholesome smell, compounded of mingled damp, dirt and decay, which one often notices in close old houses. The wallpaper was defaced, in spots, by slops of beer and wine; or garnished with chalk memorandums, and long sums footed up, as if somebody had been practicing arithmetic there.

The reference to chalk marks makes clear that Legree regards his sitting room as merely a place to do business, a point underscored by the fact that the room is a jumble of "saddles, bridles, several sorts of harness, riding-whips, overcoats, and various articles of clothing" (p. 370).

Legree's callous violation of the cult of domesticity is matched by the more subtle damage dealt to the ideal family by Augustine St. Clare, the gentle, handsome, almost effeminate slave owner, and his wife, the vain and selfish Marie. Of the two, Augustine is the more sinned against, and his unhappiness flows from violations of the cult of romantic love. He fell in love with a beautiful woman, but her guardian forbade marriage, for he had another match in mind for her. In despair, Augustine threw himself into a "whirl of fashionable society," and there met Marie. He did not love her, but he was persuaded to propose by a "fine figure, a pair of splendid eyes, and a hundred thousand dollars." In Marie he married a woman who violated every tenet of virtuous womanhood and the cult of motherhood:

> As the glosses and civilities of the honeymoon wore away, he discovered that a beautiful young woman, who has lived all her life to be caressed and waited on, might prove quite a hard mistess in domestic life. Marie never had possessed much capability of affection, or much sensibility, and the little that she had, had been merged into most intense and unconscious selfishness; a selfishness more hopeless, from its quiet obtuseness, its utter ignorance of any claims but her own. (p. 156)

To the problems of this unpromising union were added the burdens of slave-owning, which troubles Augustine's conscience but which he cannot bring himself to oppose. The evil of the system is brought home to him through his child, Eva, who, improbable as it may seem with a mother like Marie, is the most saintly child in American fiction. Eva possesses a spiritual perfection denied her parents, and as she grows older she begins to witness and absorb the evils of the slavery system around her. Heartsick, she speaks of dying, and tells her father that she longs to go to heaven, for "it's so sweet and peaceful there—it is all so loving there!" (p. 279). Too saintly to endure the evil world, she expires, providing the readers with the most heartrending death in all of American sentimental fiction.

Mrs. Stowe reserved her highest literary explosive, however, for the awful destruction wrought by the system of slavery on the families of blacks. In addition to experiencing numerous slave auctions, the reader suffers along with Uncle Tom in his separation from his family, feels a mother's love and terror as she flees across the ice of the Ohio River with her child in her arms, and learns from the quadroon, Cassy, what it is like to be the mistress to a succession of white men, one of whom sold his own children. Mrs. Stowe, well acquainted with the literary tradition of which she was a part, knew that these tales of the forcible separation of mothers and children would have their effect. She addressed frequent asides to the reader:

> And you, mothers of America,—you, who have learned, by the cradles of your own children, to love and feel for all mankind—by the sacred love you bear your child; by your joy in his beautiful, spotless infancy; by the motherly pity and tenderness with which you guide his growing years; by the anxieties of his education; by the prayers you breathe for his soul's eternal good;—I beseech you, pity the mother who has all your affections, and not one legal right to protect, guide, or educate, the child of her bosom! By the sick hour of your child; by those dying eyes, which you can never forget; by those last cries, that wrung your heart when you could neither help nor save; by the desolation of that empty cradle, that silent nursery—I beseech you, pity those mothers that are constantly made childless by the American slave trade! (p. 447)

Harriet Beecher Stowe's indignation was genuine, and through her art she lifted the sentimental revolution out of the cloying falsity that mars such lesser work as Warner's *Wide, Wide World*. For our purposes, however, the significance of Stowe's novel lies in its fundamental adherence to the cults of romantic love, domesticity, motherhood, and childhood. That *Uncle Tom's Cabin* proved to be the most popular book of the latter half of the nineteenth century bears testimony not only to Stowe's skill in exploiting the moral issue of slavery, but also to the popularity of sentimental ideals among Americans in the Victorian era.

Coming of age just as *Uncle Tom's Cabin* appeared, Louisa May Alcott occupied a particularly strategic position from which to comment on the sentimental revolution and to trace its relevance to life in nineteenth-century America. Her parents—Bronson and Abigail—were among the cultural avant-garde who embraced sentimental views about domestic life even before Louisa May was born, and they worked zealously to live by them. Growing up in such a sentimental family and then coming to know the humiliation of poverty as an adolescent, Louisa was also in a position to assess the sentimental revolution and its relevance to a dynamic, restless, materialistic society. Finally, in her art, she drew upon her experience to sort out the meaning of the sentimental revolution, attempting to salvage its strengths and strip it of its ludicrous excesses.

The Contradictions of a Sentimental
Childhood: Louisa's Early Years

The sentimental revolution provided the cultural context within which Louisa May Alcott came to maturity. Her parents were in crucial respects adherents of the sentimental revolution, attempting to make the Alcott household a model by the emerging standards of the sentimentalists.[1] It was a family formed in 1830 by the union of a man and a woman who had repudiated conventional standards of a courtship and who married without regard for prudential advantage. During the succeeding years, Amos Bronson and Abigail May Alcott struggled, as the cult of domesticity demanded, to make their household into an enclave against the materialism and conformity of Jacksonian society. As for sex roles, Bronson played a larger role in the internal affairs of the family than the sentimental literature contemplated, and both he and Abigail endorsed a somewhat less conservative position on the subject of sexual equality than the sentimentalists would allow. Nevertheless, Louisa's mother confined herself to the home during the children's earliest years, and, though she did not relish household chores, she genuinely delighted in her role as mother to Anna, Louisa, Elizabeth, and May, who appeared respectively in 1831, 1832, 1835, and 1840. Both she and her husband struggled to provide an atmosphere of warmth and intimacy which the sentimental ideal demanded, and much of this quality of family life suffuses Louisa May's fiction.

THE LITTLE PARADISE

In 1843, when Louisa was ten years old, Bronson wrote his four daughters:

I will show you what is beautiful, beautiful, indeed—surpassing all other things in beauty. . . . It is a pure and happy; a kind and loving family—a house where peace and joy, and gentleness and quiet, abide always, and from which sounds of content, and voices of confiding love, alone ascend—around whose hearth gather serene and loveful countenances; where every hand is quick to help, every foot swift to serve, every eye to catch the wishes, and every ear, the wants of the other.[2]

By then, with thirteen years of married life behind him, Bronson should have known how far actual experience departed from his ideal, but if there was a disparity between the ideal and the real it was not for want of trying on Bronson's part. He set out to be the most sentimentally ideal husband and father.

Born in 1799 the son of an impecunious Connecticut farmer, Bronson spent much of his youth engaged in farming and peddling, acquiring more formal learning only through primitive rural schools and by dint of his efforts at self-education. At the age of twenty-three he became a district schoolteacher, which in itself was not so unusual. What else could a young man with bookish inclinations and no advantages aspire to? But though poorly educated, he possessed both intelligence and demonic energy, and he threw himself into the role of an educational reformer. He also made two discoveries during his years as a Connecticut schoolmaster: first, that he had a way with children, especially with the little ones; and, secondly, that his talent was appreciated. His impressive work in the schools of Connecticut won him no friends in the local districts, to be sure, but he did manage to attract the attention of Boston's avant-garde, who proved willing to tolerate an educational reformer. In 1828 Alcott accepted an invitation to conduct an "infant" school in America's intellectual capital and within two years he had acquired a reputation as a reformer of schools for young children.

Even then Bronson was moving toward opinions that would place him at the center of a movement which represented a highly sophisticated version of the sentimental revolution. Like so many of the reformers who were gathering in Boston during the decade of the 1830s, Alcott was intrigued with the mix of philosophic idealism, romantic imagery, and native religious sentiment that was to become known as transcendentalism. Alcott had arrived, by dint of strenuous self-education, at the persuasion his friend, Ralph Waldo Emerson, would expound in his seminal essay, "Nature," and that another friend, Henry David Thoreau, would explore in his classic book, *Walden*. Like Emerson and Thoreau, Alcott harbored a radical dissatisfaction with the culture of Jacksonian America, believing that Americans were far too materialistic and too conformist. The charge of materialism was made by transcendentalists at two levels, one philosophic and the other practical. The philosophic charge was that Americans—if they thought about such things at all—tended to view ultimate reality as totally a combination of matter in motion, hence denying a more ultimate reality that was divine and spiritual. The more practical charge was that Americans, in harboring these materialistic assumptions, were much too preoccupied with such worldly goods as wealth, status, and power, and much too enamored of mere creature comforts. "Things are in the saddle and ride mankind," Emerson complained, and Alcott agreed with him.[3] As for conformity, this was a failing that flowed from materialism. Preoccupied with the goods of this world, Americans were too inclined to ride with the herd, ignoring the higher reaches of reality and hence denying their individual genius. Again to quote Alcott's friend Emerson, "who so would be a man must be a nonconformist."[4] Celebrating spirituality and individualism, transcendentalists like Alcott and Emerson often spoke of a universal order, embracing both man and nature, but transcending both, to which men can refer their aspirations for the ideal. Above all, transcendentalists possessed a belief in man's essential divinity, which consists in the power to transcend the limitations of human nature and human society.

Such were Bronson's ideas when in 1828 he met Abigail May, who, far from resenting his odd notions, was fully taken with his ideas and actually seemed to understand what he was talking about. Coming from a respectable Boston family, she was a highly perceptive and intelligent woman, who had read widely—if informally—in philosophy and history. Before making Alcott's acquaintance, she had acquired decided convictions about the need for educational reform, for a more liberal theology, and for equality for blacks and women, views similar to Bronson's. The attraction between Bronson and

21

Abigail grew out of these shared convictions more than it did out of either passion or prudence. Certainly, Bronson would not have been regarded as a "catch" in fashionable Boston society, as he himself well recognized: "Popular manners, the chief requisite to success, I do not possess, and my appearance in public assumes so much of the rustic awkwardness and simplicity of natural life that I am often offending the more cultivated tastes of those with whom I sometimes come in contact."[5] Some of Abigail's relatives wondered if she should marry a man of Bronson's doubtful origins, and it was clear even to Abigail that he would never be a rich man. His lack of fashionable graces only endeared him in her eyes, however, for it was his mind more than his manner that attracted her. Shortly after meeting him she observed:

> He shall be my moral mentor, my intellectual guide. He analyzes my mind with care and judgment, my character with discrimination and charity, my heart with love and confidence. He is my benefactor, he shall see that he does me good, that I am not only his lover, his mistress, but his pupil, his companion. It shall be my business to secure his respect and affection, not my boast that he loves me.[6]

Like so many who knew Bronson well, she was awed by his apparent serenity of spirit, which, she thought, would provide a beneficial check on her own volatile temperament.[7]

Bronson approached the relationship with equal highmindedness. Abigail was neither rich nor beautiful but she possessed, he thought:

> Intelligence, sympathy, piety, exemplified in the tenderness of the eye, in the beauty of moral countenance, in the joyousness of domestic performance. . . . We conversed on a variety of subjects. She had thought for herself. She had thought liberally. Her views compared with ours. Her sentiments were also ours. Her purposes were like ours—the instruction of the young. Everything seemed to favor the commencement of an acquaintance of a pure and sentimental kind.[8]

In the end, Bronson decided, he loved her because she was good, and because she loved him.[9] It was hardly a passionate avowal, and Bronson seemed to recognize that Abigail was capable of a deeper, more unqualified love than he, a fact which he attributed to her sex: "Man's love in general is a selfish and exacting sentiment; it demands every sacrifice, and refuses all. There is in the heart of woman so deep a well of love, that no age can freeze it. . . . In love, man, be he ever so generous, is always outdone."[10]

Consequently, Bronson hesitated "with fear and trembling" before making a proposal, as if he doubted that he could make the full commitment of devotion that he believed marriage required.[11] Abigail, however, seemed to have no qualms, and she pressed the shy and doubting Bronson to declare himself, brushing aside the objections of relatives. In any event, her faith overcame his doubts and they were married in the spring of 1830. It was, Abigail later declared, a union of "principle, not passion," a marriage based on the hope of mutual self-improvement, morally, intellectually, and spiritually.[12]

The way was thus prepared for an experiment in ideal family life. Seven months after their marriage, Bronson accepted an invitation from a wealthy Quaker farmer to open a school in Germantown, Pennsylvania. Accompanied by his pregnant wife, he sailed from Boston for Philadelphia, where they spent the winter preparing for the new ventures in school and home, both of which Alcott trusted would launch his reputation among men of influence. The first order of business was to find an appropriate physical setting. Required, he thought, was something ideal, which meant something antiseptic. He could imagine the setting, far removed from the corrupt world. It would be a cottage set in a "romantic" valley, beside a bubbling brook, and surrounded by steep precipices and lofty mountains. Here, under the supervision of a mother who had renounced fashionable society and of a father who had repudiated worldly ambition, children would be reared as they ought.[13] As the cult of domesticity required, the Alcott family would provide a moral refuge from the sinful world without.

Germantown possessed no lofty mountains, and bubbling brooks were difficult to come by, but the Quaker farmer provided the Alcotts with a cottage, recently painted, neatly furnished, and rent-free. Situated on a main road, with more than an acre of grounds and garden, the setting was very close to ideal, in Abigail's opinion. The house would compare favorably with her father's residence in Boston for neatness and order, while the garden was charming, lined with raspberry, currant, and gooseberry bushes. The grounds featured also a lovely walk shaded with pine, fir, cedar, apple, pear, peach, and plum trees. It was, Mrs. Alcott reported to her brother, a "little paradise."[14]

In this ideal setting, the Alcotts set about their experiment in child-rearing, and Bronson kept a voluminously detailed record.[15] In keeping with the cult of childhood, the proper care and nurture of the young was the heart of family life, and in the spring of 1831 Anna appeared, to become the most important member of the new family. One hour after the birth, her father recorded his feelings: "How delightful were the emotions produced by the first sounds of the infant's cry—making it seem that I was, indeed, a father! Joy, gratitude, hope and affection were all mingled in our feeling."[16] Abigail was in no condition to write about her feelings just then. It had been a difficult pregnancy, casting her often into periods of gloom and anxiety, and she had endured thirty-six hours of labor in giving birth. Nevertheless, eleven days after Anna's arrival, she proved no less ecstatic than her husband. Writing her brother, Abigail was eager to convey her joy, and to assure him that it made not the least difference that her first child had not been a boy. Anna was in good health and perfectly quiet, while nursing and caring for her was delightful. "I would not," she said, "delegate it to an angel."[17]

As Anna grew, it became evident to the Alcotts that a domestic sanctuary required more than an isolated physical setting. The ideal of family life required also that the parents provide for Anna a cocoon which would exclude harmful influences. Relatives would present no threat; the move from New England to Pennsylvania ensured little interference from that quarter. Servants might, however, become a problem, for Alcott thought too many parents failed by consigning their infants to the care of a nurse, who was usually ignorant, selfish, and lazy. It seems that the Alcotts could not do without household assistance, and the record reveals that servants usually worked in the home during these early years, but the danger was kept within bounds. The Alcotts insisted that the domestic help take care of the house, while they kept Anna to themselves. After the first four weeks, Anna remained under the sole charge of her mother and father during her first year, and Abigail rarely left the house without Anna on her arm. She even developed the habit of retiring with Anna in the evening, holding the infant until she fell asleep in her arms. Neighbors were more of a problem, and Alcott complained about the effect on his daughter of "distorted faces," "harsh sounds," sudden movements, loud voices, baby talk, and "incessant prattle."[18] After Louisa May's appearance in November 1832 the protective screen which the Alcotts erected was expanded to include her as well. As the two girls grew, their parents began to monitor their friendships and, of course, the books they read.

This idealistic regime proved demanding on both parents. Abigail did not care much for housework, and if she had a choice, she left it to a maid or, in later years, often chose lodging in a boarding house. Motherhood, however, suited her exactly, and she shared Bronson's fascination with observing the growth and development of the girls. As Bronson reported at the occasion of Louisa May's birth, his wife "lives and moves and breathes for her family alone."[19] As the girls grew older, Abigail established herself as their chief confidante, rarely too busy to listen to their complaints or to sympathize with their difficulties. The girls were not lacking in attention from their father either. Despite his duties as a breadwinner during the early years, he devoted an extraordinary amount of attention to his offspring, motivated in part by his hope that the publication of his extensive observations of their development would eventually establish a reputation for him in philosophy.

By the time Anna was four and Louisa May two and one-half, their father had devised an orderly schedule which he adhered to more or less faithfully. The schedule called for him to rise at 6:00 A.M., with the children. He washed and dressed them, frequently over their protest, although the nursery was kept warm during the night to make the task a bit more pleasant. The girls were then permitted to play in the nursery until 7:00, when the maid brought in breakfast. Afterward they spent some time with their father in the study, or resumed play in the nursery. At 8:30 the girls separated, Louisa to spend the morning with her mother, until lunch at 11:00 and a nap at 12:00. Anna would pass the morning at the school with her father from 9:00 until 2:00 in the afternoon, playing with the other children, looking at pictures, listening to stories, and marking letters on her slate. By 2:30 Anna and her father had returned home, where Anna and Louisa would have dinner together, and afterward take a walk, either with their father or with the maid. The remainder of the afternoon they spent playing in the nursery, taking a light supper at 6:00 followed by more play in the nursery, or, perhaps, by conversations with their father in the study. At 7:30 they were put to bed.

Given Bronson's bent for educational reform, it was not surprising that he shaped his encounters with his daughters to educational ends. When Anna became interested in the alphabet, her father devised a game of imitating the letters with his arms and legs, much to Anna's delight. On still another occasion, Bronson brought home an educational game consisting of circular pieces of pasteboard, with a letter drawn on one side and an appropriate animal picture on the other, together with a box into which the discs could be placed. Louisa was not excluded from these educational games. She frequently joined her sister and father in his study after supper to enact little dramas, adapted from stories they knew, with a bit of music and dancing added for good measure. Louisa enjoyed one game especially: her parents permitted the girls to run about the room naked for a time before they were dressed for bed, with Louisa "running riot," as her father put it.[20] Above all, Alcott made use of conversations and stories with his daughters just before bedtime. He prepared this evening hour with great care and surrounded his little narratives with caresses and kisses, taking pains to associate the stories with frequent demonstrations of parental warmth and affection. Quickly, the tales became something of a bedtime ritual, enjoyed not only by Anna but also by Louisa, who could summon a patience for stories that she could not command for her father's conversations.

While Alcott intended that those intimate exchanges with his daughters would foster the skills of reading, writing, and arithmetic, the major object was the development of their moral character. While establishing an intimate bond of affection with his offspring, he then proceeded, quite deliberately, to make this bond the basis for the perfection of their conscience. Every story, every conversation contained a moral lesson, and the point of the lesson was the obligation of self-sacrifice. The most mundane occasion might give rise to such a lesson. One day, for example, Anna was sitting in a rocking chair, nursing a sprained ankle. Louisa wanted the chair and used tears, pleas, and blows to make her point. Father intervened and suggested that Anna, because she was older, should give in to Louisa's demands. Anna promised to try, but an hour later fresh outcries brought Alcott back to the nursery, where he discovered Anna sitting in the chair once again and Louisa standing beside her in tears.

"Anna, what is the matter with Louisa?"

"She wants to sit in the rocking chair, where mother told me I might sit because I am lame, while she puts the room in order."

"But will you not let her sit in it, if it will stop the tears from running down her cheeks. Will you not get up to make your sister happy?"

"I want to sit here. Mother said I might."

"So does your sister. And don't you know that you said you would give up your wants to Louisa's. And now you can do so. Mother is willing that Louisa should sit in the chair. Are you, Anna?"

"I want to sit in it."

"Well, Anna, I see you do not mean to be *very good*. Very good little girls give up their own wants to the wants of their little sisters whom they *love*. Love makes us give up our own wants. If you love your little sister, you will give up the chair to her."

"I love her but I want to sit in the chair."[21]

Alcott then asked Anna to go down with him to the study. When she refused, he turned to Louisa and asked her to go. Louisa agreed, and he picked her up in his arms, but as he was leaving the room, he said to Anna:

"Now, you are not a very good girl. If you were, you would give up the chair to Louisa. I shall not give you the apple that you were to have if [you had been] good when I came up again."

"I will let her sit in the chair." Anna said, moving herself to the floor to make room for Louisa.

"Now, Anna, did you give up the chair because you loved your sister, or because you wanted the apple."

"Because I wanted the apple." After a reflective pause, she added, "and I like sister too."[22]

It was, Alcott admitted, not a "perfect" example of self-sacrifice, but he hoped Anna would soon perceive the superiority of acting out of love for Louisa to acting out of love for apples. His comment points up the high expectations he entertained of his daughters. The principle was one of ascetic self-sacrifice for the sake of sacrifice, resting on the commands of love. It was also clear that love, as Alcott used the term, was not spontaneous impulse, but rather the result of a heroic exercise of will-power. The techniques he employed to secure these results would be called by later generations a "love-oriented discipline," which includes reasoning with children, giving praise and affection as a reward, and practicing isolation and withdrawal of affection as forms of punishment. Alcott already sensed what later investigations would confirm, that a love-oriented discipline is usually associated with the early appearance of conscientious behavior. As we shall see, Alcott's child-rearing strategy proved in this regard to be extraordinarily successful, not only with Anna but with Louisa May as well.

Louisa May's recollection of these early years were for the most part happy ones. She recalled playing with the books in her father's study, building houses and bridges with them, and scribbling on blank pages with pen or pencil. She recalled fondly her father's teaching:

> I never went to school except to my father or such governesses as from
> time to time came into the family. Schools then were not what they are
> now; so we had lessons each morning in the study. And very happy
> hours they were to us, for my father taught in the wise way which
> unfolds what lies in the child's nature, as a flower blooms, rather than
> cramming it, like a Strasburg goose, with more than it could digest. I
> never liked arithmetic nor grammar, and dodged those branches on
> all occasions; but reading, writing, composition, history, and geogra-
> phy I enjoyed, as well as the stories read to us with a skill peculiarly
> his own.[23]

Even the lessons in self-sacrifice, which she received at the hands of her mother as well as her father, were remembered with stoic acceptance, if not delight. One incident in particular stuck in her mind. Louisa was allowed to celebrate her fourth birthday at Bronson's school, with all her father's pupils present:

> I wore a crown of flowers, and stood upon a table to dispense cakes to
> each child as the procession marched past. By some oversight the

cakes fell short, and I saw that if I gave away the last one I should have none. As I was queen of the revel, I felt that I ought to have it, and held on to it tightly till my mother said, "It is always better to give away than to keep the nice things; so I know my Louy will not let the little friend go without." The little friend received the dear plummy cake, and I a kiss and my first lesson in the sweetness of self-denial.[24]

Louisa did not, as we shall see, always find self-denial sweet. And, if she remembered her childhood as happy, it was because she had forgotten or suppressed the difficulties that arose when a nineteenth-century American family attempted to put into practice the sentimental vision of the family. To these difficulties we now turn.

SAINTS AND DEMONS

In 1846, when Louisa was fourteen, Bronson said of her and his wife, "Two devils, as yet, I am not quite divine enough to vanquish— the mother fiend and her daughter."[25] This startling comment might be explained in part by the fact that the family was experiencing extraordinary difficulty at the moment, but it provided as well the hint of a tension that had been flowing for some time under the surface of family life. The tension consisted of two elements: the actual behavior of mother and daughter, both being volatile in temperament; and Bronson's notions of what was proper behavior, notions which, as his use of the word *divine* indicates, favored calmness and serenity. Louisa was rarely calm or serene and had not been since she was at least two years of age. Two-year-olds, then as now, were notorious for their obstreperous ways, and even Anna had proved difficult for her parents at that age, but Louisa persisted in being stubborn and aggressive long after her older sister had adopted more decorous ways. Bronson wished saints for daughters, but Louisa was turning out to be a devil in his eyes, a fact which created difficulty for both father and daughter and left Louisa with a wound that never healed.

It was not that Bronson was blind to positive traits in his second-born. When he put aside his notions of proper child behavior, he could be a shrewd and sympathetic observer. He noted in two-year-old Louisa an unusual force of mind, as well as of body, and he found that she was making unusual progress for her age in building her vocabulary. Moreover, she exhibited, he believed, an unusually vivid imagination:

> I had a long interview with her after she had lain herself in bed. Her thoughts came rushing after each other, with a vivid celerity; so fast and so evanescent, both in idea and expression, that 'twas almost impossible to fasten them in the mind. . . . They were all clear and vivid to her. Her associations are *dramatic*.[26]

Nevertheless, while appreciating Louisa's positive qualities, he found her temper tantrums difficult to deal with and he blamed them on Abigail. She resembled her mother in appearance as well as in temperament, for both were dark in complexion, in dramatic contrast to Bronson and Anna, who were both fair. It was popularly believed—and Bronson shared the belief—that dark people were less inclined than fair people to serenity of temper. There was also the fact that Abigail was feeding Louisa meat, which Bronson's growing inclination toward vegetarianism led him to believe contributed to her "ferocity" of spirit. Finally, he complained that Abigail was entirely too indulgent with Louisa. "Young as she is," he said, "it is not too early to soften down her guideless nature to docility, and sustain it by habits of obedience."[27]

Since he could do nothing about Louisa's inheritance, and since Abigail insisted on feeding her daughters meat, Bronson took it upon himself to attempt some "softening" of Louisa's spirit. His preference was, as it had been with Anna, to punish her by the withdrawal of affection, followed by calm conversation: "I punished her by the loss of the kiss, with some kind sympathy in her weakness, and she went to bed in a happy mood."[28] But such tactics did not work as well with Louisa as they had with Anna. Soon Bronson found himself resorting to physical punishment, with traumatic results for both father and daughter. When three-year-old Louisa wanted to sit on her mother's lap at dinner, Bronson insisted that she sit in a chair:

> I placed her little chair by her mother's side and invited her to seat herself in it. She refused. I repeated the wish; she again showed disinclination to comply. . . . I told her that I should place her in the chair if she did not get in herself; she refused, saying, "No. No." with

her usual force of expression, raising her tones and giving me to understand that the decision was made in her mind. I placed her in it, notwithstanding her struggles. The cry was heightened, and prolonged; the persistence more decided and obstinate. I told her she must stop crying and sit in the chair or—I should punish her—hurt her, for she "must" mind father. "No. No." she exclaimed with more decided vehemence than before. I said, "Father must *spank* Louisa if she does not do as he says—will she?" "No. No. Sit with mother," she reiterated. I *spanked her*. She cried the louder. I then told her that she must sit on her little chair by the side of her mother, and be still; or I should punish her more. She was unwilling to give up her purpose; and set up crying again. I repeated the punishment, and did not attain peace and quiet for her, till I had repeated it again.[29]

Louisa subsided into obedience, but Bronson was shaken by the experience, for Louisa had succeeded for a moment in shattering his carefully maintained composure, leading him, moreover, to violate his principles. In reflecting on this incident, he reasserted his belief that physical punishment was "barbarous in the extreme," but he put the blame not on himself but on Abigail for failing to enforce obedience on Louisa.[30]

With redoubled energy, Bronson repeatedly told Louisa that she was a "naughty girl," and continued the practice of withdrawing affection when she misbehaved. Abigail, apparently worried about Bronson's criticism of her indulgent ways, also took a firmer hand with Louisa, tying her once to a bedpost after she ran away, but nothing, it seemed, could quell her fiery temperament. After the birth of Elizabeth, the Alcott's third child, Louisa told her mother: "I don't like Baby. I wish she was dead. I will throw her out the window and kill her."[31] Her mother expressed astonishment, saying she was ashamed of her, which seemed to have the desired effect: "O, mother, I am a naughty girl. I am very naughty. I will lie down on the bed and hide myself." And to her father she said, "I am very naughty. I feel bad. Nobody will love me. God will not love me."[32]

All her life Louisa carried with her the feeling that she was inexpressibly bad and that she would not be loved unless she was especially "good," but at the same time, she was unable to quell a temperament that labeled her, in her own eyes and even in the eyes of

31

her mother, as "peculiar."[33] While Anna grew into a little girl who dressed neatly, disliked fighting, feared to walk in wet grass, and loved tending her baby sisters, Louisa was both physical and aggressive. As she later recalled:

> Active exercise was my delight, from the time when a child of six I drove my hoop around the Common without stopping, to the days when I did my twenty miles in five hours and went to a party in the evening. I always thought I must have been a deer or a horse in some former state, because it was such a joy to run. No boy could be my friend till I had beaten him in a race, and no girl if she refused to climb trees, leap fences, and be a tomboy.[34]

When the Alcott family moved from Boston to Concord, Louisa had more scope for her boundless energy, climbing trees and on one occasion "borrowing" a sleigh and horse from a neighbor without permission. Bronson could take no comfort in telling himself that this was merely a stage in Louisa's development, for at the age of thirteen she was still earning a reputation among playmates for her odd ways. As one recalled:

> Louisa was thirteen years old, tall and slim—limbs predominated and were used freely, so that she was the fleetest runner in school, and could walk, run and climb like a boy. At one time she trundled her hoop from her home to the foot of Hardy's Hill, the distance of a mile, turned and came back without stopping. She had dark brown hair, pleasant gray eyes with a peculiar twinkle in them and a sallow complexion. She was not prepossessing in personal appearance, and in character a strange combination of kindness and perseverance, shyness and daring; a creature loving and spiteful, full of energy and perseverance, full of fun, with a keen sense of the ludicrous, apt speech and ready wit; a subject of moods, than whom no one could be jollier and more entertaining when geniality was in ascendancy, but if the opposite, let her best friend beware.[35]

What her friends did not recognize was that beneath her tomboyish ways and volatile temperament lay an undercurrent of melancholy, accompanied by desperate attempts to measure up to the family's expectations. During the period when the family was experimenting with the beneficial effects of cold water baths, ten-year-old

Louisa professed to "love cold water," expressed her resolve to be kind to poor people, to stop teasing her mother so much, and, above all, to control her temper: "I made good resolutions, and felt better in my heart. If I only *kept* all I make, I should be the best girl in the world. But I don't, and so am very bad."[36]

As Louisa grew older, her father became more baffled by her behavior, and he could only resort to warning her of the terrible consequences of not obeying her conscience. As he told the seven-year-old: "You feel your conscience, and have no real pleasure unless you obey it. You cannot love yourself, or any one else, when you do not mind its commandments. . . . How it smiles upon you and makes you glad when you resolve to obey it! How terrible its punishments! It is God trying in your Soul to keep you always good."[37] Three years later he was still admonishing her about the evil effects of her temper and pleading with his second-born to obey him and allow him to influence her.[38] By the time she was fourteen he had decided that she was "possessed."

Abigail was more understanding, for she recognized in Louisa many of her own traits, but even she was beginning to accept the notion that her second-born was peculiar. She attributed Louisa's odd ways to the fact that she had been "unusually" depressed while pregnant with Louisa, "which accounts to me for many of her peculiarities and moods of mind, rather uncommon for a child of her age." But Abigail recognized Louisa was much like herself, and saw that beneath Louisa's boisterous ways and sometimes violent temper were also moods of frequent melancholy—"no hope, no heart for anything, sad, solemn, and desponding." Abigail also detected qualities that Bronson seemed too preoccupied to notice, for she found in her daughter "fine generous feelings, no selfishness, great good will to all, and strong attachment to a few."[39] In dealing with Louisa, Abigail adopted a delicate blend of admonition and sympathy, together with expressions of trust in her potential. As she told the fourteen-year-old: "Your temperament is a peculiar one, and there are few who can really help you. Set about the formation of character and, believe me, you are capable of obtaining a noble one."[40]

Louisa gratefully turned to her mother, who seemed the only one capable of sympathizing with her struggle. "People think I'm wild

and queer," she wrote, "but Mother understands and helps me."[41]
She also found, at age thirteen, some solace in religion and seems to
have experienced something like an epiphany while walking in the
woods:

> It seemed like going through a dark life or grave into heaven beyond.
> A very strange and solemn feeling came over me as I stood there, with
> no sound but the rustle of the pines, no one near me, and the sun so
> glorious, as for me alone. It seemed as if I *felt* God as I never did
> before, and I prayed in my heart that I might keep that happy sense of
> nearness all my life.[42]

That sense often deserted her in future years, but for the time being,
at least, she felt that she might be near enough to God to control her
wayward temperament and to please Him—and her father. As she
expressed it in a poem written at the age of fourteen:

> Dear Father, help me with the love
>   That casteth out my fear;
> Teach me to lean on thee, and feel
>   That thou art very near,
> That no temptation is unseen,
>   No childish grief too small,
> Since thou, with patience infinite,
>   Doth soothe and comfort all.[43]

As the ambiguity of the word *Father* suggests, Louisa was struggling
to make Bronson's standards her own. It would not always be so, and
once she had begun to question her father's principles, she was compelled to search for God in other directions. Never, however, was she
able to eradicate the feeling that she harbored within her something
of the demonic.

From a feminist perspective, it might appear that Bronson was
shaping his daughters to conform to the sentimental stereotype of
sacrificial womanhood, but the difficulty with this point of view is
that Bronson imposed the same ethic on himself. Ascetic renunciation
of the "animal appetites" was for him not merely a sentimental gesture reserved for women but a standard that he adhered to in his own
life. Boston merchants might despise his innocence of worldly values
and his strange notions, but Thoreau thought him one of the sanest

men in America. Anna paid her tribute by observing—without prompting—that she thought her father nearly as good as Jesus. He did shout at her occasionally, and he often provoked her to anger and resentment, but by practicing what he preached he may have invested his stern demands with sufficient meaning to save them from the taint of hypocrisy. In short, Bronson's child-rearing practices may have been foolish, but they were not sexist.

The real difficulty was not that Bronson looked at women as different, but that he lived in such a realm of distant abstraction that he could only with effort relate honestly with other human beings— whether male or female. He lacked altogether a sense of humor, which was a sure sign that he lacked perspective. His search for human perfection led him to expect too much of others, and he was not always aware of his own failings. Abigail sensed that he was asking too much of his daughters and, despite her awe of Bronson and his principles, she sometimes attempted to put a brake on his transcendental ambitions for their offspring. By 1848, eighteen years after their marriage, she was willing to acknowledge that beneath Bronson's serene surface there was a good deal of agitation and excitement; "more so than I thought," she said. She was also prepared to admit to herself that though Bronson was intolerant of the weaknesses of others, he "does not see his own."[44] By then, however, it was too late to shield Louisa from Bronson's expectations. Even as he sought to liberate childhood from barbarity and indifference, Bronson imposed on Louisa a burden that could prove more crushing to the human spirit. That Louisa did not succumb altogether is a testimony to the support she received from her mother as well as a measure of her own inner strength.

There is evidence, admittedly speculative, that in later life Louisa harbored resentment toward her father for his seemingly distant and abstract way of dealing with her. Her sensational novel, *A Modern Mephistopheles*, portrays a man, Jasper Helwyze, who, like Bronson, was consumed by psychological curiosity, but with none of Bronson's saintly qualities. Louisa arranges for one of the characters to speak indignantly of "the want of love and reverence for the human soul, which makes a man pry into its mysterious depths, not with a hope or purpose of making it better, but from a cold philosophical curiosity.

35

This would be the separation of the intellect from the heart: and this, perhaps, would be as unpardonable a sin as to doubt God, whom we cannot harm; for in doing this we must inevitably do great wrong both to ourselves and others."[45]

The Vulnerable Sanctuary

On one occasion Bronson signed a letter to his daughters with the phrase, "your present friend and careful provider."[46] It was an irony, however unintended, and pointed to a major contradiction that marked Louisa's experience of the family. If the family was to be an emotional refuge for its members it required a "careful provider," but in 1843, when Bronson described himself as such, nothing could have been further from the truth. From this contradiction flowed a series of difficulties for all of the family, and especially for Louisa. Her remarkable parents, committed to the notion of the family as a place radically apart from the world, had forged between themselves and their offspring an intimate bond which no subsequent experience could break. But if the family was intimately woven into her being, it also proved a highly vulnerable institution, largely due to Bronson's failings as a breadwinner. Consequently, Louisa and her mother and sisters came to know the disparity between the sentimental model of family life and the reality of genteel poverty to which they were exposed.

The difficulty began, coincidentally, with the arrival of Louisa May. The "little paradise" of which Mrs. Alcott spoke lasted only six months. In the fall of 1831, a year before Louisa May's birth, Bronson's wealthy patron died, and support for his school dwindled. Abigail was forced to take in a child as a boarder, the first invasion of the intimate fortress which the Alcotts hoped to make of their family. Soon the child was joined by four others who, according to her parents, were exercising a bad influence over Anna. It is, Abigail observed, a "thankless employment to take care of other people's children," and she longed for the intimacy of "as small a circle as possible."[47] Meanwhile, the patronage for Alcott's school continued to plummet, and finally in the spring of 1833 the family was forced to abandon their little cottage and move to Philadelphia, where Alcott attempted a second school. Taking up lodging in a boarding house, the Alcotts restricted Anna's movements, for they were convinced that urban life was dangerous for her. The effect on Anna was bad. As her father observed: "She suffers . . . from confinement. Denied the free, unrestricted range afforded her while in the country, she sometimes finds it difficult to content herself with the few objects of the nursery and the attentions of her mother and nurse."[48] Louisa suffered also from Anna's unhappiness, as Anna took to striking or scratching her. Mrs. Alcott was distraught, and she worried about her skills as a mother. The father, too, was beginning to find the familial sanctuary more of a prison:

> It is absolutely necessary to the natural unfolding of the infant mind, as well as the tranquility and progress of the parent, that Space should be enjoyed. . . . Before this, both myself and companion got time for reflection and study. This is of the first importance to us both. To me, it is a positive want of my being. I pine, and lose my Spirits, my hopes and aspirations without it. During the last few months, our arrangements were such that opportunity for free, uninterrupted thought was almost impossible. My companion suffered from the same cause. We were thrown in each other's way. The children were thrown in our way. The effect on all was depressing.[49]

As if these domestic troubles were not enough, Alcott was again having difficulty with school patrons and enrollments were dwindling. In 1834 he closed the school and gathered up his wife and two daughters and returned to Boston, where, in September, he opened his most successful venture, the Temple School. The Temple School was, however, a success only in comparison with the failures that preceded and followed it. The school enjoyed patronage for a time from some of Boston's most wealthy and influential citizens, but once again Alcott's quixotic temperament landed him in difficulty. As a teaching technique, he developed the notion of "conversations" with the children, convinced that children were founts of divine wisdom, which could be elicited from them with the proper approach. In 1836 he began publishing the results of these conversations under the title, *Conversations with Children on the Gospels*, which scandalized proper Bostonians. Alcott offended conservatives by his contention that children were sources of moral wisdom, and he offended others by publishing the results of a conversation with children about child-birth. Enrollment dwindled and once again Alcott was forced to close a school. He opened another but, ever the idealist, admitted a black girl as a pupil, a move sufficient to bring down on his head again the wrath of popular opinion. In 1839 he closed his last school. For the next twenty years he lacked regular employment, because no one offered him the kind of work for which he felt himself qualified.

Thoreau and Emerson admired Alcott for sticking to principle, but other friends like Elizabeth Peabody hinted that Alcott was going too far, refusing to make distinctions between greater and lesser causes, and, as a result, taking on battle with the entire world at once. Parents who might have tolerated racial integration could not tolerate religious heresy, while others who could stomach both might not accept violation of sexual taboos. There was about Alcott's behavior during the entire series of difficulties a stubborn idealism and a studious innocence that was childish. Alcott accepted the charge, but he would substitute the word *childlike* for *childish* and take it as a compliment. To see the world with the eyes of a child was to see the world with the eyes of an uncompromising radical, and Alcott would make no apology for it. "My style or method," he commented, "is simpler than that of my predecessors. I do not except even the Prophet of Nazareth. I keep closer to Nature. I take the childlike soul as ideal."[50]

After the failure of his Boston school his interest in public issues increased, and it was during this period that he cultivated friendships with Emerson, Garrison, George Ripley, Theodore Parker, Horace Mann, and Margaret Fuller, and began those series of conversations which provided the seedbed for the transcendentalist movement. There was involved here no dramatic abandonment of the family. He kept himself tethered to his wife and daughters, the latter soon to number four. He earned a bit of money from odd jobs, which together with help from Mrs. Alcott's relatives kept them all from starving. Clearly, however, the family no longer commanded his highest loyalty. Anna's diary was recording more frequent and lengthy departures by her father, and Alcott confided to his brother-in-law in 1840 that more than father or mother or wife and child, he must love justice.[51]

38

But Alcott had not given up the vision of an enclave within which the individual could live and remain true to his higher principles. The family would not do, as he had discovered, but neither was he prepared to tamper with the basic union of man, woman, and children. The solution seemed to be to expand the family and bring it into closer relation with other families. The plan, fixed in final form during a six-month visit to England, led to the formation of the Fruitlands community in 1843. Alcott's journal for the period was lost, but a letter, written shortly after the end of the experiment in ideal living, recorded his attitude. "I cannot," he said, "consent to live solely for one family. I would stand in neighborly relations to several, and interpose an internal check to all selfish and narrow interests: institute a union and communion of families, instead of drawing aside within the precincts of one's own acres and kindred by blood."[52] Upon his return from England, therefore, he brought with him two reformers, Charles Lane and Henry Wright, and Lane's son William. Subsequently he lured several more men and one woman to share a Spartan life on a farm purchased by Lane.

As is well known, the Fruitlands community collapsed in six months, although it might be counted as lasting a full year if one includes the initial period during which the English visitors crowded into the Alcott cottage in Concord. The failure of the "consociate family," as Alcott called it, may be laid in large part to that same economic innocence which had kept Alcott's own family in difficult straits during the dozen preceding years. Even when the community restricted its diet to apples, potatoes, and water, Alcott's hopes for economic self-sufficiency could not be realized when he and Lane absented themselves from work to commune with reformers elsewhere. But the more serious difficulty, and the one which defeated the experiment, arose from Alcott's efforts to widen the circle of family intimacy by including the Englishmen. There emerged a quiet but deadly war between Abigail and Charles Lane. Even as Alcott was groping for an ideal community larger than the family, his wife was discovering how much she yearned to lose herself in concern for her children alone. Earlier she had declined an invitation to move in with the Emersons, commenting that she could not "Gee and Haw in another person's Yoke."[53] Charles Lane revived her old fears. He was in fact a poor choice for the consociate family life, for, as Emerson observed, he was not one to confuse society with sociability.[54] To Lane's cold exterior and dictatorial manner must be added Mrs. Alcott's discovery that Lane regarded the family itself as an outmoded form of social organization. He displayed great interest in a nearby Shaker community and tried to persuade Alcott that the only spiritual life was a celibate one. Alcott was caught in the middle, but one must wonder how this man, who should have been well acquainted with his wife and Lane, could have ever supposed they could live together under one roof.

With the failure of Fruitlands, Bronson sank into a deep depression which may have nearly cost him his life. Louisa later recalled that he lay down upon a bed, turned his face to the wall and refused both food and water.[55] For Abigail, the threat that her husband would lose his mind was worse than the possibility of death, as she told her brother at the time: "I do not allow myself to despair of his recovery, but oh, Sam! that piercing thought flashed through my mind of insanity, and a grave yawning to receive his precious body would be to me a consolation compared to that condition of life."[56] As Louisa recalls, it was Abigail who persuaded Bronson to give up his mortal fast, and soon he recovered his physical strength, but the experience left a wound. Alcott seemed to lose all heart for experiments in social organization. He had asked much of himself and others and no one quite measured up. He searched about, looking at other Utopian communities, but all, in one way or another, fell short of his ideal. Neither could he revive any enthusiasm for his family as a spiritual sanctuary. "I will not," he said, "abide in a house set apart for myself and family alone."[57] But there seemed no choice, and so he resided with the family without really being a part of it. He noted in himself a declining interest in his children and, while he regretted the loss of the companionship and intimacy he had enjoyed with them in earlier days, he found his thoughts drifting toward the ideal, which it was evident children no longer represented as they once had. "I am," he said, "not as I once was. I am become recluse and thoughtful in the extreme, and an idealist, from having been a socialist and sentimentalist as extreme in days past."[58] With his thoughts went his energies, and the family fell deeper into poverty, with the eventual result that Mrs. Alcott was forced to seek employment and to send her adolescent daughters out to labor also.

If the family and the community had failed Alcott, it was equally evident that he had failed them. Both the troubles of his family and the failure of Fruitlands may be traced to the fact that he was unsuited for the leadership of any form of social organization. His quest for perfection, which initially led him to deify the family, excluded the calculation and compromise without which no institution can long endure. It was to Alcott's credit that he recognized the dilemma. As he saw it, the world afforded him no honorable work to do, but he noted the effect on his family and believed that his transcendental conscience, which commanded him to follow the ideal, would be unlikely to forgive him for failing to manage the things of the world also. For himself he did not regret the want of sympathy, support, and success, for that is often the lot of the philosopher. But, he added, "to the thinker's family, if he have one, it is no small matter, but a serious one, and for the wrongs it suffers there is, nor can be, no recompense."[59]

Bronson Alcott's concern for the welfare of his family was well justified and it was a concern fully shared by his wife. It was not that Abigail thought her husband's principles were wrong. She fiercely defended him against his detractors. To her brother she wrote:

> If I do not mistake the spirit as well as the letter of your remark, you would have us believe that a righteous retribution has overtaken us (or my husband, and we are one) and that the world is justly punishing him for not having conciliated it by conforming to its will and ways. . . . Is he to sell his soul, or what is the same thing, his principles, for the bread that perisheth? No one will employ him in this way; he cannot work in theirs, if he thereby involve his conscience.

She and her children were, Abigail admitted, "necessarily implicated" in this decision, and they were determined to make all sacrifices necessary to see it through.[60]

The girls found poverty difficult to bear, though they, like their mother, stood in awe of their father's principles. Anna, at age eight, found her father to be "the best man in the world," and she struggled to obey her conscience as he had taught her.[61] It was especially hard, however, not to have Thanksgiving dinner, and it became increasingly difficult for the girls to maintain a brave front, especially as it became evident that the Utopian experiment at Fruitlands was turning into a disaster.[62] Louisa, no more than her mother, could abide Charles Lane, and she became aware that there was talk of her father's abandoning the family to join Lane in a Shaker community. Suddenly, the vulnerability of the family became evident to the ten-year-old girl: "I did my lessons, and walked in the afternoon. Father read to us in dear Pilgrim's Progress. Mr. L was in Boston and we were glad. In the eve father and mother and Anna and I had a long talk. I was very unhappy, and we all cried. Anna and I cried in bed, and I prayed God to keep us all together."[63]

Louisa's prayer was answered, but although the family remained together, it was on the basis of charity from friends and relatives, from a small legacy which Abigail received from her father, from such small pay as Bronson could earn from odd jobs and from his philosophical "conversations," and most important of all, from the labor of Abigail and the girls. For Louisa the family's financial trouble was yet another wound to her already low self-esteem. From the time she was seven until she reached adulthood she was to share with her mother and her sisters the humiliation of poverty, made even more complex by her confusion about her role as a woman. She reacted first with despair and finally with a deep anger that made its way into her writing, sometimes in disguised ways. As a result, her literary portrait of family life, while conforming in important respects to the sentimental vision, ultimately broke free of this vision and projected a new ideal of relations between husbands and wives and between parents and children.

Growing Up Female and
the Family Claim

In 1860, at the age of twenty-seven, Louisa witnessed her sister Anna and her husband in their honeymoon cottage and commented, "Very sweet and pretty, but I'd rather be a free spinster and paddle my own canoe."[1] Louisa thus revealed an identity that put her at odds with what antebellum America thought proper for a woman. It was, as she fully recognized, an identity that matched her temperament. Never, even as a small child, had she gladly played the role that society considered proper behavior for a girl. As a woman, she admitted that she thoroughly enjoyed the feeling of independence that she had achieved. But Louisa was no twentieth-century feminist, at least not in her early years, and she did not justify her lonely course in life by referring to any right of "self-fulfillment." Always she must explain her independent life and her growing fame and fortune as a matter of duty to the family. Certainly, the needs of the family were real enough before she found fortune in her children's books, but even after she became wealthy she continued to portray herself as a galley slave chained to her obligations. Nineteenth-century America cut women out for self-sacrifice, not for self-fulfillment, and Louisa was in this regard thoroughly a product of her time.

Both parents contributed much to Louisa's eccentric course. Her debt to her mother was obvious and acknowledged, for Abigail provided her daughter both encouragement and a model for imitation. Abigail was a writer of considerable talent, and although she never wrote for publication, her letters and diaries possess a vigor of expression that is reflected in the best of Louisa's writing. Bronson's influence on his daughter's emerging identity was more complex and ambiguous but nonetheless real. He could provide no model for his daughter as a writer for, unlike Abigail, Bronson had no ear for words, a fact which he came to recognize with considerable regret.[2] If he could supply no example as a writer, he nevertheless provided a powerful and constant model of ambition itself. It was, to be sure, no petty ambition and it had nothing to do with money. Bronson yearned for fame as a philosopher, and he hungered for nothing less than spiritual perfection. As we have seen, he would sacrifice himself and even his family in an effort to achieve it. Louisa herself renounced Bronson's "principles," as she called his reform ideas, especially once she witnessed the price they exacted, but ambition itself remained a constant lure and this urge alone marked her as her father's daughter. In 1856, at the age of twenty-four and a full twelve years before she won acclaim with *Little Women,* Louisa announced with ferocity, "I'll be famous yet."[3]

None of this was apparent during Louisa's teenage years, when the family was struggling for survival, but it was evident that Abigail even then was giving hard thought to the matter of woman's role generally and to the futures of her daughters in particular. As she attempted to view her offspring objectively, she concluded that they would turn out to be neither "wits" not "beauties," and so they must have a trade of some kind.[4] The object should be, she thought, "putting the girls in a way to do something for themselves, without being driven from home for support and to be spared that most afflictive of all conditions—dependence on relatives."[5] Much of the problem, she thought, lay in the education of girls:

> Many of the evils of Woman's life may be traced to the want of education of the Senses. They do not see clearly, hear distinctly, feel deeply. Thus, when they describe anything, they are not quite sure of the distance or color. When they tell anything it is quite certain their statement is a good deal modified, and inaccurate—and their sensations are false or feeble. Girls are taught to seem, to appear, not to be and do. Costume, not armour, dress, not panoply, is the covering for woman.[6]

Abigail attempted to convey some of her thoughts to Bronson, but when she spoke of their daughters' need for "some trade, art or accomplishment by which they can get support," he responded merely by directing, "Make no arrangements for them. The place or work will come when they are prepared."[7]

All the talk about improving the education of girls did little, of course, to solve the immediate needs of the family, and Abigail reluctantly concluded that she would have to take over direction of the family's practical affairs. As she told her brother: "I have taken the Ship into my own command but whether I shall do better as captain than I have as mate, the revenue and record of the years must decide. At least I think I shall keep better soundings, and ascertain oftener and more correctly whether I am sailing in deep waters or in shallows."[8]

Somehow or other the older girls must be put to work earning money, which meant sewing, housekeeping, and above all, teaching. Anna, the oldest, was the first to respond to the family's needs. By the age of thirteen she was "keeping school" for her younger sisters in the home, and by the age of fifteen she added neighboring children to the group. Enrollment was small, and it became evident to both Anna and her mother that she would have to leave home in order to make any money at teaching. Bronson disliked the idea, since he could not stand the thought of his daughters leaving home, but Anna and her mother persisted, and when she was sixteen Anna had departed for Walpole, New Hampshire, to live with a relative and keep school. For the next ten years, she labored at schoolkeeping, sending most of her money home to the family.

Despite her efforts, Anna proved to be a slender reed for Mrs. Alcott to lean on. She was given to moodiness and dreaming, losing herself in imagining how things might be for her if she were rich. When she spoke of education, she dreamed of a fashionable girls' school, and when she spoke of beautiful things, she meant fine clothes and elegant surroundings. She suffered under the necessity of laboring in the homes of others and, on occasion of her family visits, she resented the shabby gentility into which the Alcotts had fallen. As Abigail explained in a letter to her brother:

Home has fewer attractions than ever [for Anna], as labour with many privations, and some hardships is the only promise winter makes us in prospect. Lizzy and Louisa are rather higher metal. . . .

Anna suffers when there is not order, gentleness and genteel surroundings. Her big eyes see the battered furniture, the odd chairs,
mother's unkempt head at the breakfast table. I often threaten to
banish her from the premises until our ship arrives, or at least until
it's telegraphed.[9]

Here at least was evidence that Alcott had failed in his effort to
transform his oldest daughter into a self-sacrificing saint who found
in poverty a virtue. Anna allowed that poor people perhaps love one
another better than rich ones, but, as she wrote from Walpole:

I never realized how very poor we are as I do here with everything
beautiful and abundant around me, and everyone seems to be comfortable, easy and free from the care and constant struggle which has
for so many years been ours to feel and bear, and it seems like a lovely
dream to me to have time to enjoy myself, rest and do most what I
like.[10]

Eventually, in 1860, Anna was to settle happily into marriage with
John Pratt and rear two children. It was not what she had dreamed of,
but the modest security which Pratt (and later, Louisa) provided
suited her notions of the good life.

Despite Anna's efforts the family continued to flounder, and Mrs.
Alcott resolved that she would have to do more herself, which meant
work outside the home, although neither her husband nor her daughters were happy about the decision. Her initial experiment in the
marketplace occurred in the summer of 1848, and consisted of a job
as a matron in a health resort in Waterford, Maine. Upon her return,
she decided that she would move the family to Boston, where she
would take a post as charity agent for the women's societies of several
Unitarian churches. Her job consisted of distributing food to the
poor and finding employment for poor women, a problem with
which she was all too familiar. Unfortunately, as it turned out,
Abigail shared with her husband a temperamental difficulty in sur-
viving in the marketplace. She was a dedicated, efficient organizer,
but she could not resist giving lectures to her employers for not doing
more to cure the causes of poverty. As a result, she lost her job in
April of 1850. A short time later the crowning blow was delivered.
The entire family, with the exception of Anna, was stricken with

smallpox. It was without doubt the nadir of the Alcott family fortunes.

Although never swerving in her loyalty to Bronson's principles, Abigail began to betray signs of impatience with her idle husband. Apart from his various reform activities, Bronson had busied himself with tinkering and gardening at the family home in Concord, and by giving instruction to his daughters. In 1849 he conceived the idea of holding "conversations" with adults on philosophical topics, but the activity, while intellectually stimulating, earned the family no income. In 1852, a genealogical impulse seized him, and he spent time visiting his boyhood home conducting research on his family. It was during one of his visits that Abigail wrote him, confessing her embarrassment at being asked by so many, "What is Mr. A. doing?"[11] In response, Bronson bestirred himself and actually earned some money by his conversations. Pleased, Abigail pointed out to him, "With all the efforts of the female part of the family, they could not produce in six months much more than you have in six weeks." "This shows," she added, "the incompetent wages paid to all female labor and proves the greater value of intellectual labour over manual or any service performed by women." "It is evident," she concluded, "the great advantage of your being in the market rather than the wife or maids."[12] Besides, Abigail took her duties as a mother seriously, and, as she told her brother, her place was in the home with her children.[13]

What the Alcott family evidently needed was someone tough enough and shrewd enough to survive in the marketplace, and that person proved to be Louisa. There seemed never any doubt that she would play the role, for the family claim was laid on her at a very early age. Already at the age of eleven, Louisa received from her desperate mother a picture which showed a daughter taking care of her aged mother. The picture was accompanied by a note: "I enclose a picture for you which I always admired very much, for I have imagined that you might be just such an industrious daughter, and I such a feeble but loving mother, looking to your labor for my daily bread."[14]

Louisa, always the closest of the daughters to her mother, responded to her mother's appeal, sometimes with resentment but always with determined resolution to fill the role which her father had vacated. In large measure it was a determination born out of gratitude to the one person in her life who accepted her "peculiar temperament." At the age of thirteen Louisa wrote: "I have made a plan for my life, as I am in my teens, and no more a child. I am old for my age, and don't care much for girl's things. People think I'm wild and queer; but Mother understands and helps me. I have not told anyone about my plan; but I'm going to *be* good. . . . Now I'm going to *work really*, for I feel a true desire to improve, and be a help and comfort, not a care and sorrow, to my dear mother."[15]

In the face of such resolution, marriage never became a matter of serious consideration to Louisa. It was not that she felt no attraction to men, but they were always much older or younger than herself and therefore ineligible as husbands. She developed a childish infatuation for her father's friends, first Thoreau and then Emerson:

> My romantic period began at fifteen, when I fell to writing poetry, keeping a heart-journal, and wandering by moonlight instead of sleeping quietly. About that time, in browsing over Mr. Emerson's library, I found "Goethe's correspondence with a Child," and at once was fired with a desire to be a Bettine, making my father's friend my Goethe. So I wrote letters to him, but never sent them; sat in a tall cherry tree at midnight, singing to the moon till the owls scared me to bed; left wild flowers on the doorstep of my "Master," and sung Mignon's song under his window in very bad German.[16]

For years she clung to her worship of Emerson. When, at the age of twenty-eight, she saw him kiss the bride at Anna's wedding, Louisa remarked, "I thought that honor would make even matrimony endurable, for he is the god of my idolatry, and has been for years."[17] Less openly acknowledged was her admiration of Henry Thoreau, but he was unmarried and therefore dangerous. The most she could permit herself was to make him the model for several of the heroes in her novels, and, on the occasion of his death in 1862, to compose a poem which contained the following lines:

> We sighing said, "Our Pan is dead;
> His pipe hangs mute beside the river;
> Around it wistful sunbeams quiver,

48

> But Music's airy voice is fled.
> Spring mourns as for untimely frost;
> The bluebird chants a requiem;
> The willow-blossom waits for him;—
> The Genius of the wood is lost."[18]

If Louisa was attracted to men, it was also true that she had her male admirers, despite her peculiar ways and despite the fact that, being unusually tall, she did not conform to popular notions of petite femininity. Always, however, she refused to take seriously their interest in her. At the age of twenty-eight she wrote:

Had a funny lover who met me in the cars, and said he lost his heart at once. Handsome man of forty. A Southerner, and very demonstrative and gushing, called and wished to pay his addresses; and being told I didn't wish to see him, retired, to write letters and haunt the road with his hat off, while the girls laughed and had great fun. . . . He went at last, and peace reigned. My adorers are all queer.[19]

Louisa's rejection of potential suitors lay in the fact that she possessed extremely high standards when it came to judging men, while her mother's suffering had not provided her with much optimism about marriage itself. As she once remarked, though she knew little of married life, she well knew that there were very few happy marriages.[20] Marriage meant subservience, and if her mother's experience provided any guide, it would be subservience without the compensation of financial security. Marriage also meant children, and Louisa was beginning to learn that she, unlike her sister Anna, had little patience with small people. Consequently, as she reached marriageable age, she talked more of independence. At the age of twenty-four she told her father, "I like the independent feeling; and though not an easy life, it is a free one, and I enjoy it. I can't do much with my hands; so I will make a battering ram of my head, and make a way through this rough-and-tumble world."[21] Necessity and the call of family duty made it easier and easier for her to embrace the temperament that made her a tomboy and to forge out of it her adult identity: "I was born with a boy's spirit under my bib and tucker. I *can't wait* when I *can work*."[22]

If marriage was never a serious option for Louisa, it was altogether a different matter with regard to the question of making a living. As she struggled to fulfill the family claim on her energy and talent, the real issue became to prevent necessity from dragging her into a mere job when what she desired was a career. In 1850, when Louisa was only seventeen and the family's fortunes were at a new low, the prospects for a career did not appear promising. For a young woman with no connections and no training, the opportunities included only factory work, domestic service, sewing, and, following in Anna's footsteps, teaching. Louisa seems never to have considered factory work, but she had always liked sewing, and kept at it over the next decade, though she knew it was not thought respectable. Teaching paid better and was more respectable, but she quickly discovered that she was not temperamentally suited for the job: "I like it better than I thought, though it's very hard to be patient with the children sometimes. They seem happy, and learn fast; so I am encouraged, though at first it was very hard . . . for as a *school-marm* I must behave myself and guard my tongue and temper carefully, and set an example of sweet manners."[23] "Sweet manners" were never Louisa's strong point, as she well recognized, and a month later she confessed that "school is hard work, and I feel as though I should like to run away from it. But my children get on; so I travel up every day, and do my best."[24] It is a measure of Louisa's determination that she stuck with the unpleasant task for another nine years, off and on, though hating every minute of it.

Working in other people's homes provided still another source of income for Louisa, although it proved to be even less congenial than teaching. At the age of eighteen, Louisa discovered the degradation confronted by women who were poor, and out of this experience came a major theme in her writing. In 1851 a bachelor lawyer came to Abigail seeking a companion for his sister and his father, promising only "light" housework. Louisa persuaded Abigail to allow her to take the job, but it proved to be a mistake. As her mother commented at the time, "Louisa has gone to do housework for a small family in Dedham, but every instinct of her being revolts against it and I am not sure how long she will remain."[25] As it turned out, the employer expected her to be more of a companion to himself than to his sister or his father, and when Louisa discouraged his advances, he doubled her housekeeping duties. The ultimate degradation in her eyes came when he ordered her to black his boots, whereupon she quit, carrying home only a pittance for seven weeks of insult and hard labor. The experience only confirmed Louisa's low estimation of most men and strengthened her resolution to make money by any means other than service. Even teaching and serving as a governess, distasteful as she found these tasks, were more welcome. These duties, together with sewing, enabled her to place an average of over a hundred dollars annually in the family coffers over a period of eight years.[26]

While struggling to make a living, Louisa kept one eye out for the elusive chance for a career. For a brief time she thought of nursing, but acting was the only profession that seriously rivaled writing for Louisa's loyalty. As a girl she had written plays and performed in them, usually playing the male roles. At the age of eleven she confessed an admiration for the singer Jenny Lind and, at the age of eighteen, she suffered from a serious case of stage fever: "Anna wants to be an actress, and so do I. We could make plenty of money perhaps, and it is a very gay life. Mother says we are too young, and must wait. A. acts often splendidly. I like tragic plays, and shall be a Siddons if I can. We get up fine ones, and make harps, castles, armour, dresses, water-falls, and thunder, and have great fun."[27] The lure of acting struck again from time to time, and as late as the age of twenty-seven Louisa was wondering to herself if she was not meant to be an actress more than a writer. The difficulty with a stage career was that it provided an uncertain source of income, and it was not yet considered by the family as a proper activity for a young woman. When it became known that she was seriously considering a dramatic role, "the dear, respectable relations were horrified at the idea," Louisa commented. Reluctantly she agreed to put aside her ambition, but she was desperate to find a way to discover and use her talent. "Nature," she said, "must have a vent somehow."[28] She loved the theater all her life, but as she began to think of herself more and more as a writer, she contented herself with writing plays (one of which was produced), and with peopling her stories with actresses and would-be actresses. Perhaps, as she suggested in her autobiographical novel, *Work*, she simply decided that she might "make a clever actress, never a great one."[29] Like her father, she was not one to be satisfied with half-measures.

In retrospect, therefore, it appears that a writing career was inevitable. Both parents insisted that the girls keep diaries, but it was Abigail who provided constant support and encouragement. At the age of eight Louisa wrote a poem, and it may not have been mere maternal pride that led Abigail to prophesy, "You will grow up a Shakespeare!"[30] Further encouragement from Abigail included a pencil case at the age of ten, a pen at the age of fourteen, and always a stream of praise and admonition, usually delivered in comments in Louisa's diary or in letters to her daughter.[31] In response, Louisa composed more poetry and turned to writing blood and thunder dramas for production by her sisters and herself. She won from Anna the admission that Louisa was the better writer.[32] By the age of sixteen, Louisa was setting down fairy tales and poems with the thought of publishing a children's book.[33]

The humiliation of domestic service galvanized Louisa into action to further her career. She realized that she would have to get something into print, although she was not yet prepared to offer anything to the public with her name on it. Within a few months after the unhappy experience as a servant in Dedham, she devised a compromise, sending a poem to *Peterson's Magazine* with the name "Flora Fairfield" attached. The appearance of the poem in September 1851 made her, at the age of eighteen, a published author. Encouraged, Louisa next sent off a story which she had written three years earlier. Entitled "The Rival Painters," it told of two Florentine painters who competed for the hand of a lovely lady. "Great rubbish," Louisa called it, and it earned her only five dollars, but it was her first prose composition to be published, and it appeared this time over her initials, providing her with needed reassurance that she was, indeed, becoming a writer.[34]

Two years later Flora Fairfield earned twice as much publishing a story for the *Saturday Evening Gazette* under the title "The Rival Prima Donnas," a story which revealed that this daughter of the serene transcendentalist philosopher nourished a fascination for violence; the tale ended with one singer crushing the head of her competitor with an iron ring. Something of a milestone was reached in her slowly evolving identity as a writer when she decided to append her own name to a work called *Flower Fables*, which consisted of a collection of poems and fairy tales for children. Sure that her mother would approve, she made of her book a Christmas present to Abigail in 1854: "Into your Christmas stocking I have put my 'first-born,' knowing that you will accept it with all its faults (for grandmothers are always kind), and look upon it merely as an earnest of what I may yet do."[35] *Flower Fables* earned her thirty-five dollars, not as much as she made by teaching that year, but more than she could earn by sewing. Encouraged, she threw herself more into writing, retreating to the house garret and surrounding herself with papers and piles of apples while she wrote in her journal and planned stories. With satisfaction, she reflected: "My book came out; and people began to think that topsey-turvey Louisa would amount to something after all, since she could do so well as housemaid, teacher, seamstress and story-teller. Perhaps she may."[36] Within a short time, she had completed nine stories for the *Saturday Evening Gazette*, each of which earned her ten dollars, and for the first time, at the age of twenty-three, she earned as much money in a year from her writing as from sewing and teaching combined.

Having established to her own satisfaction her identity as a writer, she began to seek some degree of independence from her parents. Although she would continue to work for the family, she would do it at a distance if at all possible. She left home for the first time to take up lodging with a family in Boston, working furiously on writing and selling her stories. Another and more subtle declaration of independence came in her effort to secure more perspective on her father. Bronson had, in fact, decided in 1857 that he would attempt to "take the reins a little more firmly in hand" and, as he told his daughters, they could rely upon him for "labour and money."[37] It was beginning to rankle Bronson that Louisa had been forced into service. As he told Anna, "I don't relish *the Governess* in proud people's palaces for any child of mine. There is no better blood nor more noble, to pride upon in any family in Boston into which she may enter or serve, than flows in her own veins and holds itself to the old nobilities still."[38]

Bronson's resolve came, however, a bit late—seven years too late, in fact—and Louisa was beginning to lose the awe with which she, like the other Alcott women, had regarded him. Shortly after putting some distance between herself and her father, she wrote him a loving but condescending letter:

I know you were a serene and placid baby when you began your wise mediations in the quiet little Spindle hill farm house (I believe that's where you descended from on high) looking philosophically out of your cradle at the big world about you and smiling as seriously and affectionately at the young motherly face bent over you, as now when you bend over that same kind face. . . . Fifty-six years have passed since then, and that peaceful baby's golden head is silver now, but the man looks as serenely at the big foolish world and meditates as wisely as he did in his cradle, and nothing but the lines on his face where troubles have been, and four tall women at his side, shows that years and trials have changed the wise little child into a wiser old man. Surely, dear father, some good angel, an elf, dropped a talisman in your cradle that gave you power to walk through life in quiet sunshine while others groped in the dark.[39]

Thus she was able to find some acceptance of herself as well as to grant a kind of forgiveness to her father. Nevertheless, she was not above delivering a barbed reminder to her father that she had taken on the task as the family breadwinner: "Things go smoothly, and I think I shall come out right, and prove that though an *Alcott* I *can* support myself."[40]

Only once did Louisa falter in her resolution, and that only momentarily. At the age of twenty-five, she walked over the milldam in Boston and thought of throwing herself into the water. Two events had set the scene for this terrible impulse. One was the death of her angelic sister, Elizabeth, who was stricken by scarlet fever. The other was the engagement of Anna to John Pratt. The death and the engagement threatened Louisa's as yet fragile identity, which was forming around the idea that she was the sole salvation of the family. Beth had needed her and now Beth was gone. Anna's engagement then reinforced a feeling that Louisa would be alone and possibly useless: "I moaned in private over my great loss, and said I'd never forgive J. for taking Anna from me; but I shall if he makes her happy, and turn to little May for comfort."[41] When she stood on the milldam, thoughts of her duty to the remaining members of the family helped her put down the suicidal impulse. It seemed, she said, "so cowardly to run away before the battle was over I couldn't do it." She told herself firmly that there was work for her, and so, she "went home resolved to take fate by the throat and shake a living out of her."[42]

For the rest of her life she labored for the family until ill health forced her to retire from that duty. Shortly before her death she commented: "The learning not to do is so hard after being the hub to the family wheel so long. But it is good for the energetic ones to find out that the world can get on without them."[43] She died two days after her father, and was buried across the feet of her father, her mother, and her sister Beth.

Although Louisa's dedication to her family was awesome, and although it provided her life with meaning, it did not sum up her ambition. She wished to make money and she wished to be famous, but above all she wished to be known as a serious writer. The publication of her first story in 1852 fired her ambition to read "fewer novels, and those only of the best."[44] Keeping herself busy with the publication of poems, plays and stories for children, nevertheless she longed, as she told her mother, "to pass in time from fairies and fables to men and realities."[45] She continued to publish what she called "rubbish," but she began to dream of writing a novel. Having surmounted the emotional crisis that led her to the milldam, Louisa took new heart and plunged once again into writing, but with more at stake than a mere living, important though that continued to be. Soon she was dreaming of her "great book," something that would earn her prestige as well as profit.[46] The book would not appear for another seven years, but she had in mind a more immediate project which, she hoped, would win the attention of literary circles. She set her sights on a story for the *Atlantic Monthly*, recently launched under the direction of no less a personage than the poet James Russell Lowell. "There's ambition for you!" she exclaimed, and set to work.[47] When her story was accepted, she was ecstatic:

> Hurrah! My story was accepted; and Lowell asked if it was not a translation from the German, it was so unlike most tales. I felt much set up, and my fifty dollars will be very happy money. People seem to think it a great thing to get into the "Atlantic;" but I've not been pegging away all these years in vain, and may yet have books and publishers and a fortune of my own. Success has gone to my head, and I wander a little. Twenty-seven years old, and very happy.[48]

Such admissions of joy in achievement and recognition were rare for Louisa and became rarer still as she grew older. In part her growing pessimism resulted from the fact that the literary acclaim she sought constantly eluded her. In part also it was due to the poor health from which she suffered constantly after an illness incurred while serving as a nurse during the Civil War. In larger measure, however, Louisa found it difficult to admit the naked desire for self-fulfillment, and she fell into the more comfortable and more familiar role as martyr to the family's needs. It seems, then, that Bronson had made two entirely inadvert contributions to Louisa's career as a writer. In the first place, his failings as a breadwinner had provided his daughter with a series of painful experiences as she made her way alone in a man's world, a theme that dominates much of her writing. If an unhappy adolescence is a prerequisite for success as a writer, then Louisa's life amply illustrates that relationship. There was, however, a second and still more ironic sense in which Bronson's refusal to play the role of breadwinner fostered Louisa's ambitions. By laying on her the duty of supporting the family, Bronson provided his second-born with the outer justification for an inner impulse. Even after success made self-sacrifice no longer a necessity, Louisa clung to the family claim as proof that she was no mere self-seeker, thus legitimizing her pursuit of fame and fortune. Such was the legacy of growing up female in the midst of the sentimental revolution.

4

Three Audiences and Three Images
of Young Womanhood

For thirty-seven years, from 1851 until her death in 1888, Louisa May Alcott ushered into print a total of two hundred and seventy publications, including sketches, poems, travel books, plays, stories, and novels.[1] Virtually all of this prodigious output dealt with domestic themes, set usually in the kitchen or the parlor or the drawing room, and concerned mostly with courtship, marriage, and family life. The most popular and best-known works were, of course, those written for a juvenile audience, but eighteen years passed after the first publication of her writing before she won fame and fortune with *Little Women.* Those eighteen years were spent, for the most part, in efforts to reach an audience of adults. On one hand, as we have seen, she set off in pursuit of literary acclaim. The publication of "Love and Self-Love" by the *Atlantic Monthly* was followed by a valiant bid to reach an adult audience of the cultural elite in the hope of placing her name among the ranks of respected authors. One result was the publication of *Hospital Sketches,* based on her experience as a nurse in an army hospital during the Civil War, and another was her first novel, *Moods,* published in 1865. Meanwhile, out of necessity, she continued to mine for popular magazines the sensational ore that she had struck with her early stories. From 1863 until 1869 she turned out a series of thrillers, always without her name attached.[2] After the success of *Little Women* she gave up the production of sensational stories and concentrated her efforts on juvenile fiction, making only two major efforts after 1869 to reach an adult audience—the first being her autobiographical novel, *Work,* which was published in 1872, and the second being *A Modern Mephistopheles,* which appeared anonymously in 1877.

57

As a writer, Alcott was a consummate professional. She kept firmly in mind the character of her audience as she wrote, and each type of literature—literary, juvenile, and sensational—reflected an aspect of her family experience. Each also projected a different image of young womanhood. Surprisingly, it was not her juvenile fiction that proved to be the most conventional. For her literary audience she created stock, sentimental heroines who inevitably fall victim to their own passivity and weakness. In her sensational fiction, on the other hand, she indulged herself with the portrayal of a series of *femmes fatales* who are more inclined to inflict suffering than to endure it. Assured of anonymity, Alcott allowed herself to run riot, and produced a set of decidedly unsentimental heroines. For the children she created an entirely new image of woman, neither sentimental nor sensational, but rather a compound of her victimized literary heroines and her vengeful sensational women. The surprising result was the achievement in her children's fiction of a woman who resembled most closely the complexity that was herself.

THE LITERARY VISION: EFFIE AND SYLVIA

It was in her literary fiction that Alcott conformed most closely to the sentimental heritage of antebellum America in a vain effort to win favor from her literary peers. Here one finds in full flower the cult of romantic love, replete with innocent young women who suffer because they enter into marriage with men they do not love, or with men who do not love them. A hint of the literary vision was contained in "Love and Self-Love," which presents a set of characters straight out of sentimenal fiction.[3] Here we find a tender maiden, Effie, who is an orphan and an angel-child: vulnerable, loving, and self-sacrificing. A man, Basil Ventnor, is the source of Effie's difficulties, and he describes himself as a "cold, selfish man, often gloomy, often stern."[4] Basil has redeeming features, however. He is himself a victim, having been wronged by Agnes, a vain and beautiful woman who rejected his love and married another. Moreover, though Basil is selfish, he is capable of compassion. When Effie's dying guardian pleads with him to marry the young girl so that she will have a home, Basil agrees, although he does not love her. This rash decision, made out of misplaced pity, is the source of subsequent unhappiness. Basil, his mind still on the unfaithful Agnes, is unable to return Effie's love and she gradually wilts under his cold indifference. Alcott does not, however, deprive her readers of a happy ending, for "love," in the person of Effie, ultimately conquers "self-love," in the person of Basil. Coming to love Effie for her self-sacrificing devotion, Basil finds her to be "a household spirit the daily benediction of whose presence banished sorrow, selfishness, and gloom, and, through the influence of happy human love, led me to a truer faith in the Divine."[5] Although the story rings false and superficial to modern ears, it accurately reflected the taste of respectable readers in the mid-nineteenth century.

Even as she was enjoying the reception accorded "Love and Self-Love," there was fermenting in Alcott's imagination a much more ambitious work, which would present a more somber though no less sentimental view of marriage. Begun in the summer of 1860, *Moods* was to be her "great book," and the writing of it became for her an obsession.[6] She noted that "Genius burned so fiercely that for four weeks I wrote all day and planned nearly all night, being quite possessed by my work."[7] Unfortunately, the fruits of this obsession did not appear in print for another five years and represented, in its final version, a tug of war between Alcott and her family, on one hand, and Alcott and her publishers on the other. Eager to produce a book that would win the approval of the respectable, she consulted the members of her family at every step, and made drastic cuts in obedience to her publisher's demands. She revised it several times, omitted ten chapters from the final version, yet suffered agonies that she may have "ventured too much."[8] In a thinly disguised comment on the entire episode, she observed in *Little Women*: "So, with Spartan firmness, the young authoress laid her first-born on her table, and chopped it up as ruthlessly as any ogre. In the hope of pleasing everyone, she took everyone's advice, and, like the old man and his donkey in the fable, suited nobody."[9] We shall never know just what the story might have been had Louisa ignored family and publishers, but the published version provides at least a clue to the compromises that the desire for respectability entailed.

The central character in *Moods* proved to be a more subtly shaded character than Effie, stripped of her infallibility and resembling more Alcott herself. The title of the work provides the key to the heroine's faulty character. Sylvia Yule is a volatile young woman, easily swayed by impulses which frequently lead her astray. As the novel opens, she is a young girl who is given to naughty pranks and who dislikes lap dogs, novels, and lovers—a clear harbinger of Jo March. Unlike Jo, however, Sylvia is a member of an affluent family, and she is the pampered favorite of her father, her brother, and her older sister Prudence. As is the case with so many of Alcott's heroines, Sylvia has no mother, which is part of her difficulty. But, as the reader eventually learns, blame must be assigned in greater part to her father. John Yule might have been a poet, painter, or philanthropist—might have been more like Bronson, in other words—but instead he settled for making money as a merchant. Worse, he married out of greed a woman he did not love, in defiance of sentimental canons. The resulting marriage was an unhappy one for both and led eventually to the death of Sylvia's mother, presumably the victim of a broken heart. Somehow—the exact mechanism is never made clear—this unholy union of conflicting temperaments saddled Sylvia with her unstable character. There was in her, "mysteriously blended, the two natures that had given her life, although she was born when the gulf between regretful husband and sad wife was widest. As if indignant Nature rebelled against the outrage done her holiest ties, adverse temperaments gifted the child with the good and ill of each."[10] From her father she inherited pride and intellect; from her mother passion, imagination, and the "fateful melancholy" of a woman disappointed in life. "These two masters ruled soul and body, warring against each other, making Sylvia an enigma to herself and her life a train of moods."[11]

In Sylvia one finds, then, the sentimental stereotype of woman: romantic, confused, inept, impulsive. She is unable to accept a practical, old-fashioned view of marriage, like that held by her aptly named sister, Prudence. Prudence is unburdened by Sylvia's sensitivity and emotional complexity. At the ripe age of thirty-five she accepts the proposal of a portly widower who has outlived three wives and is looking for a fourth to care for his nine children, discipline his unruly servants, and bring some order into his chaotic household.

Dismissing considerations of love, Prudence defends her decision by telling Sylvia, "I shall be happy, for I shall be busy."[12]

Sylvia, on the other hand, is doomed to fall madly in love with a man unsuited for marriage. In Adam Warwick she finds the "perfect man"—tall, broad-shouldered, manly, strong-limbed, a lover of nature, bronzed by wind and weather, possessed of a beard, an "eminent" nose, and piercing eyes. Clearly modeled on Henry Thoreau, Adam is also "violently virtuous," as Sylvia's brother tells her, and "much given to denunciation of wrong-doing everywhere, and eager to execute justice upon all offenders high or low." Adam is also an adventurer who values his liberty and scorns the hypocrisy and deceit that he believes characterize relationships between men and women.

A conventional plot would have Sylvia marrying Adam and living to regret it. Alcott, however, poses for Sylvia a different set of complications. Adam is already engaged to another woman, whereupon Sylvia commits the cardinal violation of sentimental standards: in a fit of impulse and disappointment, she marries a man she likes but does not love. To make matters worse, Sylvia's husband is also a friend of Adam and is, without doubt, the most patient and long-suffering male Alcott ever created in her fiction.

Although Sylvia was a young woman familiar enough to nineteenth-century American readers, Alcott provided in her first novel a twist that set her book apart from most sentimental fiction, and that stirred considerable agitation among the reading public. Sylvia has sinned and Sylvia must suffer, to be sure, but Louisa raised in a frank manner the possibility of ending unhappy marriages by separation. Embedded in the novel is a conversation involving Adam, Sylvia, Sylvia's sister Prudence, and a close woman friend, Faith, who speaks for the author. The conversation concerns a young girl who married an old man for his money and then ran away from him when she realized that she did not love him. When Sylvia finds excuses for the girl, Prudence, faithful to her name, is shocked: "You young girls think so much of love, so little of moral obligations, decorum, and the opinions of the world, you are not fit judges of the case."[13] When Adam sides with Sylvia, Prudence appeals to Faith for support, but she agrees with Sylvia, at least in part. It is wrong to marry out of any motive but love, she advises, and yet, once the fatal mistake has been committed, and assuming that one partner wishes to continue the relationship, the other is obligated to abide by the contract until it is apparent that love cannot be awakened. Then and only then is separation permissible.

In obedience to Faith's advice, Sylvia tries to remain faithful to her husband, but at last he senses that a secret mars their intimacy. She inadvertently reveals a hint of it in a sleepwalking episode and he forces her to confess fully her deception and her love for Adam. Furious, he leaves her. Sylvia flees to Faith for advice, and she warns against marriage to Adam. Love, although a necessary condition for marriage, is not sufficient, and Faith quite candidly tells Sylvia that she is not good enough for Adam. For one thing, she is too confused, both mentally and emotionally, to take on the sacred responsibilities of marriage and children. In any event she is not a strong enough person to deal with Adam.

Sylvia accepts this advice and, since she believes she can no longer live with her husband, she resolves to repent of her sins alone, and then dies. In an aside, the author sounds the sentimental theme of melancholy and suffering, which is the fate of women:

> She had joined that sad sisterhood called disappointed women; a larger class than many deem it to be, though there are few of us who have not seen members of it. Unhappy wives; mistaken or forsaken lovers; meek souls, who make life a long penance for the sins of others; gifted creatures kindled into fitful brilliancy by some inward fire that consumes but cannot warm. These are the women who fly to convents, write bitter books, sing songs full of heartbreak, act splendidly the passion they have lost or never won. Who smile, and try to lead brave uncomplaining lives, but whose tragic eyes betray them, whose voices, however sweet or gay, contain an undertone of hopelessness, whose faces sometimes startle one with an expression which haunts the observer long after it is gone.[14]

The autobiographical elements are apparent, but Sylvia is altogether too passive to resemble the author. Although Alcott, like Sylvia, feared marriage, she did not permit herself to drift into it because she had nothing else to occupy her mind.

With pride, Alcott presented *Moods* to her parents on Christmas Day 1864, accompanied by a note of gratitude to her mother:

I am happy, very happy tonight, for my five years work is done, and whether it succeeds or not I shall be the richer and better for it because the labor, love, disappointment, hope and purpose that have gone into it are a useful experience that I shall not forget. Now if it makes a little money and opens the way for more I shall be satisfied, and you in some measure repaid for all the sympathy, help, and love that have done so much for me in these hard years. I hope success will sweeten me and make me what I long to become more than a great writer—a good daughter.[15]

Notwithstanding this pious sentiment, Alcott did care very much about the reception of the book and anxiously awaited the reviews. Her parents were, as might be expected, delighted. It is, Bronson observed, "a better book than she knows." He was pleased with the way it managed to justify ideals without lapsing into "murder and adultery," and not at all offended by the hint that the problems of young women might be laid at the door of their parents. Nor was Bronson disturbed by the book's frank avowal of separation as preferable to a loveless marriage.[16]

Others were not so kind. It was apparent that Alcott had ventured, as she feared she might, beyond conventional views of marriage. Public opinion was not yet ready for her frank portrayal of separation. As she reported, "some fear it isn't moral, because it speaks freely of marriage."[17] The harshest judgment came from the young Henry James. While acknowledging Alcott's talent as a writer, James remarked that "the two most striking facts with regard to *Moods* are the author's ignorance of human nature, and her self-confidence in spite of this ignorance." Although the tone of the review was light— "flippant" was Bronson's word for it—yet it was apparent that James did not share Louisa's admiration for Adam, nor did he agree with her views on marriage. Commenting on Sylvia's sentimental inability to remain with a man she does not love, James countered with stout defense of marriage as it was "in the fashion of the old days."[18]

Alcott attempted to joke about James's remarks. "Being a literary youth he gave me advice, as if he had been eighty and I a girl," she remarked. She was hurt by it nonetheless. Vehemently she promised herself, "My next book shall have no *ideas* in it, only facts, and the people shall be as ordinary as possible; then critics will say it's all right. I seem to have been playing with edge tools without knowing it."[19] She then denied that it was a book about marriage. This denial should not be taken too seriously, however, for she specifically defended her views of marriage in a letter to a friend: "Self-abnegation is a noble thing but I think there is a limit to it; and though in a few rare cases it may work well, yet half the misery of the world seems to come from unmated pairs trying to live their lives decorously to the end, and bringing children into the world to inherit the unhappiness and discord out of which they were born."[20] Nevertheless, the criticism stung, and five years later she remarked that she was trying to forget that she ever wrote *Moods*.

The Sensational Vision: Pauline

Alcott's sensational stories presented a far less sentimental picture of women, perhaps because they were written more for profit than for prestige. As she told a friend in 1862, it was her intention to write "blood and thunder" tales, for they are "easy to 'compoze' and better paid." In that year she published the first of her sensational stories in response to the offer of a one-hundred-dollar prize by *Frank Leslie's Illustrated Newspaper*.[21] She won the prize with "Pauline's Passion and Punishment." Leslie demanded more and she produced for him "A Whisper in the Dark." Word got around among the publishers that Miss Alcott knew how to write these nineteenth-century equivalents to soap opera, and she received offers from *The Flag of Our Union*, which published a series of her pot-boilers, including "V.V.; or, Plots and Counterplots," "A Marble Woman; or, The Mysterious Model," and "Behind a Mask; or, A Woman's Power."

The young Miss Alcott was frankly ashamed of her "necessity stories," as she called them, and kept them concealed from her father and his circle of friends. She insisted that they be published either anonymously, or, later, under the pseudonym of "A. M. Barnard." Despite pleas and bribes from her publishers, who offered her more money if she would put her name to her work, she would not be identified with this "rubbish," as she constantly referred to her sensational work. Her attitude was best captured in an exchange that occurs in *Little Women* between Jo, the authoress, and the two most important men in her life, her father and Professor Bhaer. Flushed with pride over winning a prize for her story, Jo shows it to Father March, who responds, "You can do better than this, Jo. Aim at the highest, and never mind the money."[22] She persists, nevertheless, in producing these sensational tales until she meets Professor Bhaer, whom she admires for his intellect and his goodness. Unaware that Jo is composing such stories, the good professor comments, "I do not like to think that good young girls should see such things. They are made pleasant to some, but I would more rather give my boys gunpowder to play with than this bad trash." Upon reflection, Jo agrees and resolves to burn her sensational productions: "They *are* trash, and will soon be worse than trash if I go on; for each is more sensational than the last. I've gone blindly on, hurting myself and other people, for the sake of money; I know it's so—for I can't read this stuff in sober earnest without being horribly ashamed of it."[23]

Given Alcott's upbringing, it is little wonder that she would be reluctant to take credit for the creation of her sensational heroines, who defied sentimental conventions of proper womanhood. These were no domesticated and submissive ladies, but rather *femmes fatales* who believed that the relationship beween the sexes was a battleground on which each struggled for supremacy. The man has on his side his superior physical strength and the sanction of custom and law. For her part the woman can rely only on her willpower and her guile. The opening line of "Pauline's Passion and Punishment" reveals a woman far different from saintly Effie and certainly less passive and confused than Sylvia: "To and fro, like a wild creature in its cage, paced that handsome woman, with bent head, locked hands, and restless steps."[24] The occasion for Pauline's unfeminine deportment is soon revealed in the form of a letter from her former lover, Gilbert Redmond, who, like so many of the men appearing in Alcott's sensational fiction, is part villain and part selfish fop. It seems that Gilbert has reneged on his promise of marriage to Pauline in order to marry a wealthy but plain heiress whom he does not love. Pauline does not, as sentimental convention would dictate, suffer in silence. As she tells a wealthy young friend, Manuel: "If you think that this loss has broken my heart, undeceive yourself, for such as I live years in an hour and show no sign. I have shed no tears, uttered no cry, asked no comfort" (p. 113). Pauline is, rather, a woman of action and enlists the aid of Manuel in a plan to seek vengeance. In double violation of the cult of romantic love, Pauline proposes to Manuel, not for love, but for his fortune, which will place her in a position to revenge herself on Gilbert. "Yes, it is weak, wicked, and unwomanly," she admits, "yet I persist as relentlessly as any Indian on a war trail" (p. 114). Manuel proves that he no more conforms to sentimental notions of masculinity than Pauline does of femininity, for he meekly agrees to her diabolic arrangement, taking comfort only in her promise that she will remain a faithful friend to him, and that she will try to love him once she has disposed of Gilbert.

Pauline's plan for Gilbert entails nothing as simple as murder. "Such revenge is brief and paltry," she explains to Manuel, "fit only for mock tragedies or poor souls who have neither the wit to devise nor the will to execute a better. There are fates more terrible than death; weapons more keen than poniards, more noiseless than pistols. Women use such, and work out a subtler vengeance than men can conceive. Leave Gilbert to remorse—and me" (p. 110). With the help of the submissive Manuel, now her husband, she pursues Gilbert, corners him, and discovers to her satisfaction that he is bored with his plain wife, Barbara, who did not bring to the marriage as much money as he expected. Worse, Barbara's wealth makes him totally dependent upon her whims. "Have you no power?" mocks Pauline, and she proceeds to tantalize him by frankly sensual dancing with Manuel. Entranced, Gilbert watches them, "fascinated, flushed, and excited as if his heart beat responsive to the rhythmic rise and fall of that booted foot and satin slipper" (p. 128). His love rekindled by her beauty, Gilbert confesses that he loves her still and kisses her hand. Pauline displays her contempt by removing the glove he kissed and dropping it to the floor. Although spurned, Gilbert is intrigued by the gesture, picks up the glove and tells her, "I accept the challenge" (p. 126).

There follows an intricate war between Pauline and Gilbert which elaborates the basic theme of the story, described by the author as "the tournament so often held between man and woman—a tournament where the keen tongue is the lance, pride the shield, passion the fiery steed, and the hardest heart the winner of the prize, which seldom

66

fails to prove a barren honor, ending in remorse" (p. 131). With Manuel's reluctant assistance, Pauline proceeds to strip Gilbert of his money, the affection of his wife, and his pride. In the midst of these maneuvers, the long-suffering Barbara earns no pity from Pauline, who describes her rival as "one of those spaniel-like creatures who love the hand that strikes them and fawn upon the foot that spurns them" (p. 137).

Although Alcott was ashamed of these stories and gave up writing them when the success of *Little Women* made it no longer a matter of necessity, they contain a psychological truth that is absent in her more respectable work. Under the cover of anonymity, she declared her independence of sentimental traditions, creating in the process women more like herself. She also found a way to vent her suppressed rage at the humiliations that marked her adolescence. She could not, of course, bring herself to imitate Pauline's direct action against the offending male, but she could at least dream about revenge and find catharsis in the creation of women like Pauline, whose feelings corresponded more closely to those that Alcott herself harbored than those of the submissive Effie or even the confused Sylvia. Alcott began to suspect as much as she grew older, and she began to view her sensational stories with more perspective if not more respect. She came to express regret that she had so ruthlessly disowned her sensational children, pinning the blame on the "respectable traditions of Concord," and in particular on Emerson and on her father. As she confessed to an acquaintance:

> I think my natural ambition is for the lurid style. I indulge in gorgeous fancies and wish that I dared inscribe them upon my pages and set them before the public. . . . To have had Mr. Emerson for an intellectual god all one's life is to be invested with a chain armor of propriety . . . and what would my own good father think of me . . . if I set folks to doing the things that I have a longing to see my people do?[25]

THE JUVENILE VISION: JO

Alcott published the last of her sensational stories in February of 1869, having found a way to make more money by writing books for children. Another advantage of children's stories was that she could permit herself to put her name to them. Unfortunately, however, she had difficulty in taking her juvenile fiction seriously, for it did not earn her much in the way of prestige. It was a field that had emerged only at the time of her birth, and it still bore the stigma of its beginnings as a didactic enterprise, aimed at the educational and moral uplift of the young. Literary critics ignored children's books, and, as we have seen, Louisa yearned for nothing as much as to be taken seriously as a writer. The critical reception accorded *Moods* seemed to dash her hopes on that score, and she was left at loose ends. When Thomas Niles, a publisher, first approached her with the suggestion of writing a book for girls, Alcott gave the idea the cold shoulder, exclaiming that she did not even like girls, except for her sisters.[26] Besides, she protested, she was busy with the editing of a children's magazine, *Merry's Museum*, a task she had undertaken in January 1868. Niles was persistent, however, pointing out that children's books were selling well. Consequently, in the spring of 1868 Alcott undertook the task of providing a book not only for girls but about girls. As with her sensational fiction, it was purely a matter of earning money as far as she was concerned, but, unlike the sensational stories, she did not find much joy in the composition.

Whereas *Moods* had occupied her attention for five years and had undergone frequent revisions, Alcott dashed off the first installment of *Little Women* in two and one-half months, writing on blue-lined paper, making no copies and sending the finished manuscript off to the publisher without revisions. It was to be a pattern characteristic of the way she composed juvenile fiction, explaining the incredible volume of publication that poured from her pen and suggesting a certain lack of respect for her readership. Upon completing the draft of the first half of *Little Women*, she pronounced it dull, concerned as it was with the lives of "sober, nice people" like herself and her family.[27] The immediate success of the first installment of *Little Women* caught her by surprise and set her to work on the sequel, confirming her low opinion of children's literature. If anything the sequel, completed in just two months, proved even more successful, and so she resolved to "keep the mill going," as she put it, and turned out *An Old-Fashioned Girl*.[28]

She had struck gold, and she was not going to stop until she had exhausted the mine. She found no satisfaction in her celebrity, complaining of the "impertinent curiosity" of reporters and of her adoring public, but she was delighted with the big money, which enabled her to pay off the family's debts and provide her mother with comfort.[29] The death of Anna's husband in 1871 set her to work once again, this time to earn money for the support of Anna and her two boys. The result was *Little Men*, which carried forward the story of *Little Women* another decade and brought more money into the Alcott coffers. The success of her juvenile stories aroused interest in her literary work, and led to republication of *Hospital Sketches* and *Moods*, and the commissioning of new projects, such as the writing and publication of her autobiographical novel, *Work*. Despite her achievements, she found little occasion for satisfaction. She still suffered bad health from her Civil War experience in the Union Hotel Hospital, and the writing of *Little Women* had made incredible demands on her strength: "When I had the youth, I had no money; now I have the money I have no time; and when I get the time, if I ever do, I shall have no health to enjoy life."[30] She complained constantly in private that she was a slave chained to a galley by duty, and there always seemed a need for more money, hence the compulsion to turn out more "moral pap for the young," as she called it, sometimes as many as two stories a day sandwiched between housework.[31] Even after her success made the family secure, and even after the death of her mother, she continued to write what she called her juvenile "pot boilers."[32] Her dissatisfaction finally broke into print with the publication of her last novel, *Jo's Boys,* which was actually the third part of the March family trilogy. She concluded the story with the remark: "It is a strong temptation to the weary historian to close the present tale with an earthquake which should engulf Plumfield and its environs so deeply in the bowels of the earth that no youthful Schliemann could ever find a vestige of it."[33]

In the light of these complaints, it is tempting to accept Alcott's self-assessment as a writer who did not share with children her deepest convictions about courtship, marriage, and family life. Certainly it is true that sex, violence, and drug use—themes that appear in her sensational work—do not find their way into her children's books.

For another thing, the battle of the sexes that dominates her sensational work and much of her literary fiction subsides to a few minor skirmishes in her children's books. Finally, it is true that her juvenile work is generally more optimistic about family life than the rest of her fiction. "I do think that families are the most beautiful things in the world!" Jo bursts out at the conclusion of *Little Women,* a remark very unlikely to come from either Sylvia or Pauline.[34] As one mother observed, she liked Alcott's books because she did not have to turn down any pages as a signal to her daughters not to read them. "All is so true, so sweet, so pious," she gushed.[35]

But while it is evident that Alcott was exercising a certain amount of censorship over herself when writing her books for children, it is also apparent that her blanket condemnation of her juvenile work was unfair. It is true that she banned sex, violence, and drugs from her children's work, but it is also true that these themes do not appear prominently in those works of adult fiction to which she appended her name. In other words, she was more intent on protecting her reputation than she was on protecting her juvenile audience. The truth is that much of her juvenile work was better than she herself knew or, at least, would admit. The sales of *Little Women* made it evident that the reading public had been won over, but, in addition, those reviewers who deigned to take notice of a children's book found that they liked Alcott's work. Although *The Ladies Repository* thought the book should be banned from Sunday school libraries because it presented "salvation without Christ," the *Nation* gave it mild praise and noted that it could be read with pleasure by older people as well.[36] The reviewer for *Godey's Ladies Book,* who found herself bored with themes of love and marriage, praised *Little Women* as a "lively story for the young . . . exceedingly interesting."[37] *Putnam's Magazine* recommended it "to all young people, big or little."[38] The tragedy is that the author found great difficulty in accepting such praise, as her father noted. Bronson hoped that the favorable comments heaped on the book would encourage his daughter "to estimate, as I fear she has not properly, her superior gifts as a writer."[39] Louisa's low self-esteem, however, led her to underestimate the value of her juvenile literature, just as the "respectable traditions of Concord" made her unduly ashamed of her sensational fiction. She seemed to share the view of many literary critics that any popular work, especially one aimed at children, was necessarily of poor quality. She could not accept her father's more perceptive judgment that in *Little Women* she had revealed herself as the "genius of the home and household, the orchard and garden, of childhood and youth."[40] While it is true that many of her children's books bear the mark of the haste with which they were written, her best juvenile work shows an attention to character and motivation lacking in her sensational fiction, where action and plot are all. One of the most noteworthy features of her juvenile work, marking it off from both her literary and sensational fiction, is that she permitted herself to give full play to her considerable wit.

Alcott's greatest achievement in her juvenile fiction was her ability to penetrate the inner lives of the young and to explode the sentimental stereotype of childhood that dominated the sentimental fiction of her day. Sarah Hale, the venerable editor of *Godey's Ladies Book*, noted at the time that "Miss Alcott has a faculty of entering into the lives and feelings of children that is conspicuously wanting in most writers who address them."[41] *Putnam's Magazine* perceived that *Little Women* signaled a minor revolution in literature for children, for it proved that books for children could be as "varied in their scope" as those written for adults. Evidently having in mind such insipid child heroines as Susan Warner's Ellen Montgomery, the reviewer noted that juvenile books had been dominated by "unnaturally good and pious boys and girls who, however, were not attractive enough to rouse a desire of imitation in the youthful breast."[42] Even writers of such stature as Harriet Beecher Stowe had difficulty, as we have seen, in creating children who were other than saints. But when Alcott described Meg, Jo, Beth, and Amy March as "good, bad, very good and middling," the reader is alerted to the fact that the sentimental stereotype has given way to characterization much livelier and more interesting.[43] These are real girls and not some didactic writer's notion of what girls should be like. Beth, it is true, conforms most closely to the stereotype of the saintly child, for she is the peacemaker, the quiet, shy one who is all too ready to sacrifice herself for others and who, consequently, proves too good to survive in this wicked world. But even Beth has her faults, minor though they might seem when compared to those exhibited by her sisters. Beth confesses that she dislikes housework, that she is inordinately fond of music, and that she is afraid of people. Beth has, in other words, a cross to bear also and, like her sisters, she must struggle to conquer her faults. Meg, the oldest, is somewhat further removed from the stereotype, for though she is gentle and pious—most of the time, at least—she is also inclined to be vain and a bit too fond of luxury. Like the silly, fashionable women who populate Alcott's adult fiction, Meg is the kind of girl who will say that a real lady is known by her dress (1:43). Amy, the youngest, is a selfish brat, perhaps the furthest removed from sainthood. An "affected little goose," she shows the most promise of growing up to be a shallow "queen of society" (1:11, 2:311).

If Alcott created in Beth, Meg, and Amy successful counters to the conventional image of young girlhood, she achieved in the portrayal of Jo a triumph. Drawing on her personal experience, she created the first tomboy in American fiction, a young woman more complex than Effie, Sylvia, or even Pauline, and one remembered long after they were forgotten. It was, of course, a self-portrait, and Alcott's achievement was that she did not allow publishers, family, or anticipated public response to deflect or modify the character. Jo is a good bad girl, who, like her sisters, possesses faults, but faults of an entirely different order. Meg, Beth, and Amy betray the weaknesses of femininity, especially in its sentimental guises, but Jo rejects sentimental femininity altogether. "I can't get over my disappointment in not being a boy," she says. She is tough and aggressive, a girl who goes about whistling and shouting "Christopher Columbus," and shocking the prim Meg. She despises fashion, never troubling herself about dress, hates dancing and girlish gossip, and detests sentimentality. She dislikes "prim and pokey" people and those who "put on airs," and she cannot abide the name Josephine because it is so "sentimental." Indeed, one of the most frequently occurring words in the novel is "sensible," which is what Jo likes to think she is (1:9–12, 19, 28, 46, 83–84).

But if Jo is a worshipper of common sense and a despiser of sentiment, the reader also learns that she is no practical, phlegmatic Prudence. For one thing, she possesses a hair-trigger temper, resembling in this regard not only Alcott herself but also most of her sensational heroines. It is, moreover, no minor fault but a trait that nearly leads to Amy's death. Amy has aroused Jo's fury by burning one of her manuscripts out of spite, and then tags along after her sister and Laurie on a skating expedition:

> Jo heard Amy panting after her run, stamping her feet, and blowing her fingers, as she tried to put her skates on; but Jo never turned, and went slowly zigzagging down the river, taking a bitter, unhappy sort of satisfaction in her sister's troubles. She had cherished her anger till it grew strong, and took possession of her, as evil thoughts and feelings always do, unless cast out at once. As Laurie turned the bend, he shouted back—
> "Keep near the shore; it isn't safe in the middle."
> Jo heard, but Amy was just struggling to her feet, and did not catch a word. Jo glanced over her shoulder, and the little demon she was harboring said in her ear,—
> "No matter whether she heard or not, let her take care of herself."
> (1:116)

It was a feeling that Alcott's sensational heroines would share, but unlike them, Jo is capable of remorse. When Amy falls into the icy water and comes close to drowning, Jo laments: "'It's my dreadful temper! I try to cure it; I think I have, and then it breaks out worse than ever. Oh, Mother! what shall I do! what shall I do?' cried poor Jo, in despair" (1:118). Her remorse provides a "moral" conclusion to the episode, of course, but more to the point, it proves Jo's moral complexity, for, unlike Effie, she could dream of vengeance, and, unlike Pauline, she could feel the pain of conscience. There is for her no easy resolution of this inner tension, and she sometimes longs to be free of moral obligation. As she remarks: "I almost wish I hadn't any conscience, it's so inconvenient. If I didn't care about doing right, and didn't feel uncomfortable when doing wrong, I should get on capitally. I can't help wishing, sometimes, that Father and Mother hadn't been so particular about such things" (2:172). Unfortunately, Alcott robs this superb insight of its moral force by following it with a little sermon on the enduring value of principles, but Jo's humanity survives even her author's moralizing, and the passage provides a revealing insight into the author's child-rearing.

Little Women deserves, then, the loyalty it won from generations of

73

girls, for it has the ring of truth. Having been denied the recognition of the respectable, Alcott reached out in desperation and created a character that defied sentimental conventions. The character she had been groping for in *Moods* she finally created in *Little Women*. In rare moments, Alcott herself recognized her achievement: "Jo wasn't a heroine: she was only a struggling human girl, like hundreds of others, and she just acted out her nature, being sad, cross, listless or energetic, as the mood suggested. It's highly virtuous to say we'll be good, but we can't do it all at once, and it takes a long pull, a strong pull, and pull all together" (2:281). For an author born of a transcendentalist father, in the midst of the sentimental revolution, it was a singular insight.

Feminism and the Family

*O*n 1 November 1868 Alcott began the second part of *Little Women*. Flushed with the success of the initial installments she was determined to do a chapter a day, and she looked forward to the task, hoping that she could in the sequel give her imagination more play. At the same time, however, she was vexed by a question which her readers and her publisher raised insistently: would Jo marry Laurie? With irritation, Alcott confided to her journal: "Girls write to ask who the little women marry, as if that was the only end and aim of a woman's life. I *won't* marry Jo to Laurie to please any one."[1] But, two months later, on New Year's Day, the author dispatched the sequel of *Little Women* to the publisher, and it contained what appeared to be a compromise. She did not, as she had promised, marry Jo to Laurie, but she had invented for her mate the kindly Professor Bhaer.

Those two months Alcott spent in writing the sequel to *Little Women* must have proved troublesome to her, for she had created Jo March in her image, and the temptation to end the story with Jo as a spinster must have been powerful. As we have seen, Alcott decided early in her life to steer a course away from marriage, and her early fiction did not present a happy view of the institution. Her skepticism about connubial bliss grew as she fell under the influence of feminism. Her father's failings as a breadwinner and her decision for spinsterhood made her familiar with the trials of women who must battle alone in a world dominated by men. This awareness led her to embrace moderate feminist causes and to participate eventually in the struggle for woman's suffrage. Submitting articles to *The Woman's Journal*, Alcott also attended the Woman's Congress in Syracuse in

1875. Four years later she was working for suffrage on the local scene, expressing disgust that her sisters in Concord were so "timid and slow," and finding that they were more interested in "cake and servants" than in the right to vote.[2] After fame gave her influence, she also brought pressure to bear on her publisher, urging him to issue feminist works. "I, for one, don't want to be ranked among idiots, felons and minors any longer," she warned him.[3] But Alcott was never one to join causes, being in this regard much like her hero Thoreau, who once said that if he could not go to heaven except by joining a party then he would rather not go. In like manner she found that public gatherings made her uncomfortable, and when she made an appearance for the good of feminist causes she was usually deluged by autograph hounds, much to her dismay. She contributed small amounts to the cause of suffrage, but most of her money went to the Alcott family, for it seems she believed that charity both begins and ends at home.

Alcott's greater contribution to the cause of nineteenth-century feminism came, therefore, in her fiction, which contains a strong undercurrent of feminist conviction and which resonated with the questions that some American women were beginning to ask. In its simplest form, feminism led many women to wonder if marriage were compatible with a career, but, at a more fundamental level, some women were beginning to ask if the institution of the family was inherently opposed to equality between the genders. Some were even beginning to assert that women had a right to self-fulfillment, and these same women were asking if the family, at least in its traditional forms, was compatible with this right. As the historian Carl Degler has recently put the matter, women seemed to be asking if women and the family were "at odds." Certainly it seems that many women were acting as if they believed there were a conflict, for, as Degler has pointed out, the proportion of American women choosing the single life rose during the years after the Civil War.[4] Nevertheless, few nineteenth-century feminists posed the issue in such a blatant form. As William O'Neill has pointed out, only the most militant feminists were raising the issue directly, and then only for a brief period of time.[5] *Revolution*, the journal of the militant National Woman Suffrage Association, went so far as to declare in 1870 that suffrage would do little to advance the cause of women unless the institution of marriage itself were radically changed. Similarly, Elizabeth Cady Stanton called for a change in the laws making divorce easier, for she was persuaded that marriage, as then constituted, was a form of slavery. Nevertheless, Stanton's opinions placed her outside the mainstream of feminism, and the more moderate American Woman Suffrage Association, with which Alcott was associated, strongly condemned Stanton's views. From 1870 on, most feminists placed emphasis on securing the vote and delicately side-stepped the issue of the family. It was not until toward the end of the nineteenth century that Charlotte Perkins Gilman once again raised the fundamental issue of the relationships between the family and women's equality.

In Defense of the Single Life

Given the confusion and hesitancy with which most feminists in post–Civil War America addressed the issue of the family, it was hardly surprising that Alcott failed to adopt a clear and consistent position, but her fiction proves that the issue of feminism and the family was much on her mind. As her irritation over the matter of Jo's marriage makes clear, Alcott gave a good deal of thought to the question of career and marriage, and, more particularly, to the issue of spinsterhood. Even before the readers of *Little Women* began pressing her to marry Jo to Laurie, the author had taken a public stand in favor of the single life for women. Shortly before undertaking the novel, she had published an article which was a patent effort to persuade young women that the single life could be a happy one. Entitled "Happy Women," the article consisted of sketches of spinsters like herself who led busy, useful, independent lives. As Alcott put it in her diary, "Liberty is a better husband than love to many of us."[6]

Little Women itself, for all of its reputation as a conservative document, defied the stigma that convention attached to spinsterhood. Marmee, that embodiment of motherly virtues, advised her daughters that she would rather see them remain single than to compromise their integrity by marrying men they did not love: "Better be happy old maids than unhappy wives, or unmaidenly girls, running about to find husbands."[7] And, in a justly famous passage, Jo makes clear that she harbors a raging ambition that has nothing to do with marriage and family life. Beth might be satisfied to stay home and take care of her mother and father, and Meg might be content with husband and children, but Jo tells her sisters of her dream:

> I'd have a stable full of Arabian steeds, rooms piled with books, and I'd write out of a magic inkstand, so that my words should be as famous as Laurie's music. I want to do something splendid before I go into my castle—something heroic or wonderful, that won't be forgotten after I'm dead. I don't know what, but I'm on the watch for it, and mean to astonish you all someday. I think I shall write books, and get rich and famous.[8]

Finally, of course, Jo marries the kindly Professor Bhaer, and leaves behind her a trail of confusion. At the end of *Little Women*, Alcott provides the reader with at least three different versions of Jo's attitude toward marriage and a career: first that she finds it difficult to "give up her own hopes, plans and desires, and cheerfully live for others," as she puts it; secondly, that she is happy to renounce ambition because "the life I wanted then seems selfish, lonely and cold"; and, thirdly, she hints that she may yet find a way to combine marriage and family life with her career as a writer.[9] Jo's ambivalence continues through the remainder of the March trilogy as she settles down to rear two children of her own and assists her husband in the operation of Plumfield, a school for boys. In the second novel, *Little Men*, Jo is fully occupied with her tasks as mother to her own offspring and housemother to the other boys, but in *Jo's Boys*, which appeared sixteen years later, the heroine seems to be having second thoughts. Although it is evident that she has pursued her writing career, and although she boasts that she enjoys "money, fame and plenty of work I love," she also expresses regret for not having remained single. Unburdening herself to a group of female students at Plumfield College, Jo lectures them on the importance of careers, and pointedly reminds them that there is nothing wrong with being a spinster, for "a woman isn't a half but a whole human being and can stand alone."[10]

The defense of spinsterhood is also reflected in her creation of

"Naughty Nan," a girl who occupies a good deal of attention both in *Little Men* and in *Jo's Boys*. It is as if Alcott regretted submitting to the pressure of her publishers and her readership by having Jo marry, and resolved to make amends by creating a new Jo in Annie Harding. She is, like Jo, a spirited tomboy, who is sent to Plumfield as the black sheep of her family. Although generous and warmhearted, she is the kind of girl who accepts dares in order to prove that girls can do most things as well as boys, and some things better. Obviously reaching back to her childhood experience for the creation of this character, Alcott also incorporated her experience as a Civil War nurse by giving Nan the ambition to study medicine and become a doctor. From this ambition, formed at the age of sixteen, Nan never wavers, although, being attractive to boys, she finds it necessary from time to time to "rout the lovers," and she announces her determination to be "a useful, happy and independent spinster." She combines this deter-mination with stout defense of women's rights. Nan, unlike more timid girls, has no fear that she will be regarded as a "strong-minded" woman. The tentative air with which Alcott discussed spin-sterhood in *Little Women* had given way by the time of *Jo's Boys* to a calm acceptance of the role as entirely proper to women like Nan. Moreover, it is evident that the author takes delight in the character she has created, calling Nan the "pride of the community," a young woman who is handsome, self-poised and purposeful, in contrast to the more domestic Daisy, Meg's daughter, who is described as being a bit "inclined to be an old fogy."[11]

Further evidence of Alcott's attitude toward the issue of woman's role is supplied in the fragment of a novel, only recently published under the title *Diana and Persis*. Apparently composed in the winter of 1879, the work features two women artists who wrestle with the issue of marriage and career. Diana is a sculptor with an unhappy past and a fierce ambition to succeed in art, a character closely modeled on Alcott's perception of herself.[12] Diana's sole friend is Persis, a beau-tiful young painter whose past presents a dramatic contrast to the experience of Diana. "Percy," as Diana calls her, has led a happier, easier life than her friend. This favored child has bloomed into beautiful womanhood and is much pursued, for "she could no more help having lovers than a clover can forbid the bees and butterflies from coming for its honey." The blessed Percy is, in fact, yet another version of Louisa's youngest sister May, who first appeared as Amy in *Little Women*. The spoiled brat has now become, however, a beautiful and talented woman, bent on pursuing an artistic career and yet attracting lovers without effort. The danger for Percy, as Diana sees it, is that she will encounter the fate of many young women, especially beautiful ones, who believe "that women were born to be wives only, and finding out too late that every soul has its own life to live and cannot hastily ignore its duties to itself without bitter suffering and loss" (pp. 65–66).

Consequently, Diana is delighted to learn that Percy has rejected her latest marriage proposal and instead will travel to Paris to study art. Here the parallel with the life of May is exact. Always the favored one of the Alcott family, May became Louisa's special charge after the death of Elizabeth, and she took special pride in seeing to it that her youngest sister received artistic instruction. After she became a wealthy author, she financed several European trips for May, who sat at the feet of the masters and in the 1870s won minor notoriety as a copyist. Like May, Percy accepts these opportunities as if they were her due, and soon she is sending Diana letters from Paris describing her joy in sharing housekeeping with other "merry spinsters, doing most everything for ourselves in the simple, free and easy way best suited to our professions and our purses." She is liberated enough in Victorian terms to join a studio for women which features live nude models, both male and female. Percy reveals that she has an appreciative eye for the male physique, and she speaks of having male acquaintances, although she hastens to assure Diana that "we are all too busy for sentiment, and are just good comrades." Soon she is telling Diana of her triumphs in art and sharing her joy in achievement (pp. 69–77).

Diana, too, has achieved at least one of her objectives by traveling to Rome, but there she has an unsettling encounter with a five-year-old boy, Nino, and through him an acquaintance with the boy's widowed father, a famed sculptor. Both provide her with the uncomfortable reminder that artistic success may not supply all her human needs: "At times she was conscious of a deeper want, an unconquerable yearning, a bittersweet regret for something lost or never found"

80

(p. 90). Usually she was the kind of woman who "looked straight forward above the level of the little heads of children," but the chance encounter with little Nino on a Roman street opens for her a new experience. They quickly become friends, and she kisses him—"involuntarily"—and discovers "a new pleasure in the mere touch of this chubby elf, so velvet soft, so full of life that thrilled her sensitive hands chilled by long contact with cold marble and damp clay." Through Nino she meets his widowed father, the sculptor, who praises her work. Having won recognition from a man she much admires, Diana can then "permit the softer side of her character to assert itself without fearing the accusation of weakness, which she hated like a man" (pp. 91, 95, 101).

This acquaintance with males is only a brief interlude for Diana, and she remains dedicated to the single life. Not so, however, with Percy, who surprises Diana by marrying and giving birth to a daughter. Again the parallel with the life of Louisa's sister May is striking. In 1878, at the age of thirty-eight, May met a Swiss businessman fourteen years her junior and promptly married him. At the time Louisa was composing *Diana and Persis*, May was pregnant and very happy. Unlike her violent reaction years earlier upon hearing of the engagement of Anna, Louisa took the news calmly, commenting only that May is "old enough to choose for herself," and admitting to a bit of envy: "How different our lives are now!—I so lonely, sad and sick; she so happy, well and blest. She always had the cream of things and deserved it."[13] Diana, on the other hand, is portrayed as disappointed and skeptical. If Louisa really believed that May could manage to combine both a marriage and a career, Diana was not so sure about such prospects for Percy. Accepting an invitation to visit her friend in Paris, Diana says, "Now I will go and see how well Percy's experiment succeeds. If she can combine art and domestic life harmoniously she will be a more remarkable woman than even I think her" (p. 109). Diana's eye takes in every detail of the domestic scene, and finds that it is indeed a charming home, admits that Percy looks well and happy, and even discovers to her own surprise that she likes both the baby and its father. On the other hand, Diana notes the dust on Percy's easel and the dried paint on the palette, and she observes a subtle change in Percy also, for "something of the youthful

81

audacity was gone, and the eyes that had looked so fearlessly into the future for herself began to wear the tender anxiety that mother's eyes take on when peering hopefully, prayerfully into the unknown future of a child" (p. 113).

If Diana is concerned that Percy may be surrendering her artistic ambitions for motherhood, Percy's husband harbors an uneasiness that Diana's appearance might arouse his wife's old ambitions, disturbing the "beautiful repose which had possessed her for a year." Out of these conflicting interests emerges a debate between husband and friend. When Diana lightly remarks that "the wiseacres say we women cannot have all, and must decide between love and fame," the husband attempts to reassure her: "I believe a woman can and ought to have both if she has the power and courage to win them. A man expects them, achieves them, why is not a woman's life to be as full and free as his? Love alone is not enough for any large and hungry soul, it should have all it can hold, else it has thwarted the purpose of its Maker" (pp. 121–22, 127). In fact, he argues, she will be a greater artist for being a happy woman. Diana, for her part, is not one whit convinced, "for her opinion on this point was as firmly fixed as Mont Blanc" (p. 228).

If, indeed, Diana speaks for Louisa, it would appear that she believed an irreconcilable conflict existed between feminism and the family. The tragic death of May in childbirth, which occurred only a few months after Louisa began the novel (and which may account for the fact that it was never finished), certainly underscored the terrible price that women sometimes pay for family life. In any event, it prevented Louisa from ever learning if May could have both "love and fame," and may have reinforced her skepticism about combining marriage and career.

A Loving League of Sisters

If Alcott remained skeptical of marriage for women of ambition like herself, she was not indifferent to its attractions, for she pictured Diana as being "conscious of a deeper want, an unconquerable yearning." Even as she celebrated the single life, Alcott was troubled by its implications, for she knew from personal experience that spinsterhood could mean a lonely life, leaving a woman shut off from both men and women. Consequently, she explored in her fiction still another feminist theme, namely, the possibility that the future might produce a union of women that would transcend not only the boundaries of the traditional family but also the barriers of social class. This dream of sorority, what Alcott once called the "loving league of sisters," held out the hope that women might assuage their loneliness and poverty and find forms of feminine self-fulfillment outside the bonds of matrimony.

In treating the sentiment of sorority, Alcott established that she was very much in touch with a significant trend among nineteenth-century American women. The feminist movement of the last decade has prompted several historians to explore the question of women's consciousness of themselves as a group—a feminist version, as it were, of the doctrine of Karl Marx concerning the importance of class consciousness as a crucial factor in historical change.[14] These historians have uncovered striking evidence that many nineteenth-century American women were beginning to think of themselves as a "sisterhood," and, in fact, one such historian has even speculated that this group consciousness achieved the status of a subculture within Victorian society. Carroll Smith-Rosenberg has uncovered extensive correspondence between nineteenth-century women that reveals a depth of emotional intimacy that convention had sought to confine to relations between men and women. Moreover, the emotional intimacy often persisted among women even after marriage.[15] The cause of this sororial subculture remains a puzzle, but it may, ironically, have been a product of the sentimental revolution itself, which had so sharply segregated the social position of men and women while at the same time asserting the moral superiority of women.[16]

For Alcott, as doubtless for many other nineteenth-century American women, the bond of sisterhood was rooted deeply in economic deprivation, which spawned in turn a sense of oppression. As we have seen, the financial disasters that fell upon the Alcott family when Louisa was yet an adolescent had the effect of drawing Abigail and her daughters closely together for mutual support and protection, and doubtless accounts for the extraordinary loyalty that Louisa felt toward them in later life. It was this sense of female loyalty and intimacy that provided a major theme in *Little Women*, where the four sisters comprise what Alcott called a "little nunnery," under the direction of Marmee, and where, despite their differences and their rivalries, they learn to pull together for their mutual benefit.[17] It is, however, a league doomed to dissolution, first by Beth's demise, and then by Meg's engagement to John Brooke. The emotional intimacy which the sisters have shared accounts for Jo's outburst on learning of Meg's betrayal:

> I see it all! They'll go lovering around the house, and we shall have to dodge; Meg will be absorbed, and no good to me any more; Brooke will scratch up a fortune somehow,—carry her off and make a hole in the family; and I shall break my heart, and everything will be abominably uncomfortable. Oh, deary me! Why weren't we all boys? then there wouldn't be any bother![18]

Eventually Amy follows Meg into marriage and even Jo, despite her protest, surrenders to the marital fever.

Far from giving up the sororial theme, however, Alcott returned to it in her autobiographical novel, *Work*, which gives an account of a young woman struggling to realize her ambitions in a world made by men. It is the most feminist of Alcott's literary work, for the heroine, Christie, is capable of putting into action what even Jo March had not dared. Christie, a slightly older version of Jo, possesses a hatred of dependence equal to that felt by Jo and by the author herself. An orphan, like most of Alcott's heroines, Christie is reared by a kindly aunt and a curmudgeon uncle, but her early life has left her with none of the temperamental difficulties that marred Alcott's more sentimental protagonists. At the age of twenty-one she is a young woman of "intelligence, courage, and common sense, many practical gifts, and, hidden under the reserve that soon melts in a genial atmosphere, much romance and enthusiasm, and the spirit which can rise to heroism when the great moment comes."[19]

The story opens with Christie issuing her personal declaration of independence. She spurns marriage to a country bumpkin, for she is persuaded that she is capable of much grander things. As she tells her stingy Uncle Enos: "You say I am discontented, proud and ambitious; that's true, and I'm glad of it. I am discontented, because I can't help feeling that there is a better sort of life than this dull one made up of everlasting work, with no object but money" (p. 9). Consequently, Christie leaves her rural home, bound for the city in pursuit of "success," a word which provided, in fact, the title Louisa originally assigned to the novel.

In the course of her struggle for independence, Christie meets a rich assortment of men, women, and children. As in her sensational fiction, Alcott confronted the reader with villains, villainesses, fops, and vain belles, but here also are types of nobility and kindness. For the first time she gave sustained attention to racial prejudice and social class bias in America, giving full recognition to the fact that the world is divided not only into male and female, but as well into white and black and rich and poor. As befits its title, *Work* also provides a richer description of urban life as the setting for the struggles of poor females who are compelled to work outside the home for a living. Finally, the novel presents to the reader an impressive array of family types, ranging from fashionable social climbers and doomed madwomen to happy working-class wives and serene Quaker mothers.

After a series of unhappy employments in the households of the rich, Christie decides to ply her talent as a seamstress, joining other poor women in an urban sweat shop. There she meets Rachel and discovers that there are poor women suffering a harder fate then her own. Christie is attracted to the girl and remains her friend even after it is revealed that Rachel is a fallen woman. It seems that Rachel made the fatal mistake of giving herself in love without marriage, a sin far worse in nineteenth-century America than marriage without love. It appears that she then drifted into a life of prostitution. Even Christie acknowledges the enormity of Rachel's transgression, but when Rachel is ostracized and threatened with the loss of her job, Christie is willing to forgive her: "I don't reproach you, dear: I don't despise or desert you, and though I'm grieved and disappointed, I'll stand by you still, because you need me more than ever now, and I want to prove that I am a true friend" (p. 137). Despite Christie's pleas with the employer, Rachel is fired, and Christie, true to her word, quits in sympathy, finding herself reduced to scrambling for piecework to pay her rent. Her gesture of sympathy for a poor sister has exacted a high price, and her brave bid for independence has become a mock-

85

ery. She compares her miserable, lonely existence with that of a happy bride, a glimpse of whom she catches during one of her desperate rounds to collect money owed her: "Yes, I'm growing old; my youth is nearly over, and at thirty I shall be a faded, dreary woman, like so many I see and pity. It's hard to come to this after trying so long to find my place and do my duty. I'm a failure after all, and might as well have stayed with Aunt Betsy or married Joe" (p. 151).

The elements that make up the novel are heavily autobiographical, and just as Alcott experienced much of Christie's frustration and despair, so she arranged for her heroine to contemplate suicide, as she herself had done. Unlike Alcott, however, Christie is not required to pull herself by her own efforts from the brink of self-destruction. Instead, she is rescued by a woman. As she prepares to plunge into the water, Rachel suddenly reappears, dissuades her from suicide and sends her to seek refuge among a circle of philanthropists that surrounds the Reverend Thomas Power, a character modeled on Alcott's friend and counselor, the Reverend Theodore Parker.

Christie goes on to experience a happy if short-lived marriage, but with the death of her soldier husband during the Civil War, she once again reaches out to the sisterhood. The final chapters form an epilogue in which Christie faces the world alone, now with a small daughter to support, inherits some money from her miserly Uncle Enoch, and, at the age of forty, turns her attention to women's causes, particularly the plight of working-class women. Christie sees herself as supplying a bridge between the needy working women and the "ladies" who would help them but who are ignorant of their needs.

While *Work* concludes by exploring feminist issues, Alcott's analysis of the plight of poor women is as vague as her program for its alleviation, establishing beyond doubt that she was more a storyteller than a social philosopher. Speaking before a group of working women, Christie reminds them that she has been a working woman all her life and advises them: "No matter how hard or humble the task at the beginning, if faithfully and bravely performed, it would surely prove a stepping-stone to something better; and with each honest effort they were fitting themselves for the nobler labor, and larger liberty God meant them to enjoy" (pp. 428–29). Equally vague was a casual reference to a "new emancipation" for women. As for concrete action, the best that Christie can offer is an appeal to a wealthy woman to reform the upper classes by making her fashionable home into a center for the discussion of serious issues. "Give them conversation instead of gossip; less food for the body and more for the mind," Christie advises (p. 436). The novel ends with a gathering in Christie's home of women she has befriended. A "loving league of sisters, old and young, black and white, rich and poor," they join hands and resolve to "know and help, love and educate one another" (p. 442).

A more sophisticated and elaborate treatment of feminist issues was contained in Alcott's juvenile fiction, further proof that she was not bent on protecting her young readers from more "radical" opinions. The second half of *An Old-Fashioned Girl* contains, in fact, Alcott's most vigorous assault on the sentimental image of woman to appear to her published work. Polly, who appears during the first half of the novel as a self-sacrificing saint, returns to the city in the second half, now six years older and somewhat matured in Alcott's imagination. At the age of twenty she is still single, and she seems determined to make a living on her own, much like Christie. Attempting to support herself by giving music lessons, Polly soon discovers that the life of a single woman is hard and lonely.[20]

Worse still, Polly finds herself snubbed by many fashionable people once they discover that she is a working girl. Fortunately she establishes contact with a group of young single women who are earning their own way in life. This "little sisterhood" consists of teachers like Polly who are working hard for little pay, young writers and singers who dream of fame, and artists who long to study in Rome. One of them is Becky, an assertive artist who is sculpting a female figure that is supposed to represent the "coming woman." As Becky ponders what she shall place in the hands of the figure, she receives many suggestions from the sisterhood, suggestions which include a child, the hand of a man, and a scepter to symbolize woman's reign over the home. Not surprisingly the militant Becky rejects all such suggestions and expresses her preference for a ballot box.

This episode is remarkable in two respects: first, that such radical feminism found expression in one of Alcott's juvenile books, going beyond, in fact, the sentiments expressed in her literary fiction; and secondly, that Alcott's imagination ultimately failed her when she tried to describe the woman who might emerge in the future. In selecting the image of the unfinished sculpture, she acknowledged her puzzlement, leaving the matter of woman's role much as it is described by the militant Becky. When it is suggested that the new woman will be "strong-minded," Becky responds: "Yes, strong-minded, strong-hearted, strong-souled, and strong-bodied; that is why I made her larger than the miserable, pinched-up woman of our day. Strength and beauty must go together. Don't you think these broad shoulders can bear burdens without breaking down, these hands work well, these eyes see clearly, and these lips do something besides simper and gossip?" (p. 264).

It is evident that Alcott's fiction paralleled in many ways the themes of her life. She began in her teenage years to believe that there was a link between celibacy and autonomy, for if there could be no marriage without subservience, there could be no sex without marriage. The humiliating poverty of her adolescence, which emphasized the liabilities that women labored under, stiffened her resolve to avoid entanglement with men—those "lords of creation," as she called the opposite sex. She regarded marriage as a surrender, and resisted it with determination, setting out to achieve fame and fortune in a man's world on a man's terms. But it is misleading to pose the issues of Victorian domesticity as a simple confrontation between women and the family. Alcott recognized that the period was marked by a variety of family forms, even though historians might speak of nineteenth-century family life in monolithic ways. She might suggest, in her more feminist moods, that the single life is preferable to any form of marriage, but she was persuaded also that not all forms of family life are equal. Certainly some forms of family were more compatible with Becky's dream of a new strong-minded woman than others, and the body of Alcott's writing provides a fascinating picture of the variety and complexity of household arrangements that comprised Victorian domesticity in her day. To this complex picture we now turn.

From Old-Fashioned Families to

Families of Fashion:

The Curse of Success

A *lthough Alcott's feminism* led her on occasion to defend the single
life and sorority, the bulk of her fiction described the world of
families. Even if she rejected for herself the roles of wife and mother,
she recognized that most women would find themselves embedded in
a family, and most of the women she portrayed would eventually
marry and have children, including the feminist Christie. But if
Alcott regarded family life as inevitable for most women, she left
with her readers decided impressions of the kind of families that were
unsuitable for the new kind of woman she hoped would emerge.
Surprisingly, it was not the sentimental family that attracted her most
scathing judgments, even though she was aware of its shortcomings.
Nor was it the traditional family, for which she preferred the label
"old-fashioned." Instead, she reserved her bitterest remarks for the
"family of fashion," that style of domestic life which she perceived to
be making such disastrous inroads among urban, affluent Americans. It was this type of family life that robbed women of their
purpose in life and left them, as Alcott told her readers, "restless,
aimless, frivolous and sick."[1]

In delivering this indictment of fashion, she performed in a sense
the function of historian, constantly reminding her readers that
American families were not what they used to be. Repeatedly jux-
taposing old-fashioned families and families of fashion, she presented a nostalgic portrait of family life and relationships in a
simpler, rural America, where husbands and wives labored together
to ensure the common survival of the household, and where children
grew up sharing the duties of the household and paying respect to

89

their elders. The sources of this portrait, it should be emphasized, lay not in her own experience, but rather in the stories she had heard about the families in which her parents had been reared—Bronson's boyhood on a Connecticut farm and Abigail's girlhood in the respectable but conservative May household in Boston.

The old-fashioned family may be perceived in Alcott's fiction only in tantalizing glimpses, serving only as background and contrast to sentimental or fashionable families. One such hint occurred in her first novel, *Moods*, providing a bucolic interlude in an otherwise somber tale. Sylvia and Adam are caught in a rainstorm in the midst of a summer outing. They seek refuge in a "red farm-house standing under venerable elms, with the patriarchal air which promises hospitable treatment and good cheer." The soaked travelers are welcomed and invited to participate in the family's celebration of a golden wedding anniversary. They join in the festivities, which have brought together the old couple's ten children and their "wilderness" of grandchildren. Sylvia is delighted and envies the "happy grandmother with fresh faces framing her withered one, daughterly voices chorusing good wishes, and the harvest of half a century of wedded life beautifully garnered in her arms." Equally impressive is the old patriarch, "rugged and white atop as the granite hills," who rules his clan with strength and benevolence. Even Adam, who is not at all cut out for the joys of domestic bliss, is impressed. He confesses that to rear ten such virtuous children is better than "winning a battle or ruling a state."[2]

In *Work* Louisa returned to the nostalgic theme by introducing the reader to the household of Cynthy Wilkins, a person with whom the destitute Christie finds refuge. The portrait is Dickensian. The Wilkins family is not rich, and it is evident that both husband and wife have to labor hard to keep themselves and their children fed, a fact signaled by a sign on the door:

> C. Wilkins, Clear-Starcher
> Laces done up in the best style.[3]

Mrs. Wilkins is clearly no candidate for fashionable society, being a large, plump woman with fuzzy red hair and no front teeth. Christie discovers that she has entered a most unfashionable household, smell-

ing suggestively of soapsuds and warm flat-irons, and enlivened by
the presence of six children who are quite unlike the timid and proper
children she has cared for in fashionable homes. Soon after Christie's
arrival, several of the Wilkins children appear in red and yellow
flannel nightgowns, darting "like meteors across the open doorway of
an adjoining room, with whoops and howls, bursts of laughter, and
antics of all sorts" (p. 166). Although Cynthy is casual with her offspring, it is evident that she adores them. When Christie offers to
mind the children for her, Mrs. Wilkins observes, "You needn't
werry about the children, only don't let 'em git lost, or burnt, or
pitch out a winder; and when it's done give 'em the patty-cake that's
bakin' for 'em" (p. 177).

It is evident that Mrs. Wilkins is a happily married woman and an
intelligent one in the bargain, a combination that the skeptical Christie finds hard to believe. Her disbelief is heightened by the appearance of Elisha, the head of the household, a taciturn shoemaker
of unprepossessing appearance who smokes and (Christie suspects)
tipples on the sly. In short, the "small, sallow, sickly looking man" is
hardly Christie's ideal of a proper mate, and yet, Mrs. Wilkins not
only loves him but professes to be proud of him: "It's redick'lus my
bein' so proud of Lisha, but ef a woman aint a right to think wal of
her own husband, I should like to know who has!" (p. 176). Her
curiosity aroused, Christie urges Mrs. Wilkins to divulge the secret
of her happy marriage. Glad to oblige, for she loves to talk, Mrs.
Wilkins tells her the story of their early married life and reveals, too,
their rural origins. There was a time when she and her husband lived
on a farm, she explains, and, while she should have been content, she
was in fact unhappy with the confinement of domestic life. She liked
to remember the freedom she enjoyed before marriage, when she
worked at "millineryin'," and her discontent was fueled by a Miss
Bascum, who advised her to stand up for her rights. Whereupon
Mrs. Wilkins persuaded Elisha to hire a serving girl to take care of
the house and children while she went "pleasurin'" and ran Elisha
into debt with the purchase of "my sinful gowns and bunnets." Soon,
the serving girl left, the household degenerated into chaos, the children "seemed to git out of sorts," and the bread burned while Mrs.
Wilkins trimmed a new bonnet. Elisha, his patience at an end,

quarreled with his wife and slapped her, whereupon she fled to Miss Bascum for comfort and advice. Soon there followed a tug of war as to which party would give in first, but Elisha "had the best on't you see, for he'd got the babies and lost a cross wife, while I'd lost everthing but Miss Bascum, who grew hatefuler to me every hour, for I begun to mistrust she was a mischief-maker—widders most always is—seein' how she pampered up my pride and 'peared to like the quarrel." Feeling ever more repentant and miserable for shirking her duty and scorning her blessing, the errant wife's resistance at last collapses and she and Elisha are reunited, creating a household suffused with "contentment, piety, and mother-love" (pp. 186–95).

Alcott's fondness for the old-fashioned family was evident, even to the extent that she would suspend for a time her feminist distaste for its patriarchal politics. Such was not the case, however, with the family of fashion, which far from waning in strength, seemed to be growing in influence among affluent Americans. Like the old-fashioned family, the family of fashion was patriarchal in politics, but in Alcott's opinion it degraded women more. In the fashionable world men are plunged into cutthroat business competition, while their wives are robbed of meaningful work, reduced to mere symbols of their husbands' success and valued the more as they have less to do. These pampered ladies filled their hours thinking only of parties and foolish finery, gossiping about their friends and engaging in petty intrigues. Rigid barriers of class separate them from their unfortunate sisters, the working women, who are either spinsters or are saddled with husbands who are unable to compete in the dog-eat-dog world of commerce. The world inhabited by families of fashion is one devoid of warmth, justice, or charity, and it corrupts all whom it touches—men and women, rich and poor, old and young.

Alcott's sweeping indictment of fashionable families sprang not only from her feminist sympathies; it shows also how well she had imbibed the lessons of growing up in a transcendentalist household. For all of her differences with her father and mother—and they were many—she was profoundly influenced by their transcendentalist convictions. Not that she had much patience for philosophy as such, having once described a philosopher as a man aloft in a balloon while his family attempted to pull him back to earth. She ridiculed Bronson's Fruitlands experiment in "Transcendental Wild Oats," and in her career set out to beat the world on its own amoral terms. But while it would be a mistake to think of her as a transcendentalist philosopher, nevertheless she had absorbed the central message, delivered by both parents, that the good life consisted of plain living and high thinking. She sought both fame and fortune, but her transcendentalist conscience forbade her to enjoy it, and she took a certain grim satisfaction in denying herself the luxuries that her wealth made possible. Her fame opened the doors of many wealthy homes formerly closed to her, but she entered only reluctantly and as infrequently as possible. She hated to be lionized, and after a brief exposure to the doubtful joys of popularity, she retreated to the bosom of the family or isolated herself in furnished rooms, giving herself over to the hard labor of writing. Whatever difficulties Bronson's child-rearing created for Louisa, it is evident that it had proved effective in shaping her character.

Out of this fusion of feminism and transcendentalism, Alcott drew her devastating portraits of the rich, portraits which appear in all of her fiction, but most especially in her sensational stories. Since the sensational stories usually occur in a European setting, Alcott strongly implied that this unhappy family style was spawned by a decadent European aristocracy. It is a world of arranged, loveless marriages in which women are mere pawns in a game of lust, greed, and ambition. Take, for example, "A Whisper in the Dark," a tale in which an innocent young heiress falls into the clutches of her greedy guardian-uncle. After she spurns his advances, the bounder imprisons her in an insane asylum for the purpose of making her fortune his own. The subsequent events are entirely implausible, including the young woman's miraculous escape, but there could be no doubt of Alcott's major point, which is that relationships between the sexes in families of fashion are an act of war.[4]

Sexual warfare is also the theme of "Behind a Mask," which appeared in 1866 in *The Flag of Our Union*, a weekly publication devoted, according to one scholar, to "violent narratives peopled with convicts and opium addicts."[5] The story features perhaps the most intriguing and full-bodied of Alcott's sensational heroines, much more convincing than Pauline of "Pauline's Passion and Punishment." It is also the best constructed of her sensational stories, for the plot unfolds persuasively in response to the temperament of her chief characters and without much help from miraculous accidents. Jean Muir, like Pauline, is a woman victimized, and like Pauline she is bent on revenge. The source of her victimization is, however, delineated with more subtlety and complexity, indicating Alcott's increasing power and skill as an author. Pauline's problem is a selfish man. Jean Muir has to deal with such a man also—several of them, in fact—but the story manages to convey as well the idea that Jean is the victim of a rigid English social class structure, which degrades her not simply because she is a woman but because she is also a woman without wealth and position. She appears in the story first as a young, timid, pale-faced applicant for the position of governess to a girl in the wealthy Coventry household: "All felt a touch of pity at the sight of the pale-faced girl in her plain black dress, with no ornament but a little silver cross at her throat. Small, thin, and colorless she was, with yellow hair, gray eyes and sharply cut, irregular but very expressive features. Poverty seemed to have set its bond stamp upon her, and life to have had for her more frost than sunshine."[6] The younger members of the Coventry household—Bella, Jean's charge, and Bella's brother Edward—feel compassion and treat Jean with respect, a kindness for which they are subsequently remembered, but the older brother, Gerald, who is heir and head of the household, makes no attempt to disguise his contempt for Jean, nor to conceal his boredom at the prospect of having her in the house. His contempt is evident in his neglect to send a carriage to the rail station to pick her up. As he explains, "I forgot it. But it's not far; it won't hurt her to walk" (p. 4). Equally contemptuous of the governess is Lucia, Gerald's fiancée, who is as beautiful as she is snobbish. From Gerald and Lucia it is clear that Jean will receive none of the respect due a human being. As an added humiliation, Jean is forced to endure a searching examination of her qualifications as a governess, including an audition at the piano. In sketching such scenes it is evident that Alcott was drawing heavily upon her long years of experience as a servant and governess in the households of the rich.

Despite Jean's unprepossessing appearance, the reader soon learns that there exists another, entirely different Jean Muir "behind the mask," a fact that the Coventry family will eventually learn to their sorrow. Having claimed that she is but a girl of nineteen, Jean Muir is in fact a worldly-wise woman, having behind her a career on the stage and a failed marriage to an unsuccessful actor. Alone in her room, the real Jean Muir is revealed to the reader:

> When alone Miss Muir's conduct was decidedly peculiar. Her first act was to clench her hands and mutter between her teeth, with passionate force, "I'll not fail again if there is power in a woman's wit and will." . . . Kneeling before the one small trunk which held her worldly possessions, she opened it, drew out a flask, and mixed a glass of some ardent cordial, which she seemed to enjoy extremely as she sat on the carpet, musing, while her quick eyes examined every corner of the room.
>
> "Not bad! It will be a good field for me to work in, and the harder the task the better I shall like it. *Merci*, old friend. You put heart and courage into me when nothing else will. Come, the curtain is down, so I may be myself for a few hours, if actresses ever are themselves."

Whereupon the governess removes the abundant braids from her head, takes out several teeth and reveals herself to be "a haggard, worn, and moody woman of thirty at least." Once having been "happy, innocent and tender," she is now a woman "brooding over some wrong, or loss, or disappointment which had darkened all her life" (pp. 11–12).

If the sources of Jean's degradation are more complex than those that wounded Pauline, her revenge is also more subtle and carefully planned, aimed at achieving a position of wealth and power, and subduing those who have shown her such contempt. To this end she proceeds to bring to bear all of her natural talent as a woman and her training as an actress. Gradually revealing to the family her accomplishments at the piano, in singing, and in storytelling, she easily wins the allegiance of the young Edward and Bella. Discovering that Edward is an ardent horseman, she makes friends with Edward's stallion, Hector. Soon her natural talent as an actress makes her the lively center of the household, but she is careful to shut Gerald and Lucia out of the charmed circle of gaiety, and they are made painfully aware that they have nothing to amuse them but their mutually boring company. Soon Jean has won Edward's affection, and then she begins to exercise her influence on Gerald, first by ignoring him, which arouses his interest, and then by allowing him to discover, as if by accident, the supposed fact that she is the daughter of a Scottish noblewoman who ran away with a poor minister. "Coventry felt his interest in his sister's governess much increased by this fact; for, like all wellborn Englishmen, he valued rank and gentle blood even more than he cared to own" (p. 48).

The conquests of Edward and Gerald were, however, mere preludes to Jean's real goal, which is to marry Gerald's uncle, the elderly, wealthy, and titled Sir John Coventry, who lives on a nearby estate. Arranging a chance meeting, she praises him while pretending not to know his real identity, thus appealing to his vanity. Although it seems only a matter of time until Jean has added Sir John to her list of conquests, Alcott had no intention of depriving her readers of a strong dose of suspense involving threats of exposure and Jean's race to snare the old man before the truth of her checkered past comes to light. In the end, Jean succeeds through luck and guile. She marries Lord Coventry and taunts the enraged relatives: "Hands off, gentlemen! You may degrade yourselves to the work of detectives, but I am not a prisoner yet. Poor Jean Muir you might harm, but Lady Coventry is beyond your reach" (p. 103). In her triumph Jean betrays not the least trace of remorse, and she suffers not the least punishment. She accepts the fashionable code and turns it to her advantage, on the principle that two wrongs do, after all, make a right. Such is the corrupting influence of fashion.

In her literary and juvenile fiction, Alcott brought the fashionable family closer to home, making clear that Americans of wealth were beginning to ape the worst features of decadent European aristocrats. By transferring the setting to the American urban scene, she was able to draw more heavily on her personal experience to bolster her imagination, and in particular to make use of her many years as a servant, governess, and companion in the homes of the wealthy. Consequently, the fullest portrayal of American families of fashion occur in the autobiographical *Work*. Christie, having left her old-fashioned aunt and uncle, ventures into the city to work for the rich. Her first employment is with Mr. and Mrs. Stuart, who are rich, vain, and shallow: "Mrs. Stuart possessed some beauty and chose to think herself a queen of society. She assumed majestic airs in public and could not entirely divest herself of them in private, which often produced comic effects" (p. 19). Finding Christie's name too long, Mrs. Stuart promptly gives her a new title of "Jane," only the first of a series of humiliations. Mr. Stuart is no more respectful of servant girls than his wife, ordering Christie on one occasion to clean his boots—echoes of Alcott's humiliation at Dedham. Moreover, it is clear that this foolish couple have no interest in establishing and maintaining a real family, for their home serves only as a setting for fashionable parties, a strategy in their campaign to pursue "that bright bubble called social success." Christie, who loves to retreat to her room and read books, soon tires of the weekly soirees hosted by the Stuarts: "Night after night the wag told his stories, the poet read his poems, the singers warbled, the pretty women simpered and dressed, the heavy scientific was duly discussed by the elect precious, and Mrs. Stuart, in amazing costumes, sailed to and fro in her most swan-like manner; while my lord stirred up the lions he had captured till they roared their best, great and small" (p. 27).

After fleeing the Stuarts, Christie attempts a career on the stage, but she discovers that she is not really talented nor beautiful enough to attain the first rank, and she worries that the life of an actress might turn her hard, selfish, and vain. She turns once again to service in a rich family, this time as a governess, and finds there fresh humiliation. Mrs. Saltonstall is cut from the same mold as Mrs. Stuart, with the exception of the fact that she is a mother—not, in Christie's opinion, a very good one: "Her time was spent in dressing, driving, dining and dancing; in skimming novels, and embroidering muslin; going to church with a velvet prayer-book and a new bonnet; and writing to her husband when she wanted money, for she had a husband somewhere abroad, who so happily combined business with pleasure that he never found time to come home" (p. 65). Her children she finds to be "inconvenient blessings," whom she turns over to Christie. It is not, however, either the mother or the children who prove to be the source of Christie's difficulty, but rather Mrs. Saltonstall's brother, Philip Fletcher, who is rich, handsome (if somewhat overweight) and withal a dandy. He takes a fancy to Christie and she is tempted to consider seriously the idea of marrying him, for the idea appeals to her vanity and ambition. As she puts it: "If he really cares for me I will listen, and not refuse till I know him well enough to decide. I'm tired of being alone and should enjoy ease and pleasure so much. He's going abroad for the winter, and that would be charming. I'll try not to be worldly-minded and marry without love, but it does look tempting to a poor soul like me" (pp. 78–79).

Christie is saved from such a cynical arrangement by Fletcher himself, who inadvertently wounds her pride and reminds her of the barrier of class that remains between them. Aware that he is considered quite a catch, Fletcher has little doubt that he can have Christie for the asking, and manages to insert into his proposal of marriage a tone of condescension. Specifically, he generously offers to overlook the fact that Christie has been an actress. He thus reveals himself as falling far short of the ideal man that Christie has in mind for a husband: "He was not the lover she had dreamed of, the brave, true man who gave her all, and felt it could not half repay the treasure of her innocent, first love. This was not the happiness she had hoped for, the perfect faith, the glad surrender, the sweet content that made all things possible, and changed this work-a-day world into a heaven while the joy lasted" (p. 83). Sylvia, who had destroyed her marriage out of love for Adam, would have agreed, and we may be certain that both Sylvia and Christie speak for the author.

The contrast between old-fashioned families and families of fashion is drawn most sharply and most explicitly in Louisa's juvenile fiction, and there she traces the impact of the two family styles on the young. Like *Little Women, An Old-Fashioned Girl* was written hurriedly, for both Alcott and her publishers were eager to strike while the iron of popularity was hot. Now the didactic side came more insistently to the fore, eager as Alcott was to lay before her young readers a moral lesson about the kind of family life to be avoided. The heroine of the story, Polly, is a somewhat subdued version of Jo March, combining Jo's independence and forthrightness with a bit of Meg's beauty and gentleness. As the title makes clear Polly has been reared in an old-fashioned rural family, where she has learned to dress simply and deal with people honestly. At the age of fourteen, she is still "not a bit of a young lady," and still approaches others with the innocence and the gaiety of a child.

The plot turns around her visit to the city and exposure to a wealthy family of fashion, the Shaws, who frequently challenge her simple rural integrity. Fannie Shaw, the older daughter of the family, is a vain, urbane, sophisticated young lady of sixteen who loses no time in pointing out Polly's shortcomings and criticizing her "countrified" ways. For one thing, Polly dresses "like a little girl" in her simple blue merino frock and stout boots. When Polly protests that she *is* a little girl, Fannie begs to differ:

> "You are fourteen; and *we* consider ourselves young ladies at that age," continued Fannie, surveying, with complacency, the pile of hair on the top of her head, with a fringe of fuzz round her forehead, and a wavy lock streaming down her back; likewise, her scarlet-and-black suit, with its big sash, little *pannier*, bright buttons, points, rosettes,—and, heaven knows what. There was a locket on her neck, earrings tinkling in her ears, watch and chain at her belt, and several rings on a pair of hands that would have been improved by soap and water. (p. 9)

Fannie sets out to improve Polly by introducing her to her fashionable set of friends and exposing her for the first time to the theater. There the entertainment is "very gorgeous, very vulgar, and very fashionable," but Polly's delight quickly changes to shock as she hears actors talking slang. A group of girls, dressed as jockeys, comes "prancing on to the stage, cracking their whips, stamping the heels of their topboots, and winking at the audience." Worse, another set of painted girls appears in costumes consisting of nothing more than gauze wings and a bit of gold fringe around the waist. "I don't think it was proper," Polly protests, but Fannie dismisses her complaint with the observation that she will soon get used to it (pp. 15–17). Aside from attending such spectacles, Fannie's time is taken up with primping, shopping, reading sensational novels, and attending a fashionable school where she indifferently studies French, German, and Italian, but fails to learn how to speak good English. Above all, Fannie is preoccupied with boys.

Alcott makes clear the source of Fannie's conduct, of which she so clearly disapproves, providing a devastating portrait of Fannie's mother and father. Mrs. Shaw is introduced as a "pale, nervous woman," who has made herself into an invalid at the age of forty. Having nothing to do, she is much preoccupied with her imagined ailments, and presides over a household in which there is little affection between parents and children. She encourages Fannie to copy her fashionable follies and has no time for her younger daughter Maud: "When Mrs. Shaw came home that day in her fine visiting costume, and Maud ran to welcome her with unusual affection, she gathered up her lustrous silk and pushed the little girl away, saying, impatiently, 'Don't touch me, child, your hands are dirty'" (pp. 11, 123–24). Mr. Shaw has better instincts, and he wistfully wishes that his Fannie would be a little more like Polly. Moreover, when a young would-be lover sends Fannie flowers, Mr. Shaw attempts to put a stop to this "nonsense," threatening to send Fannie away to a convent in Canada. But while Fannie is afraid of her father, she receives encouragement from Mrs. Shaw, who regards her daughter's precocious ways with indulgence. In any event, Mr. Shaw is much too preoccupied with business affairs to pay much attention to his children, "who had always found him busy, indifferent and absentminded" (p. 57).

That the Shaw family represents a descent from an old-fashioned golden age is made evident when Polly meets Mr. Shaw's mother, who clings to her old-fashioned ways and thus takes a great liking to their country visitor. Madame Shaw prefers Polly to her own granddaughter because, as she explains, Polly is still a little girl and not a young lady, because she is respectful of her elders, because she knows how to make bread, and because she delights in hearing the old lady reminisce about her youthful escapades in an earlier, simpler day. There follows an "in my day" lecture from Madame Shaw, but it is significant that Alcott did not choose to lampoon the elderly lady's views: "In my day, children of fourteen and fifteen didn't dress in the height of fashion; go to parties, as nearly like those of grown people as it's possible to make them; lead idle, giddy, unhealthy lives, and get blasé at twenty. We were little folks till eighteen or so; worked and studied, dressed and played, like children; honored our parents; and our days were much longer than now, it seems to me" (pp. 11–14).

Grandmother Shaw dies halfway through the novel, and her old-fashioned ways die with her, making clear a point that Alcott only hinted at in her literary fiction, namely, that the clock cannot be turned back. Likewise, the golden wedding anniversary in *Moods* remains only an interlude, for it is a world closed to the likes of Sylvia and Adam. Having caught in the rural household a glimpse of Camelot, Sylvia must turn to meet the fate to which her temperament condemns her. As for Cynthy Wilkins, Christie is impressd with the intelligence of this simple working woman, but Christie is not Cynthy. She is too independent in her ways to tolerate a man like Elisha. After all, she had already renounced her rural background with its limited horizons, and she had specifically rejected the prospect of marriage with a farmer who, most likely, would have turned out to be another Elisha. Christie finds that the Wilkins household is a bit too patriarchal to suit her taste, for she notes that Elisha does not really pull his weight in family chores. In short, for a strong-minded woman like Christie, there can be no return to the old-fashioned family, notwithstanding its undeniable charm.

The decline of the old-fashioned family as Alcott portrayed it serves to shed light on a dispute among historians which centers around the matter of whether the new kind of family emerging in the nineteenth century had the effect of enhancing or depressing the power and status of women, particularly when compared with the position of her ancestors in Colonial America.[7] Alcott might be puzzled by the debate, for she was aware that the old-fashioned family, based on paternalistic politics, was actually giving way to several alternative models, each of which held in store a different fate for women. The sentimental family model would rob women of their roles in productive labor, to be sure, but at the same time it emphasized her significance within the home, and especially in her role as a mother. Alcott entertained reservations about this model, as we shall see, but her greatest indignation was reserved for the family of fashion, which not only stripped women of their economic tasks but also rendered them incapable of performing as housekeepers and mothers. From Alcott's vantage point, the real warfare within Victorian domesticity was not between women and the family, but rather between the family of fashion and other forms of family life that would square with the aspirations of women like Christie, which is to say, women like Alcott.

Companionate Marriage and the Androgynous Ideal

*I*n 1870 Alcott told the readers of *An Old-Fashioned Girl* that the heroine had "early learned what it takes most women some time to discover, that sex does not make nearly as much difference in hearts and souls as we fancy. Joy and sorrow, love and fear, life and death bring so many of the same needs to all that the wonder is we do not understand each other better, but wait till times of tribulation teach us that human nature is very much the same in men and women."[1] Even if she reserved her greatest contempt for the family of fashion her androgynous insight clearly implied criticism of the sentimental family as well. It also proved that for all of her complaints about the pressure of public and publishers, Alcott could summon the courage to dissent from the sentimental revolution, which had emphasized differences between the masculine and the feminine temperaments to the point of caricature.

Alcott's insistence on the bond of humanity that transcends the divisions of male and female lent, of course, powerful support to a feminist demand for equality of opportunity for women in the marketplace. Anyone able to put aside for a moment a sentimental perspective would not be shocked to discover that the Dianas of the world might harbor a "masculine" hunger for public recognition. Beyond this feminist persuasion, however, Alcott's emphasis on the common needs of male and female held implications for the private sphere of marriage and the family. If, indeed, men and women had much in common, then a consciousness of that fact might point the way toward transcending the battle of the sexes and finding a new kind of marital relationship, one based not only on mutual affection, but also on a sharing of privilege and duty.

In describing such a relationship, Alcott was forced to draw heavily on her imagination, but she was provided some assistance in the example of her parents, who, despite their troubles, loved one another deeply and maintained a mutual respect over the difficult years. For all his failings as a breadwinner, moreover, Bronson was unusual in his willingness to shoulder the burdens of nurture within the home. Alcott's recollection that her father played a major role in her education was no mere exaggeration born of nostalgia. By the same token, Abigail displayed considerable "masculine" strength by venturing into the employment marketplace when it became apparent that her husband was not up to dealing with his conventional responsibilities as a provider. If a companionate ideal of family life required considerably more flexibility in sex roles than sentimental notions allowed, then Bronson and Abigail had paved the way for Louisa's endorsement of companionate marriage.

Manhood in Alcott's Imagination

While Alcott's parents provided an example of companionate marriage, they did not by any means resolve all of the difficulties their daughter encountered in portraying such a relationship, for she was compelled to struggle with her skepticism about the ability of most men to adapt to such a novel role. In her portrayals of "the lords of creation," as she frequently termed the opposite sex, she was also handicapped by the fact that her acquaintance with men was extremely limited, consisting of Bronson and his transcendentalist friends—hardly a representative group—and the unsavory types she encountered in her years of domestic service. Consequently, her early fiction suffers from a tendency to assign men to one of three stereotypes. There are, as we have seen, selfish fops and villains who populate her sensational world, the Gilberts and Geralds whose misdeeds earn the enmity of women like Pauline and Jean. Their polar opposites appear in her literary work, men like Adam who are cast in a rebellious mold and who are so "violently virtuous" that they prove no more suited for the institution of marriage and family than the Gilberts and Geralds. Finally, she presented domesticated males like Sylvia's unfortunate husband, who seems suited for family life, to be sure, but neither Alcott nor her heroines can conceal the fact that they find such men dull. All in all, Alcott's conception of manhood in her early fiction hardly amounts to a rousing vote of confidence in the prospect of happy marriages for women of sensitivity and spirit like herself.

This stereotyped approach to men mars even some of her later work. One of the more unfortunate of Alcott's creations is Professor Bhaer, who figures prominently in her juvenile fiction as the man Jo March marries. Although Bhaer moves through three of the novels, he rarely takes on the lineaments of a flesh-and-blood human being. He is a kindly, stout, fortyish German who loves children and holds advanced theories about dealing with them, but Alcott never invests him with any problems, except the ever-present difficulty of poverty. He is a thoroughly domesticated male but with a touch of sainthood. His entire life seems to revolve around the welfare of his family and his pupils. He resembles, in fact, Jo's father, who also seems to float in a world above common human frailties. One wonders what the lively and passionate Jo sees in Bhaer, except as a substitute father who functions to restrain her more impulsive moods. Bhaer seems expressly invented for the purpose of marrying Jo off to someone other than the more interesting Laurie.

Equally unconvincing is Alcott's portrait of John Brooke, another ideal husband and father who entered the March family circle by marrying Meg. Although Brooke figures in some lively and humorous episodes in *Little Women*, he sinks into the oblivion of the Domesticated Male, despite Alcott's efforts to present him as someone to be admired. The essential problem is that Brooke is as dull as the bookkeeping occupation he follows, almost as if dullness were a prerequisite for success in family life. Brooke's death earns him a chapter in *Little Men*, a chapter devoted to an unpersuasive eulogy. The reader is led to believe that the orphan boys of Plumfield really admire Brooke despite his lack of distinction, and despite the presence of the rich and fun-loving Laurie, who would seem to provide a more exciting model for imitation. When several of the boys express admiration for the departed Brooke, another begs to differ, whereupon Professor Bhaer sets him straight:

> "He wasn't rich, was he?" asked Jack.
> "No."

"He never did anything to make a stir in the world, did he?"
"No."
"He was only good?"
"That's all;" and Franz found himself wishing that Uncle John *had* done something to boast of, for it was evident that Jack was disappointed by his replies.
"Only good. That is *all* and everything," said Mr. Bhaer. . . . "He simply did his duty in all things, and did it so cheerfully, so faithfully, that it kept him patient, brave, and happy through poverty and loneliness and years of hard work. . . . He was a good husband and father, so tender, wise, and thoughtful."[2]

Given such passages, it is little wonder that the author never attracted many boys among her readers.

Professor Bhaer and John Brooke aside, Alcott's later work is populated with increasing frequency by men who prove worthy of her heroines and who begin to match them in depth and complexity of character. In larger measure, her growing power in the portrayal of manhood reflected her increasing maturity as a writer, but in particular, it may be traced to her Civil War experience. The firing on Fort Sumter set in motion a chain of events that provided Alcott with a much wider experience of men and, ultimately, enriched her literary portrayal of the opposite sex. Characteristically, the first emotion aroused in her by the onset of the Civil War was envy for the adventures now open to men. The conflict stirred her blood, and she longed to be a man so that she could do battle. "But as I can't fight," she said, "I will content myself with working for those who can."[3] What this resolution initially meant was the joining of a sewing circle, but she hungered for something closer to the action. In 1862 she volunteered as a nurse and journeyed to Washington, D.C., for service in the Union Hotel Hospital, with her father observing that since he could not go, he had sent his only son. There she shared with the wounded and the dying soldiers the poor ventilation and bad food and learned much about the reaction of men under stress. As she later has one of her fictional women remark about men, "See them sick as I do, then you know them."[4]

Alcott's first shock was the discovery that her supervisor expected her to bathe the patients. It was clear that the conventional proprieties were out of place:

> If she had requested me to shave them all, or dance a hornpipe on the stove funnel, I should have been less staggered; but to scrub some dozen lords of creation at a moment's notice, was really—really—. However, there was not time for nonsense, and, having resolved when I came to do everything I was bid, I drowned my scruples in my washbowl, clutched my soap manfully, and, assuming a business-like air, made a dab at the first dirty specimen I saw.[5]

The hospital experience also unsettled, as she later confessed, some of her feminist convictions. Describing herself at the outset as a "woman's rights woman," who would have declined any offer of help from a man, she soon found herself ready enough to call for assistance and even to become "a timid trembler" on occasion. She also found that the surgeons did not fit her expectations. She expected "to be treated by them like a door-mat, a worm, or any other meek and lowly article, whose mission it is to be put down and walked upon." Much to her surprise, however, she found herself treated with utmost courtesy and kindness, so much so that she was even emboldened to disagree with the doctors on occasion.[6]

The patients themselves also upset some of her expectations, presenting a wider range of masculine character than her somewhat meager experience of men had prepared her for. There were among them the whiners and the grumblers, hardly a revelation to the bitter young woman, but she was surprised to discover that many of the men possessed virtues which sentimental convention assigned to women. She discovered that men, too, could suffer in silence and endure their afflictions with patience:

> It is all very well to talk of the patience of woman; and far be it from me to pluck that feather from her cap, for, heaven knows, she isn't allowed to wear many; but the patient endurance of these men, under trials of the flesh, was truly wonderful; their fortitude seemed contagious, and scarcely a cry escaped them, though I often longed to groan for them, when pride kept their white lips shut, while great drops stood upon their foreheads, and the bed shook with the irrepressible tremor of their tortured bodies.[7]

One man, a "prince of patients," impressed her in particular, and seemed to combine within himself the best traits of manhood and womanhood. A blacksmith by trade, about thirty years of age, tall and handsome, he was slowly dying of a bullet through his lung. Under his plain speech and unpolished manner, Alcott seemed to see "a noble character, a heart as warm and tender as a woman's, a nature fresh and frank as any child's." In constant pain, he never complained, although once he cried, which seemed to Alcott not a sign of weakness but "only very touching." She sat by him as he died, "glad to have known so genuine a man."[8]

Alcott also encountered humor from such unexpected sources as the sergeant with one leg missing and an arm so shattered that it would soon be amputated. When she asked him if this had been his first battle, he replied:

> "No, miss; I've been in six scrimmages, and never got a scratch till this last one; but it's done the business pretty thoroughly for me, I should say. Lord! What a scramble there'll be for arms and legs, when we old boys come out of our graves on the Judgment Day: wonder if we shall get our own again? If we do, my leg will have to tramp from Fredericksburg, my arm from here I suppose, and meet my body, wherever it may be." The fancy seemed to tickle him mightily, for he laughed blithely, and so did I.[9]

In their simple humanity the blacksmith, the sergeant, and others like them forced Alcott to examine her stereotypes, for it was clear that they were neither villains, rebels, nor mild-mannered providers.

After only six weeks, Alcott herself fell ill, a victim of typhoid pneumonia, which cut short her wartime adventure but which also led to one of the most revealing insights into her confused erotic life. Upon returning home to Concord, she experienced what she called some "strange fancies," induced, no doubt, by a feverish delirium. In her diary she recorded one of the most troubling:

> The most vivid and enduring was the conviction that I had married a stout, handsome Spaniard, dressed in black velvet, with very soft hands, and a voice that was continually saying, "Lie still, my dear!" This was Mother, I suspect; but with all the comfort I often found in her presence, there was blended an awful fear of the Spanish spouse who was always coming after me, appearing out of closets, in at

windows, or threatening me dreadfully all night long. . . . A mob at Baltimore breaking down the door to get me, being hung for a witch, burned, stoned, and otherwise maltreated, were some of my fancies.[10]

The sexual significance of the hallucination is apparent, and it should be interpreted in the context of her recent experience in nursing wounded men. For more than a decade, as we have seen, she had repressed her sexual feelings toward men, a defense threatened by the requirement that, as a nurse, she handle the bodies of men. The experience doubtless aroused sexual feelings and, consequently, considerable anxiety as well. This disturbing experience in turn reawakened her erotic feeling for her mother, all of which was made more complex by her desire for and her fear of her father. Louisa had, as we have seen, replaced Bronson by taking on his role as provider, and by developing a strong attachment to her mother. It is not surprising, then, that when she took comfort in the presence of the "stout, handsome Spaniard" (her mother), she would fear the retribution of the "Spanish spouse" (her father). Louisa, in other words, was experiencing an anxiety usually experienced by sons who replace their fathers in an intimate relationship with their mothers. The fevered dreams reveal that she was a seething caldron of sexual energy that was seeking but not finding an approved outlet. The resulting guilt might then explain her further delusion that she was being hung for a witch, a fit punishment in her eyes for her illicit and confused passions.

This traumatic episode seemed to help her sort out her feelings toward men and toward other women, for at least she had raised her convoluted feelings to a sufficient level of consciousness that she could record them in her diary. There is, however, a further significance to these revealing dreams. Although there is precious little evidence that she was a lesbian, it is undeniable that she felt strong erotic feelings toward her mother and toward other women. But she possessed erotic feelings toward men as well, and these were the source of much confusion in her emotional life. If a label must be affixed to her sexual orientation, it would be androgynous rather than lesbian. This androgyny was a source of much difficulty for her, but it placed her in a position unique in Victorian culture. Able to acknowledge her bisexual feelings, Alcott could penetrate the wall that sentimentality had erected between the genders, which in turn enabled her to project the ideal of the companionate family.

BOYS AND GIRLS TOGETHER

The literary benefit of Alcott's Civil War experience came in her characterization of men, which became richer and more complex. Her later work delineated men who possess nobility but who are not, for all that, infallible. One such man, still in his formative years, was Laurie, perhaps Alcott's best-known creation next to Jo March, and her characterization of him lends credence to her oft-stated belief that, except for her sisters, she really liked boys better than girls. A composite of several boys she had known, Laurie is a handsome young man who is blessed with a keen wit and shares with Jo a contempt for sentiment in all its forms. It is one of Laurie's purposes, Jo explains to her sisters, to "keep us from being too sentimental." When Meg and John Brooke fall in love (but before John has declared himself), Laurie takes it upon himself to write a passionate note to Meg, signing John's name to it. Laurie is no mere practical joker, however. When he and Jo first meet at a party, he asks her to dance a polka but she declines, explaining that she scorched her dress while standing before a fire. "You may laugh, if you want to," Jo says. "It is funny, I know." "But Laurie didn't laugh; he only looked down a minute, and the expression of his face puzzled Jo when he said, very gentle,—'Never mind that; I'll tell you how we can manage: there's a long hall out there, and we can dance grandly, and no one will see us.'"[11]

The tenderness and understanding that Laurie extends to Jo is reciprocated, as is well known to the generations who read *Little Women*. Jo employs her courage and determination in defending the scapegrace before his grandfather, and in other ways serves as a surrogate mother to a boy without parents. She also makes it one of her missions in life to save Laurie from smoking, drinking, and fashionable indolence. If Laurie tempered the sentimentality of the little women, it was their task to keep him from sowing too many wild oats. Much as Alcott might express dissatisfaction with the sentimental view of relations between the sexes, she clung consistently to the sentimental notion that women were less prone than men to the more blatant vices. Consequently, men and women can provide a healthy corrective for each other. It was a strong affirmation of the mutual value of marriage, and it is little wonder that Alcott's young readers would clamor for Jo and Laurie to exchange vows, for it seemed so apparent that they were in all respects good for each other.

Although she refused to unite Jo and Laurie in marriage, she continued to explore in her subsequent fiction the healthy and unaffected relations that young men and women can have if they are not corrupted by fashion or misled by the sentimental insistence on separate spheres. Polly, the heroine of *An Old-Fashioned Girl*, grew up in an easy and affectionate relationship with her brother, and she is consequently shocked by the often cruel sibling rivalry that divides Fannie Shaw and her brother Tom, as if they are already in training for the battle of the sexes: "Fanny, forgetful of her young-ladyism and her sixteen years, had boxed Tom's ears, and Tom, resenting the insult, had forcibly seated her in a coal-hod, where he held her with one hand while he returned the compliment with the other. Both were very angry, and kept twitting one another with every aggravation they could invent, as they scolded and scuffled, presenting a most unlovely spectacle."[12] The difficulty, as Polly soon perceives, is that the entire family has labeled Tom the black sheep and he sets out to prove it by uncouth behavior. Polly, who sees good qualities beneath Tom's rough exterior, shows him kindness and leads him to soften his raucous ways, a relationship that ultimately flowers into marriage. Alcott returns to the theme in *Little Men*, in which Plumfield is a school explicitly based on the principle of coeducation. As Jo explains to Laurie, the girls temper the boys in the direction of keeping them "gentlemen," while the boys help the girls by teaching them many skills that they would otherwise be ignorant of. Jo exclaims to Laurie: "'Dear me! If men and women would only trust, understand, and help one another as my children do, what a capital place the world would be!' and Mrs. Jo's eyes grew absent, as if she was looking at a new and charming state of society in which people lived as happily and innocently as her flock at Plumfield."[13]

CHRISTIE AND DAVID: "FAITHFUL COMRADES"

The obstacles that prevented Alcott from envisioning Jo's marriage to Laurie were overcome four years later when she imagined and described for her adult readers a marriage between a woman like herself and a man who, like Laurie, was not molded along stereotypical lines. *Work,* although autobiographical, abandons memory in favor of imagination when Christie meets and eventually marries David Sterling. David is, as his surname suggests, a man of integrity who resembles Adam, the Thoreau-like hero of Alcott's earlier novel, *Moods*: "The other face possessed no striking comeliness of shape or color; but the brown, becoming beard made it manly, and the broad arch of a benevolent brow added nobility to features otherwise not beautiful,—a fact plainly expressing resolution and rectitude, inspiring respect as naturally as a certain protective kindliness of manner won confidence."[14] Not that Christie is smitten with David immediately. When she first hears of him, David is praised for his virtue and good works, while Christie would prefer someone less virtuous and more exciting. His reputation is saved somewhat in her eyes when there is also a hint of a great sorrow in David's life, traceable to a woman.

For all of his apparent resemblance to Adam, David is a man built along more human lines. For one thing, he has a known occupation (that of florist and gardener), and for another he possesses a sense of humor, a fact which Christie finds puzzling, for she had expected someone with such a tragic past to be more melancholy. It becomes apparent that Alcott is poking mild fun at Christie's sentimental expectations, a measure of the fact that Alcott herself has tempered some of her earlier tendency to make certain men into gods. Chiding herself as well as her heroine, Alcott has Christie observe: "I never shall outgrow my foolish way of trying to make people other than they are. Gods are gone, heroes hard to find, and one should be contented with good men, even if they do wear old clothes, lead prosaic lives, and have no accomplishments but gardening, playing the flute, and keeping their tempers" (p. 246). Nevertheless, Christie cannot help wishing to reform David. Specifically she wishes to

111

fire his ambition, but he seems satisfied with "watching over his mother, reading his old books, and making flowers bloom double when they ought to be single" (p. 252).

Gradually Christie falls in love with David, despite his imperfections. She is surprised to discover that her restless ambitions have subsided, and that she is becoming quite content with her domestic duties in the Sterling household with David and his mother. Perhaps, she thinks, home is the woman's sphere after all, "and the perfect roasting of beef, brewing of tea, and concocting of delectable puddings, an end worth living for if masculine commendation rewarded the labor" (pp. 288–89).

After several twists and turns of plot, David proposes marriage and Christie accepts, without the fashionable sparring of courtship, and they come to know each other better during a year-long engagement as members of his mother's household, working side by side in the greenhouse. The firing on Fort Sumter disrupts their idyll. When it is apparent that David will enlist, they decide to marry, but it is a marriage based on an unusual agreement, one in keeping with Alcott's notion of companionate marriage. Christie agrees to his enlistment, but insists that she will enlist when he does, to serve as a nurse: "That was all: she did not offer to detain him now; he did not deny her right to follow. They looked each other bravely in the face a moment, seeing, acknowledging the duty and the danger, yet ready to do the one and dare the other, since they went together. Then shoulder to shoulder, as if already mustered in, these faithful comrades marched to and fro, planning their campaign" (p. 364). Confirming the comradeship, Christie and David are both married in uniform, he in the Union blue, she "looking very like a Quaker bride in her gray gown with no ornament but delicate frills at neck and wrist, and the roses in her bosom" (p. 378). Alcott could have found no more concrete symbol of her belief in the ideal of companionate marriage as a union of equals. The Civil War provides a testing ground for both, and each proves equal to the task: Christie as a successful nurse, with "no confounded nerves" to impair her usefulness, and David as a courageous soldier. During the course of the war she and David meet as frequently as their duties permit until, at last, David is fatally wounded and dies in her arms, leaving her only his memory and a child in her womb.

Although Alcott felt her novel was not what it should be, *Work* represents her most thoughtful and mature statement about marriage and the family, and thus serves as a standard against which to measure and evaluate her more popular work. In it she recapitulated and elaborated the theme of her sensational and literary visions, condemning the hypocrisy and contradictions of fashionable standards, which train women to be vain and foolish, deny them equality of education and opportunities for employment, and then throw them on the marriage market as if they were so much produce. *Work* is an eloquent plea for women like Christie (and Alcott) who wish, no less than men, to hold on to their integrity and independence, and who deserve men who will both love and respect them as human beings. It is, then, a feminist work, but it is not a tract against marriage and family life. While providing a sobering view of family life in Victorian America, especially among the affluent, fashionable urban classes, *Work* celebrates marriage, provided that it is based on romantic love, and provided that the union results in a genuine partnership of privileges and responsibilities. Mrs. Wilkins the laundress and Christie the nurse refuse to place themselves on the pedestal the sentimental revolution reserved for women, and each contributes to the work of the world and the survival of her family. It was, in a sense, a revival of the old-fashioned family, now shorn of its patriarchal features, and thus an ideal response to the family of fashion.

COMPANIONATE MARRIAGE: A SENSATIONAL VERSION

Given Alcott's yearning for literary respectability, her endorsement of companionate marriage in *Work* leaves room for doubt that she really meant it. *Work* was, after all, yet another bid for acceptance by the cultural elite, however autobiographical it was in outward detail. Would she adhere to this vision of marriage when, assured of anonymity, she returned for one last fling at sensational fiction during her later years? An answer is provided in an examination of *A Modern Mephistopheles,* published in 1877 at the suggestion of Thomas

Niles, who approached her with the idea of writing a novel for the "no-name" series, which, as the label suggests, consisted of an elaborate literary game in which readers and critics attempted to guess at the identity of the authors. Fascinated with the intrigue, and assured of anonymity, Alcott agreed to make a contribution. She thought of Goethe's *Faust*, which she had recently read, and set about revising one of her manuscripts, rejected a decade earlier by Frank Leslie as too sensational. "Tired of providing moral pap for the young," as she put it, she set to work on *A Modern Mephistopheles*, keeping her association with the project secret from all save her publisher, her mother, and her sister Anna.[15] She did not show the story to Bronson.

A Modern Mephistopheles is the most ambitious of her sensational work and, in her own opinion, the best of her novels.[16] As the title indicates, it is an updated version of the Faust legend, in which a representative of diabolic forces seduces a young man into selling his soul in return for worldly prizes. Set exotically in a vine-clad villa filled with sumptuous furnishings, the tale provides little hint of domestic tranquility, and the plot is marked by intrigue, sensual passion, drugs, illicit liaisons, and attempted murder. It is little wonder that Frank Leslie had rejected it as too sensational or that Alcott would insist on anonymity. At the same time, however, she attempted more in this novel than in her other sensational stories, and for the first time in her sensational work she celebrated romantic love and companionate marriage.

The story is dominated by Jasper Helwyze, the most utterly villainous of Alcott's creations. He is an invalid, pale and frail, with a beardless, thin-lipped, "keen" face, and dark, penetrating, "burning" eyes. In character he appears nearly superhuman, a fit representative of diabolic forces, possessing great talent yet incapable of passion, love, or conscience. Nevertheless, the author attempts to provide Helwyze with human qualities, tracing the sources of diabolic temperament to an "accident which left him in incurable pain," and to the betrayal of a beautiful woman, Olivia, who married another. As the story opens, however, Olivia has left her brutal, unfaithful husband. Discovering that she loves Jasper after all, she reappears at his side to do his bidding. Her love is unrequited, for Jasper's only passion now is the worship of the god of intellect, and his only source of gratification is the sense of power he gains from manipulating his fellow human beings and gaining control over their minds.

The villain's first victim is Felix Canaris, a beautiful young man who is pleasure-loving and ambitious but lacking talent. He "thinks himself a genius and will not forgive the world for doubting what he has failed to prove," Jasper sardonically remarks. [17] Attracted by his beauty Jasper promises to help Felix with his career as a writer if he will serve him as his secretary. Felix readily agrees and offers himself "body and soul" to his patron. Jasper keeps his part of the bargain, it is ultimately revealed, by writing the books to which Felix appends his name, for it appears that Jasper is as talented as he is unscrupulous. For his part, Felix is expected to do more than serve as his master's secretary, but Jasper has no homosexual interest in Felix. "Thank heaven," Jasper tells Olivia, "my passions are all dead, else life would be a hell, not the purgatory it is" (pp. 42–43).

What he has in mind is a more subtle gratification, involving an innocent young woman, Gladys. Gladys is an orphan who has come under the protection of Olivia, and she seems to be as pure as Jasper is villainous. Resembling those ethereal virgins sentimentalists love, Gladys appears totally without vanity or guile, or bad habits. She neither smokes nor drinks, and she proves her piety by saying grace at meals, shocking the other members of the household. Her virtue is, in fact, the source of her fascination for Jasper, more so than her physical beauty. He quite frankly wishes to make her the subject of an experiment by thrusting her together with Felix. Following his insane plan, Jasper orders Felix to woo Gladys and wed her, with the understanding that Gladys will spend much of her time as a companion to himself. Felix objects, cherishing his liberty and fearing that marriage may damage his career. Besides, "though I reverence her as an angel, I do *not* love her as a woman," he protests. Jasper reminds him of their bargain, and Felix capitulates, easily winning the love of the innocent girl.

Thus is set in place a peculiar triangle: Felix busy with his career and spending increasing time away from home in carousing and gambling; Gladys torn between her adoration for Felix and her duties to serve as the companion to Jasper; and Jasper himself, who amuses himself by observing Gladys. Although the author did not use so strong a description, it is apparent that Jasper is attempting mental rape of the young woman, having her read to him from such "dangerous" works as George Sand, Goethe, Shakespeare, Dante, and Byron: "She often paused to question with eager lips, to wipe wet eyes, to protest with indignant warmth, or to shiver with the pleasurable pain of a child who longs, yet dreads to hear an exciting story to the end" (p. 122). Jasper persists in his efforts at mental seduction, resorting even to the use of hashish to undermine the resistance of the young woman and corrupt her mind.

It would appear that Jasper has triumphed over the young couple, but he has reckoned without the power of a woman armed by virtue and love. Gladys begins a counterattack by challenging her husband to give up his bad habits and late nights away from home: "I want you to be as good as you are gifted," she tells Felix. Felix reluctantly agrees to spend more time at home where, as he puts it, he will be "safest if not happiest" (p. 159). Gladys then proposes that they form together a "domestic league," an enclave, as it were, within the evil household, where they can work to make themselves independent of Jasper. She suggests that he spend some time translating a book while she takes up embroidery, and they can work together: "While he wrote she sat near, so quietly busy, that he often forgot her presence; but when he looked up, the glance of approval, the encouraging word, the tender smile, were always ready, and wonderfully inspiring, for this sweet comrade grew dearer day by day" (p. 168). As they work together and talk, Felix finds himself growing more fond of Gladys and soon he is learning from her how to love another person besides himself.

She succeeds so well that Jasper grows alarmed, commanding Olivia in the funniest line in the book: "Amuse Felix; he's falling in love with his wife" (p. 173). None of Jasper's tricks can avail now, however. Felix, his manhood aroused, attempts to murder Jasper, but Gladys stops him. Felix then confesses to her at last that Jasper has written all of the works for which he has taken credit, a confession which releases him from bondage. Gladys, true to her character, forgives him this deception and then dies in childbirth, pleading with the two men to forgive one another. Felix leaves to find "honest work," and Jasper slips toward death, suffering the agony of losing his mental faculties, his only deity.

The sad ending of the novel was, of course, entirely appropriate for a work of sensational fiction, but it should not obscure the major transformations that occurred in the characters of Felix and Gladys. Gladys, who began as a stock sentimental heroine—totally pure and unbelievably innocent—is transformed by the experience of evil into a strong, assertive, passionate young woman. She in turn rescues Felix from his selfish ambition, and, armed with their mutual love, they confront together the forces of evil represented by Jasper. It was a powerful if sensational assertion of the possibilities of mutual benefit and growth in companionate marriage.

It can be seen, then, that Alcott did not repudiate marriage and the family in her fiction, but called rather for the creation of a new kind of family which would transcend all varieties of Victorian domesticity. It would be a family marked by mutual affection and a genuine sharing of privileges and responsibilities between men and women, putting to an end the war between the sexes which she described so vividly in her portrayal of fashionable families. But the companionate family would transcend as well the sentimental model of family life, for it was not merely sexual conflict that Alcott deplored, but also the sharp separation of gender roles endorsed by the sentimental revolution. Alcott, like her heroine Jo March, was quick to ridicule woman's pretensions to spiritual superiority and she took delight in satirizing the current feminine indulgence in sentiment. She could find no higher praise for a woman than to describe her as "sensible." Conversely, as she matured in her understanding, she sought to portray men who possessed what sentimentalists might have regarded as feminine sensitivity to the needs of others. In keeping with this androgynous ideal, she also laid heavy emphasis on the value of coeducation, both within the family and without, hoping that boys and girls could grow up together, correcting one another's faults and learning the lessons of comradeship in preparation for their sharing of the burdens of adult life.

117

Victorian Manhood

Unfortunately, despite Alcott's earnest efforts, her portrait of companionate marriage remained somehow unpersuasive, because she had great difficulty in portraying men who combined in themselves the qualities of the rebellious adventurer—which she much admired—and the qualities of the responsible, conscientious nurturer and provider, which the companionate family would seem to require. Although her delineation of males improved with time, Alcott was swimming against the mainstream, for Victorian culture itself was highly confused about the subject of masculinity and in particular about the relationship of masculinity to the institution of the family. Leslie Fiedler was among the first to call attention to the problem of masculine identity as it was reflected in the American novel. As Fiedler pointed out, the greatest of nineteenth-century male novelists had difficulty portraying men as husbands and fathers, a difficulty which has persisted among the better male authors of the twentieth century. Fiedler contends that Cooper, Poe, Dana, Melville, Hawthorne, James, Faulkner, and Hemingway found in marriage and family life a threat to the male ego, for, he argues, "it is maturity above all things that the American writer fears, and marriage seems to him its essential sign." Advancing a Freudian interpretation, Fiedler speculates that fatherhood was particularly threatening to our male novelists because it meant that the hero would have to abandon his role as deliverer of the "captive mother," and assume the role of the "ogre who holds her in captivity."[18] Whatever the motivation, Fiedler calls attention to the paradox that our most honored writers rejected the values of marriage and family life which middle-class readers professed to revere. "Only by assuming an unconscious marginal rejection of the values of that society on the part of all or most of its members," Fiedler comments, "can we come to terms with its glorification of a long line of heroes in flight from woman and home."[19]

More recently, Joe Dubbert has traced similar themes, although he broadens his subject matter to include popular culture and he leans more toward a social-historical interpretation than a psychological one. Dubbert contends that the identity of American men rested on the existence of the frontier—"both as fact and as fantasy"—a place where men could be men, which meant that they could be adventurous, courageous, strong-willed, and autonomous. As the nineteenth century wore on, however, this male identity was threatened from two directions, first by the disappearance of the frontier and the advancement of urban, corporate civilization, and secondly by the new assertiveness of women, who men feared would capture and domesticate them. As Dubbert puts it:

> If the perception of progress was linked to the availability of virgin land and if the moral destiny of America depended on expanding onto new frontiers, as Turner said it did, then what was to happen when the frontier no longer existed? Here was a crisis for American males as the *space* paradigm was threatened. They now had to accept living in *place*, in a community, in a social environment, interacting with other men doing the same, and facing the very real possibility that they might become fathers with children to support.[20]

Searching desperately for urban equivalents to the frontier as an opportunity to validate their masculinity, men immersed themselves in business competition, obsessively pursuing the elusive goals of wealth, status, and power, leaving the familial responsibilities to women. The result, Dubbert contends, is that men embraced the sentimental doctrine of the two spheres with enthusiasm, and fought any effort to violate the arrangement.

The nature of the difficulty was spelled out in detail by Junius Browne, who published an article in *Cosmopolitan* just a month before Alcott's death. Asking, Are women companionable to men? Browne was pessimistic about the possibilities of companionate marriage, but, he argued, the difficulty lay not with women but with men. Browne predicted that "ages" would pass before companionate marriage could become a reality, largely because most men are still less "civilized" than women. Browne said men would never dream of being comrades of their wives, for they do not respect women, regarding them either as rogues or fools. After the passion of the honeymoon has subsided, men flee home and wife and immerse themselves in the delights of billiards, draw-poker and brandy-and-soda—all indulged, of course, in the company of males. Moreover, most men speak disdainfully of men who seem to enjoy the company of women, labeling them effeminate, weak-minded, and "Miss Nan-cyish."[21] If Browne was correct—and all indications are that he was—then Alcott's hope of companionate marriage was nothing more than a pipe-dream. Victorian males had no use for it.

Alcott was aware of these difficulties, for her own father had rebelled against familial responsibilities in the name of adventure, albeit a philosophical adventure. She filled her work with portraits of family life without men and, at the same time, with complaints about the way men neglected their duties as husbands and fathers. But no more than the male novelists of the Victorian era could Alcott project an image of masculinity that transcended the antifamily archetype. Only in her literary work did she manage to portray men who are good husbands without at the same time being dull, but David Sterling loses his life and Felix Canaris loses his spouse before the reader discovers if either possesses the stuff of fatherhood. Despite Alcott's efforts, we are left to conclude with Dubbert that in nine-teenth-century America "one searches mostly in vain . . . for a con-cept of fatherhood, or even of an opinion of what a good father might be."[22] The sharp separation along lines of gender which nineteenth-century Americans erected between the values of nurture and the values of worldly success remains one of the most troublesome legacies of Victorian domesticity.

The Nurture of the Child:
The Sentimental Legacy

Critical though Alcott might have been of the role that the sentimental revolution assigned to women, she embraced wholeheartedly the emphasis which the sentimentalists placed on nurture within the family. Her parents displayed, as we have seen, an intense preoccupation with children and with their proper upbringing, and it would be surprising indeed if their concern did not find its way into their daughter's depiction of family life. When Alcott treated the experience of childhood, parents or surrogate parents hover constantly in the background, and if the family is a good one, these adults are much preoccupied with the welfare of the younger generation. Among the many failings of families of fashion, according to Alcott, a major fault was precisely that fashionable husbands and wives did not take seriously their duties as parents. Men were too busy with their careers and their wives too caught up in the social whirl to pay much attention to the welfare of the young. The result was children who grew up too quickly and who were exposed too soon to the temptations of adult life.

THE CULT OF MOTHERHOOD EXAMINED

For the evils of the fashionable neglect of the young, the sentimental revolution had provided a ready solution in the cult of motherhood, which condemned child-neglect as out of keeping with the nature of true womanhood, but which, at the same time, laid virtually the sole responsibility for the rearing of the young on the shoulders of women. Given Alcott's endorsement of companionate marriage, it was entirely logical that she would raise serious questions about this sentimental arrangement, but, at the same time, it could not have been easy for her to regard the cult of motherhood with detachment. For one thing, the sentimental celebration of maternal love was not as offensive to her as the evil of maternal neglect, which she believed to be so much a feature of fashionable families. When it came to a comparison between a Mrs. Saltonstall or a Mrs. Shaw, who regarded their offspring as nuisances, and a Cynthy Wilkins, who adored her young ones, there could be no doubt where Alcott's sympathies lay. Moreover, the cult of motherhood was no mere literary convention for her, but rather a part of her most intimate experience. She had before her a living example of motherhood in Abigail, who was happiest when seated by the hearth, surrounded by her girls, and who ventured into the marketplace only under the lash of necessity and returned to her children at the first opportunity. Still another who exhibited the domestic temperament to a high degree was her sister Anna, who even as a little girl delighted in the care of her younger sisters, and who seemed to have the patience for children that Louisa recognized she lacked.

Nor does it seem to be the case that Alcott herself lacked maternal feelings, even if she was not exactly cut out for the tasks of motherhood. She displayed a keen interest in Anna's offspring and was delighted at their birth, on occasion making envious comparisons of Anna's offspring with her own literary creations. "I sell *my* children," she once remarked, "and though they feed me, they don't love me as hers do."[1] After the death of Anna's husband, Louisa assumed responsibility for the financial support of her sister and her children, purchased a house for them and later adopted one of Anna's boys to carry on the Alcott name. May's death in 1879 provided Louisa with an opportunity to experience at firsthand the joys of maternity when she took charge of her namesake, Louisa May Niereker. "Even lonely old spinsters take an interest in babies," she explained in her diary.[2] After "Lulu" arrived, Louisa found "unspeakable comfort" in the care of her infant niece, and found that she could "bear anything with this little sunbeam to light up the world for me."[3] Poor health forced her to turn over the care of Lulu more and more to her sister Anna, but there can be no doubt that Louisa placed high value on nurture in her private life.

But if she was acquainted with maternal feeling, she could not subscribe uncritically to the sentimental cult of motherhood. Far from treating the cult with the respect which it demanded, she undermined it with humor. The most familiar example occurs in *Little Women*, when Meg happily marries John Brooke and settles into her "dovecote." Twins arrive and Meg, as the sentimental cult required, begins to center her life around the babies. Soon, difficulties arise between Meg and her husband.

> When he went out in the morning he was bewildered by small commissions for the captive mamma; if he came gaily in at night, eager to embrace his family, he was quenched by a "Hush! They are just asleep after worrying all day." If he proposed a little amusement at home, "No, it would disturb the babies." If he hinted at a lecture or concert, he was answered with a reproachful look, and a decided—"Leave my children for pleasure, never!"[4]

Nor was the cult necessarily of benefit to the mother herself. Meg's constant preoccupation with the children leaves her worn and nervous, and her neglect of John leads him to spend more time in the home of the friend who has a lively and pretty wife. A lecture from Marmee shows Meg the error of her ways: "Don't let John be a stranger to the babies, for they will do more to keep him safe and happy in this world of trial and temptation, than anything else, and through them you will learn to know and love one another as you should" (2:223).

Proper Discipline: The Middle Way

In distributing advice about the proper rearing of children, Alcott attempted to steer a middle course between neglect and indulgence. In arriving at her notions about child-rearing, she owed, of course, a heavy debt to her parents. Her enormous popularity as a writer enabled her to serve as a vehicle for her father's theories about proper child-rearing, and he reached through her a hearing for his ideas that he was never able to achieve by his own efforts. On matters of technique, Louisa adhered close to Bronson's notions, which, in turn, were consistent with most sentimental manuals of parental advice. As Nancy Cott has noted in her review of antebellum child-rearing advice, the emphasis lay on teaching the child to adopt internal controls.[5] For the achievement of this goal, the strategy recommended by sentimental writers was a heavy reliance upon the bond of affection between parent and child, which was to supplant authority or coercion. Such a strategy was, as we have noted, consistent with the sentimental stress on the importance of mothers, who were presumed to be more temperamentally suited to the use of "gentle methods." As Cott has observed, "Recognition of the mother-child relationship, close on the heels of the new esteem for infant potential, altered childrearing norms. The innovations introduced in childrearing advice all veered toward gentler methods, more feminine by the sex-role definitions of the day."[6]

Alcott's parents, it will be recalled, adopted these sentimental strategies in the rearing of their daughters, and their second-born saw no reason to depart from their example in writing about the relations between parents and children. Throughout her fiction, Alcott advocated that parents adopt a firm, consistent, but, withal, tender and loving approach to children. Harshness had no more place in the treatment of children than neglect. One of the rare occasions in *Little Women* when Marmee is shown losing her temper is occasioned by a schoolmaster who whips little Amy on the hand. Marmee, who governs her daughters "by love alone," decides to remove Amy from school, for, she says, "I don't approve of corporal punishment, especially for girls" (1:103–5). Even where boys are concerned, Alcott arranged for their education to proceed without spur of the rod, and, in *Little Men,* Professor Bhaer makes clear his disapproval of whipping by reversing the normal order of punishment. When one of his orphan boys is caught in a lie, Professor Bhaer orders the lad to strike him, a bizarre punishment invented by Bronson in his Temple School days.

> Nat took the rule, for when Mr. Bhaer spoke in that tone every one obeyed him, and, looking as scared and guilty as if about to stab his master, he gave two feeble blows on the broad hand held out to him. Then he stopped and looked up half-blind with tears, but Mr. Bhaer said steadily . . . "Go on, and strike harder." As if seeing that it must be done, and eager to have the hard task soon over, Nat drew his sleeve across his eyes and gave two more quick hard strokes that reddened the hand, yet hurt the giver more.[7]

If Alcott, like her father, disapproved of corporal punishment, she was a believer in firmness and consistency in dealing with children, laying even greater emphasis than Bronson on these parental qualities. It should be remembered that it was Bronson, not Louisa, who subscribed to the notion that children are saintly. Louisa had no illusions on that score, doubtless remembering her own obstreperous youth. Her portrayal of youngsters—both male and female—made clear her belief that children are as capable as adults of anger, jealousy, and pride. They must be brought, by "gentle measures" to be sure, to the place where they can conquer their little sins through strength of will. Indeed, the importance of learning self-control was for Alcott the heart of proper education.

MASCULINE NURTURE

It is for these reasons that Alcott believed that the proper rearing of children required a judicious mixture of fatherly and motherly influence. Meg's obsession with her babies, which threatens to shut her husband out of her life, also has unfortunate consequences for the children. The babies, the supposed beneficiaries of the cult of motherhood, suffer under Meg's feminine regime, for they are too much with their mother and not enough with their father, with the result that the indulgent Meg spoils them (2:432). A source of constant conflict between Meg and her infant son is the boy's prejudice against going to bed at the proper hour, and Meg uses cajolery and threats to persuade him to retire. Alas, nothing helps, and the "short-sighted woman" attempts to bribe her son with a lump of sugar, which only tempts him to leave his bed once again with demands for more sugar. At last the father intervenes, his patience exhausted: "'Now this won't do,' said John, hardening his heart against the engaging little sinner. 'We shall never know any peace till that child learns to go to bed properly. You have made a slave of yourself long enough; give him one lesson, and then there will be an end of it. Put him in his bed and leave him, Meg'" (2:226–27). When Meg pleads that the boy will not stay in bed unless she sits by him, John assumes charge and carries his son kicking and screaming to bed:

> The minute he was put into bed on one side, he rolled out on the other, and made for the door, only to be ignominiously caught up by the tail

of his little toga, and put back again, which lively performance was kept up till the young man's strength gave out, when he devoted himself to roaring at the top of his voice. This vocal exercise usually conquered Meg, but John sat as unmoved as the post which is popularly believed to be deaf. No coaxing, no sugar, no lullaby, no story. (2:436)

John's firmness and patience are as evident as the fact that he did not resort to physical violence in dealing with the rebellion. In any event, the strategy worked beautifully, and illustrated the effectiveness of the middle way between harshness and indulgence.

Even where the rearing of girls is concerned, Alcott allowed that masculine influence might be essential. Such is the chief message conveyed by her popular juvenile story, *Eight Cousins*, which turns around the education of thirteen-year-old Rose, who stands sorely in need of help when the story opens. This orphan girl has fallen under the tutelage of six aunts, most of whom represent one or another failing of American mothers. Aunt Jane practices severity to a fault, fearing always that Rose will be spoiled. Aunt Myra, on the other hand, pampers Rose, firmly persuaded that the child suffers a mysterious malady and will soon die. Myra represents a caricature of the sentimental mother, one straight from the pages of *The Wide, Wide World*, and she spreads morbidity about her as a cloud. Aunt Plenty is an old-fashioned mother, exhibiting both the vices and virtues of that type. A stout, brisk, garrulous lady, she is well versed in the lore of housekeeping, but, unfortunately for Rose, she also has an unquenchable faith in old-wives' potions and believes a good "dosing" will cure any of her niece's problems. The author saves most ridicule, not surprisingly, for Aunt Clara, a former belle who exhibits the failings of the fashionable mother. She desires to send Rose to a finishing school "so that at eighteen she can come out with *éclat*."[8] Together, these four manage to override the sweet but ineffectual Aunt Peace and the levelheaded but outgunned Aunt Jessie. The result is that they have produced in Rose a thoroughly confused young lady: her body wracked by mysterious ailments, exacerbated by a bad diet and lack of exercise, her head filled with unaccountable fears and precocious ideas of what it is to be a lady. Able to read Greek and Latin, Rose has not the faintest idea of how to keep house, and she fears and detests her eight cousins—all male.

Enter Uncle Alec, a forty-year-old bachelor who is constructed along the lines of most of Alcott's heroes—brown, bearded, broad-shouldered, alert and strong, the kind of man who "looks as if he made people mind," Rose notes with trepidation (p. 24). Alec briefly surveys the damage wrought by the aunts and takes charge of his niece, asking only that the women give him a year to straighten out the girl. It is significant that Alcott portrayed Alec as a physician, anticipating the larger role that medical expertise was to play over the clerical in the future of American child-rearing. Alec's general prescription for Rose is sun, fresh air, and exercise, and with considerable difficulty he persuades Rose to surrender her languid ways and take up running. To the lugubrious Aunt Myra, Alec remarks, "You have put into her head that she has no constitution, and she rather likes the idea" (p. 41). He handles Aunt Plenty with more diplomacy. Knowing her predilection for pills, he devises for Rose a placebo made of brown bread. As for diet, he bans coffee, hot breads, and fried foods, and prescribes oatmeal and milk.[9] He even orders Rose to do the milking herself. On the matter of dress, he forbids corsets and tight belts, pointing out that Rose dresses too much like a fashion plate. Such notions about proper dress bring Alec into conflict with the fashionable Aunt Clara, who prefers for Rose high heels, corsets, and dresses laden with fringes, bows, and ruffles. When Alec expresses preference for a "neat, plain suit," Clara delivers what she believes to be the clinching argument: "It has not a particle of style, and no one would give it a second glance. . . . Dress her in that boyish way and she will act like a boy. I do hate all these inventions of strong-minded women" (pp. 212–13).

Despite Clara's objections, Alec has his way and turns to Rose's education. In this matter, his preferences are neither feminist nor fashionable, but decidedly practical. He allows that Rose can benefit from learning the arts of housekeeping from Aunt Plenty (p. 181). As to more formal education, Alec argues against the smattering of learning so characteristic of female finishing schools, but also against the masculine ideal of Greek and Latin. Instead, he prescribes for Rose a thorough grounding in the basics of English grammar, together with a thorough understanding of "morals" and physiology, an oblique reference to what later generations would call sex education.

MOTHERS AND DAUGHTERS

Although *Eight Cousins* concludes with the women admitting that Alec's influence has been a good thing for Rose, Alcott did not suggest that mothers might be supplanted entirely in the task of rearing girls. Aunt Jessie, although supporting most of Alec's notions about the proper education of Rose, makes clear her belief that the girl needs a mother and that Alec, for all of his virtues, cannot play that role. Mothers are indispensable, if not sufficient, in the proper rearing of the young, and it is to *Little Women* that we must turn for Alcott's views on the relationship of mothers and daughters.

Marmee is a paragon of motherhood who reproves and regulates her daughters, monitors their acquaintances and provides an unfailing source of comfort and good advice. Clearly modeled on Abigail Alcott, Marmee takes seriously her duties as a mother and has given the matter of rearing children a good deal of thought. She has elements of the old-fashioned mother about her, resembling Cynthy Wilkins in many ways, but with an added touch of sophistication. Like Mrs. Wilkins, she adores her offspring and she is charitable to her neighbors, but one finds in her child-rearing practices none of Cynthy's casual ways. Certainly she would never, like Cynthy, resort to corporal punishment, even in jest. As methods of guidance, she prefers setting a good example and delivering little sermons when she thinks her daughters are ready to listen. If possible, she lets the discipline of natural consequences take its course. When the girls decide that they would like to have a vacation from household chores, Marmee agrees to a week's experiment in allowing each to do as she pleases. The result is, of course, chaos. By the end of the week the girls are more than ready to listen to Marmee's sermon: "I wanted you to see how the comfort of all depends on each doing her share faithfully. . . . Don't you feel that it is pleasanter to help one another, to have daily duties which make leisure sweet when it comes, and to bear and forebear, that home may be comfortable and lovely to us all?" (1:172). The secret of Marmee's influence over her daughters is that she practices what she preaches and that her intimacy with them is marred by no secrets. The girls share their innermost concerns with her, and she has managed to establish an atmosphere of absolute trust. Laurie, the motherless boy next door, perceives Marmee's

128

influence and envies the girls for it. As he tells Jo: "Why, you see, I often hear you calling to one another, and when I'm alone up here, I can't help looking over at your house, you always seem to be having such good times. I beg your pardon for being so rude, but sometimes you forget to put down the curtain at the window where the flowers are; and when the lamps are lighted, it's like looking at a picture to see the fire, and you all round the table with your mother" (1:64).

Although loving, Marmee is strict, and makes perfectly clear to the girls what her rules are. She does not approve of drinking alcohol, dislikes flirting, and regulates her daughters' acquaintances. When Jo takes an interest in Laurie, Marmee tells her: "I like his manners, and he looks like a little gentleman, so I've no objection to your knowing him, if a proper opportunity comes" (1:37). The reader soon learns that the reason for this screen that Marmee has carefully thrown around the girls is so that they will not grow up too quickly. She wishes to keep them children as long as she possibly can. Much of her concern centers around her eldest daughter, and it is only with reluctance that she gives Meg permission to accept an invitation to a fashionable party, which she fears—accurately—will make her daughter dissatisfied with the modest circumstances of the March household. Meg attends the party, drinks champagne, flirts, and then overhears gossip to the effect that Marmee is plotting to have Meg marry Laurie because he is rich. When Meg returns, ashamed and angry, Marmee tells her: "I was very unwise to let you go among people of whom I know so little; kind, I dare say, but worldly, ill-bred, and full of these vulgar ideas about young people" (1:144).

Ideologically, Marmee proves to be a feminist, although decidedly a moderate one. She encourages Jo's ambitions to achieve something in the world, and she specifically warns all her daughters against the fashionable folly of marrying for money or for mere security. They should, she advises them, marry only for love (1:146). As the plot reveals, Marmee's advice strikes home. Meg falls in love with and marries a bookkeeper of modest circumstances, while Jo rebuffs Laurie's advances (with Marmee's support) because she does not love him, and later chooses a poor professor. Amy threatens for a time to stray from Marmee's moral influence, even toying with the idea of marrying a rich and titled Englishman, for, after all, she says, "one of us *must* marry well" (2:120). But at last even Amy adheres to her mother's ideals and marries Laurie only after she has convinced herself that she loves him.

Mothers and Sons: The Ambivalent Bond

When Alcott turned to examine the relationship of mothers and sons she was compelled to rely almost totally on her imagination, but it is to her credit that she sensed the complexity of the bond between women and their male offspring. This complexity, it should be noted, had little to do with the Oedipal relationship which Sigmund Freud made so familiar to later generations of Americans. The ambivalence of mothers toward their sons as Alcott portrayed it had rather to do with the fact that women wished, on the one hand, to protect their sons from the temptations which the world held for them and, on the other hand, recognized that this protective instinct might weaken their sons and make them less "manly," as Victorians understood this emotion-laden word. It is precisely for this reason, Alcott seemed to imply, that the involvement of fathers in the nurture of sons is so crucial.

Little Men and *Jo's Boys* provide the fullest description of the mother-son relationship, as Aunt Jo wavers between her desire to hold her orphan boys close to her and her recognition that they must learn to make their way in an unfriendly world. This ambiguity is evident in the way Jo deals with two very different boys—Nat and Dan. In *Little Men* Nat is a timid, somewhat effeminate boy who possesses only one talent, having learned to play the fiddle as a street musician. Aunt Jo does not really like Nat, for she prefers "manly" boys, and she is particularly distressed by his habit of lying, itself a product of his timidity. "I don't mean to," Nat explains when caught, "but it's so much easier to get along if you aint very fussy about being exactly true" (p. 59). Jo's annoyance with Nat's deviousness results in the boy coming more and more under the discipline of Professor Bhaer, who has the patience for the boy that his wife lacks.

Jo's task, as she sees it, is to instill some backbone in the timid lad.

As he nears manhood in *Jo's Boys,* Nat falls in love with Meg's daughter, Daisy, but both Jo and Meg agree that Nat must first prove himself a man before he marries. He is sent off to study music in Germany, a sermon from Jo ringing in his ears:

> I'll tell you what I should do. I'd say to myself, "I'll prove that my love is strong and faithful, and make Daisy's mother proud to give her to me by being not only a good musician but an excellent man, and so command respect and confidence." . . . Now cheer up; don't be lackadaisical and blue. Say good-by cheerfully and bravely, show a manly front, and leave a pleasant memory behind you. We all wish you well and hope much for you.[10]

As Jo fears, Nat is led astray by fashionable society and the prospect of pleasure. He hides the fact that he is a poor orphan, boasts of his wealthy family, neglects his lessons, moves to more expensive lodgings and accumulates debts. Clearly, Nat's character flaws are pushing him to perdition, but in proper sentimental fashion, the long arm of domestic influence reaches out in the form of letters to save him from himself:

> Ah, how welcome it was! how eagerly he read the long pages full of affectionate wishes from all at home! For every one had sent a line, and as each familiar name appeared, his eyes drew dimmer and dimmer till, as he read the last—"God bless my boy! Mother Bhaer,"—he broke down; and laying his head on his arms, blistered the paper with a rain of tears that eased his heart and washed away the boyish sins that now lay so heavy on his conscience. (pp. 232–33)

Nat eventually reforms himself and wins Daisy's hand, but matters are not so easily resolved for Dan, who at the age of fourteen has already become what a later generation would call a juvenile delinquent. Like Nat he has grown up on the streets, but the experience has turned him sullen and suspicious, precociously wise in the ways of the world. Contemptuous of adult authority, when we meet him in *Little Men* he defies the rules of Plumfield by smoking, drinking, playing poker, and swearing. (In portraying Dan, Alcott allows herself the only profanity to appear in all of her fiction.) Dan is, in short, a thoroughly "bad specimen," who tries even the saintly pa-

131

tience of Professor Bhaer. When his misdeeds finally result in a fire, the good professor expels him from Plumfield.

As might be expected, Jo takes a liking to Dan, perceiving virtues beneath his rough exterior. Dan is, in fact, a younger, more rough-hewn version of so many of Alcott's fictional heroes. Like Adam, the "perfect man" portrayed in *Moods,* Dan is a rebel who possesses the virtue of absolute honesty. Yet he has a tender side, carefully hidden, of course, which reveals itself in his love of animals and in his genuine affection for Jo's younger offspring, baby Teddy. More important, Jo recognizes in the lad traits of her own character. When Dan returns to Plumfield, now somewhat chastened, Jo undertakes to reform him. She pleads with her husband:

> "I tell you, Fritz, that boy is a brave lad and will make a fine man yet."
>
> "I hope so, for your sake, enthusiastic woman, your faith deserves success. Now, I will go and see your little Spartan. Where is he?"
>
> "In my room; but, dear, you'll be very kind to him, no matter how gruff he seems. I am sure that is the way to conquer him. He won't bear sternness nor much restraint, but a soft word and infinite patience will lead him as it used to lead me."
>
> "As if you ever were like this little rascal!" cried Mr. Bhaer, laughing, yet half angry at the idea.
>
> "I was in spirit, though I showed it in a different way. I seem to know by instinct how he feels, to understand what will win and touch him, and to sympathize with his temptations and faults. I am glad I do, for it will help me to help him; and if I can make a good man of this wild boy, it will be the best work of my life." (p. 161)

In proper sentimental fashion, Alcott once again endorsed the belief that children are to be "conquered" through the bond of affection, rather than intimidated by the threat of violence or overawed by the voice of authority. Here also is illustrated her androgynous ability to transcend sentimentality, enabling her to see the world the way a boy might see it.

As Dan matures, he becomes one of the most interesting of his author's creations, combining in his character elements of the rebel and the villain. As *Jo's Boys* opens, Dan has returned from a stint as a miner in California, tall, bearded, and sinewy, alert, "as big and black as a villain in a play," Jo says admiringly (p. 70). Although he has saved some money, he is an adventurer at heart, and has no interest in financial security. He will never be, Jo recognizes, a "steady young man." It is this very trait, in fact, that Jo finds so attractive in her protégé, and she recalls that when she was a girl she liked adventurous fellows like Dan—so "fresh and daring, free and romantic" (pp. 69–70). This is the woman speaking. As a mother, however, Jo cannot help wanting to "settle" all her boys, including Dan, with a good wife and a nice little home. In short, her maternal side wishes to tame her "firebrand," as she calls him, for she fears that his wayward temperament and his lawless nature will lead to trouble. Such fears prompt a farewell sermon to Dan as he prepares once again to head for the West: "Now that you are a man you can control that lawless nature better; but as a boy only great activity and much adventure could keep you out of mischief. Time is taming my colt, you see, and I shall yet be proud of him" (p. 125).

Jo's maternal fears are fully realized. Dan kills a man for cheating at cards and is sentenced to a year in prison for manslaughter. Suffering from the loss of liberty and full of remorse for having failed to live up to Jo's expectations, Dan sinks into despair. "The firebrand can't be saved," Dan laments, and he comes close to joining in a prison break. Only his memories of Plumfield and the sermon of a woman like Jo save him from participation in the desperate act. Freed at last, he heads for Montana, determined to perform some deed that will redeem him in Jo's eyes. There he acts the part of a hero in a mining accident. He returns to Plumfield, confesses his crime, and receives absolution through Jo's love. Melodramatic and sentimental though these incidents are, they bear testimony to Alcott's belief in the power of family nurture, and in particular of mother love, to reform sinners. To this extent at least she subscribed to the sentimental cult of motherhood.

THEMES OF GENDER AND GENERATION IN CHILD-REARING

Biographers of a feminist persuasion have argued that Alcott presented to her juvenile readers a sexist version of child-rearing, whereby boys are cut out for manly self-fulfillment, while girls are intended for womanly self-sacrifice.[11] As Dan's painful growth to maturity fully illustrates, however, Alcott did not subscribe to such a neat bifurcation of the goals of education between the sexes. If girls like Jo are encouraged to entertain ambitions to make a name for themselves in the world, so boys like Dan are encouraged to cultivate a sensitive concern for the welfare of others. In keeping with Alcott's notions of coeducation as prelude to companionate marriage, she makes clear that the lessons of self-denial and self-control apply equally to boys and girls, and they lead to the achievement, by both men and women, of a quality of "nobility," a word that occurs again and again in Alcott's writing. As a description of model character, the term *nobility* has gone out of fashion, but it perfectly captures the aspirations of proper Victorian parents for their offspring, whether male or female. For Alcott it represents, in the final analysis, a profoundly religious view of life's goals (albeit an unorthodox one) and it was based on her contention that the survival of family life and spiritual values require self-denial and self-sacrifice from boys as well as girls. If girls must become ladies, then boys must become gentlemen. Generations of readers well remember the saintly qualities of Beth March. Not so well remembered are boys who also attain a kind of spiritual transcendence in Alcott's fiction and who serve as models for their more fallible peers. One such is Ed Devlin, whose death adds a somber note to the otherwise lighthearted story recounted in *Jack and Jill*. In describing Ed, Alcott might have been portraying a young sentimental heroine: "Dutiful and loving; ready to help; patient to bear and forbear; eager to excel; faithful to the smallest task, yet full of high ambitions; and, better still, possessing the childlike piety that can trust and believe, wait and hope."[12] The development of such character should be the goal, and it is this goal of noble self-sacrifice and self-control, rather than the supposed division of child-rearing along lines of gender, that sets Alcott apart from the post-Victorian age.

While she did not endorse sexual segregation of the sentimental variety, she lent her fiction to another kind of segregation with unfortunate consequences for a fuller understanding of parenthood and family life. She never succeeded in integrating in her fiction the many roles that adults play within the family. Rarely do the adults of her sensational and literary fiction appear as parents, and rarely do the adults who appear in her children's books play any role other than as parents. One wonders how Gladys and Felix might have turned out as parents. Conversely, Professor Bhaer lives and breathes only for the welfare of his orphan boys, and only rarely is the reader given a glimpse of the relationship between the good professor and his wife. Similarly, Marmee performs in *Little Women* as the perfect mother, and there is provided little hint of her relationship with Father March, who, in fact, is absent during much of the story of *Little Women*. Still less is there any mention of the working life that Marmee lives so mysteriously outside the family. Only in her portrayal of the mature Jo does Alcott provide a suggestion that maternal duties might somehow intersect with more worldly ambitions. In sum, she failed to explore the way that adults orchestrate—or fail to orchestrate—their activity as husbands, wives, lovers, and workers with their treatment of their offspring. The portrait of family life that emerges is thus flawed, and it reinforces the sentimental tendency to render parents as either fashionable villains who neglect the young, or as saints who find in child nurture their sole reason for existence. Parents rarely emerge as people, in startling contrast to Alcott's impressive and sensitive portrayal of the children themselves. It is young Jo, not Marmee, who lives in our collective memory.

VICTORIAN CHILDHOOD

Americans of the twentieth century have beat a steady retreat from the kind of upbringing Alcott described and endorsed, because to many observers it has appeared that relations between the generations in Victorian America placed a great burden both on mothers and on their children. Alcott's ever watchful parents and surrogate parents seek to prolong childhood dependency by keeping children, both boys and girls, within the confines of the household far beyond the time of home leaving honored in colonial America, a trend increasingly evident among those who read her books. Moreover, good parents like Marmee seek to protect the innocence of children by shielding them from exposure to the world and its ways, for if children are not precisely saintly, nevertheless they are vulnerable.

Alcott's good parents strive therefore to protect their children from precocious experience with sex, alcohol, and sensational novels. The reason that orphan Dan proves to be such a disruptive influence in the family world of Plumfield is precisely because he brings with him the vulgar ways of the street, and though Mother Bhaer admires his adventurous ways, she cannot rest until she has converted him and has restored, in a measure, his childhood innocence. Likewise, the "old-fashioned girl," Polly, is superior to the fashionable Fanny because she has not yet lost her childlike ways.

Within this moral cocoon of family life, nurture proceeds in the fashion prescribed by sentimental convention—along the lines, in fact, already established by Alcott's father. Like Bronson, Louisa believed that awe of authority and fear of physical punishment should have no place in relations between parents and children. Instead, parents should rely on gentle methods to establish a bond of intimacy with the young, which would facilitate the children's internalization of parental values. Marmee never raised her hand or her voice, but she could rely on the fact that conscience would guide her daughters, or, if it failed, that they would feel the lash of guilt. Boys were to be treated much the same, and when Jo becomes Mother Bhaer she relies on the pull of mother love to bring both Nat and Dan back into line, even after they are thousands of miles from the family circle. The result of proper child-rearing is the emergence of self-disciplined, self-sacrificing ladies and gentlemen.[13]

Historians have been reluctant to address themselves to the subject of Victorian child-rearing because it entails venturing into the uncharted seas of psychohistory, but a few early, mixed reviews are in. On the one hand, it would seem that the new ways of arranging the experience of children, when compared to the patterns of colonial child-rearing, should have made smoother the path to adulthood, for if Victorian parents were listening to authors like Alcott, then the children suffered from neither brutality nor neglect. Moreover, one historian has argued that the emerging patterns of parent-child relations, marked by greater emotional intimacy, represented a distinct improvement in the lives of children, for there now emerged the possibility of genuine empathy between old and young.[14] As for the increasingly delayed entrance into the world of work, this would seem to have provided children more opportunity to enrich their lives and discover their talents before being saddled with adult commitments of work and family. As one historian has pointed out, the Victorian pattern of socialization made economic sense because the increasing sophistication of the workplace required a longer period of dependency and more subtle techniques of child-rearing.[15] Other scholars, while acknowledging the shifting emotional climate within affluent households, are not altogether convinced it was a good thing. John Demos, for example, has pointed to the growing insularity of the family and the corresponding intensification of emotional bonds between parents and child as one which may have caused psychological damage.[16] Likewise, practitioners of psychoanalytic biography who have examined the lives of eminent Victorians have attempted to spell out in detail some of these psychic costs, emphasizing in particular the compulsive personality that seems to have been the fruit of Victorian child-rearing.[17] Finally, scholars have speculated that the emphasis which the sentimental ideal placed on the protection of children may have exacerbated discontinuities as the children came of age, making more difficult the business of leaving home and facing life. Growing up in a domestic Utopia of warmth and affection seems hardly the best preparation for doing battle in the competitive world of the marketplace.[18]

Evidence bearing on such complex matters is obviously difficult to come by and may emerge only after an exhaustive study of the lives of Americans who grew up in Victorian households, but it is worth noting that Alcott herself entertained no doubts about the new style. If she harbored any worries about the effects of sentimental child-rearing on the young, she gave no hint of such qualms either in her private correspondence or in her published work. To have done so would have been to repudiate her own child-rearing and to call into question the very core of her existence. She took great pride in her heroic capacity for self-discipline, and she greatly admired those who were capable of renouncing pleasurable indulgence for the sake of their principles. The rigidity that later generations have detected in Victorian personality was regarded by Alcott and most of her contemporaries as a sign of "character," a Victorian code word for integrity and self-discipline. Her father possessed these virtues, and although

Alcott might have found fault with him, it was never because he stubbornly adhered to principle. Likewise, Alcott's mother was a person of firm conviction and her clear and unbending sense of right and wrong provided, as we have seen, the inspiration for the creation of Marmee. Finally, the fact that Alcott created Jo in her own image testified to her unswerving belief in the value of her parents' child-rearing practices. For all of her faults, Jo imposes discipline upon herself and is quite capable of delivering stern lectures to those, like Laurie, who are inclined toward a more casual attitude on questions of morality and self-discipline. Endorsing gentle methods of nurture, Alcott never sanctioned the permissiveness that some observers have found so characteristic of American middle-class child-rearing in recent years.

The Family and the World:

The Privatization of Utopia

*I*n *"Transcendental Wild Oats," published in 1873,* Alcott looked
back on her father's ill-fated attempt to found the Utopian community, Fruitlands, and she concluded her description with a bitter
remark: "He had tried, but it was a failure. The world was not ready
for Utopia yet, and those who attempted to found it only got laughed
at for their pains."[1] When she wrote these words the nation was in the
midst of the Gilded Age, an era noted for its brazen cupidity and
corruption. She was always proud of the part her parents had played
in the cause of abolition, and as she looked about her at the world that
had emerged in America after the Civil War she could not help
concluding that the transcendental past was superior to the materialistic present. "In other days," she commented, "men could sell all
and give to the poor, lead lives devoted to holiness and high thought,
and, after the persecution was over, find themselves honored as saints
and martyrs." "But," she added, "in modern times these things are
out of fashion. To live for one's principles, at all costs, is a dangerous
speculation; and the failure of an ideal, no matter how humane and
noble, is harder for the world to forgive and forget than bank rob-
bery or the grand swindles of corrupt politicians."[2]

Notwithstanding her condemnation of the Gilded Age, Alcott
herself entertained mixed feelings on the subject of social reform, an
ambivalence which was to have significance for her views on the
family and its relationship to the world outside it. On the one hand,
she felt concern for the problems encountered by working women.
She also made frequent contributions to the *Woman's Journal,* and
signed one of her letters to that periodical with the phrase, "Yours for

reform of all kinds."[3] As we have seen, reformist sentiments also found their way into her fiction, providing tantalizing if vague hints of a sisterhood of mutual support.[4] But if Alcott sounded sometimes as radical as her father had been, she entertained a highly selective, decidedly practical and, withal, narrow view of social reform. For one thing, she never developed further the vision of a reformist sisterhood. As her satiric history of the Fruitlands experiment reveals, she had difficulty in taking Utopias seriously. Her skepticism may have had something to do with remembered pain, for the Fruitlands period had proved a difficult time for her, hovering as she had been on the brink of puberty. More important, perhaps, the adult Louisa was beginning to conclude that her father's ideals, however noble, were simply irrelevant, not only to the facts of political life in the Gilded Age, but also to human nature as Louisa understood it. Although sharing her father's hostility to materialism, she had little patience for the construction of ideological alternatives to capitalist society. She tolerated only with difficulty her father's creation, in his later years, of the Concord School of Philosophy, commenting that though she tried to look as if she liked speculation, she actually found it a waste of time "till our poor are fed and the wicked saved."[5] It seems never to have occurred to her that speculation might be a prelude to reform rather than simply an evasion of reality, and she betrayed no interest in socialism, whether of the foreign or domestic varieties. Among the specific failings of the reform-minded ladies depicted in *Work* is that they are either too Utopian, too political, or too erudite: "One accomplished creature with learning radiating from every pore, delivered a charming little essay on the strong-minded women of antiquity; then, taking labor into the region of art, painted delightful pictures of the time when all would work harmoniously together in an Ideal Republic, where each did the task she liked and was paid for it in liberty, equality, and fraternity."[6] Still another, a fervent suffragist, sought to incite the working women to march for the ballot, "before one-half of them were quite clear what it meant, and the other half were as unfit for it as any ignorant Patrick bribed with a dollar and a sup of whiskey."[7] A third, clearly of a socialist persuasion, merely baffled and depressed her audience by quoting statistics, reading reports of labor reforms, and engaging in tirades against capitalists who wrung profits from their employees. In contrast to these learned and strong-minded ladies, Christie speaks to the working women in loving, direct, and practical ways, concluding with the hearty but vague advice to keep on and not to lose heart.

In point of fact, Alcott's notion of a reform-minded sisterhood had less to do with Utopian sentiment than it had to do with the founding of women's voluntary organizations that featured goals at once more pious and more specific. Even as Alcott published *Work*, there was emerging a movement which gave concrete form to the "loving league of sisters" she hinted at in that novel. One expression of this movement was the organization of church-related missionary societies for the salvation of foreign and domestic heathen. Still another was the effort to protect the home by outlawing sin in the community and by promoting religious and cultural "uplift." Typical of this latter approach to reform—and one of the most popular woman's organizations to appear during the Gilded Age—was the Women's Christian Temperance Union. Organized in 1874, just one year after the appearance of *Work*, the WCTU could boast a total membership of 160,000 by 1890. The WCTU membership chanted the slogan, "For God and Home and Native Land," and wore white ribbons symbolizing purity. Although the WCTU later broadened its interests to include women's suffrage, prison reform, and even labor reform, the major thrust of the movement was the banning of liquor and prostitution, for the majority of its membership subscribed to the notion that the elimination of saloons and brothels would keep husbands steady and families on an even keel. [8]

Both in her private life and in her fiction, Alcott demonstrated that her sympathies were with the goals of the movement for "social purity." She endorsed the campaign to ban white slavery, as the traffic in prostitution was then called, and she actually became active in efforts to organize a temperance movement in Concord. She had, after all, grown up in a home which religiously abstained from the use of alcoholic beverages, and, indeed, the entire campaign of the social purists against the sins of the flesh was entirely congenial to the transcendentalist atmosphere in which Alcott came of age. It was hardly surprising that she would make her juvenile fiction a vehicle for the spread of social purity, focusing particularly on the dangers of

141

dime novels, sex, and alcohol. Interestingly enough, for all of her androgynous views, Alcott clung to the belief that boys were more susceptible than girls to the harmful influences of cheap literature and strong spirits, and thus must be more carefully protected from these vices. In *Eight Cousins* the sensible Aunt Jessie speaks for the author when she expresses alarm that her two sons are reading popular dime novels. These cheap stories are marred by slang, and they acquaint boys with the "low life" found in police courts, counterfeiters' dens, gambling houses, and saloons. But that is hardly the worst of it, in Jessie's view. These books also purvey the notion that the goal of life is to be smart and become rich, and that success in life comes by luck rather than by hard work. "This love of money is the curse of America," Jessie declares, and she hugs her boys "as if she feared to let them leave that safe harbor for the great sea where so many little boats go down." Alcott's definition of cheap literature extended even to Mark Twain's *Huckleberry Finn*. Supporting the decision of the Concord library to ban the novel, Alcott told the press, "If Mr. Clemens cannot think of something better to tell our pure-minded lads and lasses, he had best stop writing for them."[9]

More dangerous for boys even than cheap literature is alcohol, for Alcott subscribed to the notion that males have a fatal weakness for tippling and that they must be saved by the influence of good women. Long before the rise of the Women's Christian Temperance Union, Alcott used her juvenile fiction as a forum to promote the temperance cause. Marmee, who metes out discipline with a good deal of tolerance and good humor, believes that the threat of alcohol to the happy home is no matter to be taken lightly. As Meg explains to Laurie when he inquires about the absence of wine at her wedding, "Mother says that neither she nor her daughters will ever offer it to any young man under her roof."[10] Meg then extracts from Laurie a promise that he will give up drinking. The novel *Jack and Jill* reveals the influence of still another good woman, Mrs. Minot, who persuades her sons to join a temperance lodge and to do battle against "the great enemy of home peace and safety."[11] In her last novel, *Jo's Boys*, Alcott fired yet another salvo at liquor, coming this time from Jo herself and aimed at one of her "failures," George Cole, who earns the nickname of "Stuffy" for his inordinate appetite. Upon entering college, Stuffy takes on a taste for wine, earning a lecture from the ever watchful Jo: "Overeating is an old story; and a few more fits of illness will teach you to be wise. But drinking is a more serious thing, and leads to worse harm than any that can afflict your body alone. I hear you talk about wines as if you knew them and cared more for them than a boy should. . . . Stop at once and learn that temperance in all things is the only safe rule."[12]

Mother Jo's lecture to Stuffy on the evils of wine accurately reflected Alcott's sincere convictions on the virtues of temperance, but her literary crusade against alcohol seems less than consistent, given her private addiction to opium. Her use of the drug was evidently habitual, for, as she confided to her diary in 1870, "I slept without any opium or anything—a feat I have not performed for sometime."[13] It is true, of course, that she justified the use of opium by the pain she suffered from an illness that could be traced back to her Civil War experience. It is also true that drug addiction seemed widespread among women at the time, indicating that popular opinion found opium use more acceptable than alcohol, provided, of course, that the practice was kept discreet.[14] To the modern eye, which is likely to see a drug as a drug, such nice distinctions have been lost, leaving us with further evidence of the moral hypocrisy of which Victorians have been so often accused.

Yet another danger to moral development, she believed, was precocious sexual activity, which threatened girls as well as boys. Fashionable families were especially careless about protecting their young from its vice, as Fannie Shaw's waywardness shows. In witnessing bawdy shows and learning the subtle arts of flirting with boys, Fannie is clearly growing up too fast for her own good. One danger is that a girl might engage in premarital sex and even fall into a life of prostitution. Alcott dealt frankly with this possibility in her adult fiction, most notably in portraying the sad fate of Rachel in *Work*. In her juvenile fiction, she was considerably more reticent, dealing with the subject in oblique ways. Marmee, for example, is ever watchful to protect the "innocence" of her daughters and to prevent them from doing "foolish or unmaidenly things," a Victorian code word for sex.[15] Boys, too, must be protected from vice, and Alcott made clear that she had little patience for the double standard which allowed more liberty for boys in sexual matters. When Jo herself becomes the mother of two boys, she explicitly condemns youthful courtship and romance, calling it an "epidemic" that infects normally sensible boys and girls. When her own son, Teddy, announces that he wishes a sweetheart, Jo is abrupt and firm in her refusal. "What are we coming to in this fast age when babes and boys make such demands and want to play with one of the most sacred things in life?" Jo asks indignantly and sends Teddy away to play baseball instead. [16]

The problem with such early dalliance is, in Alcott's opinion, that it leads to a premature and dangerous sensuality. Such is the trap awaiting Dolly, the handsome, indolent scion of a fashionable family who is sent to Plumfield for an education and quickly earns Jo's description as another of her "failures," along with Stuffy Cole. Upon entering college, Dolly takes to frequenting risqué theatres where men come to ogle the "painted girls" and then take them out to supper afterward. When Jo hears of it, she gives the hapless youth a lecture: "The society of such women will unfit you for that of good ones, and lead you into trouble and sin and shame. Oh, why don't the city fathers stop that evil thing, when they know the harm it does?" [17] Boys no less than girls must struggle to hold themselves pure by resisting fashionable vices, although Jo admits that it is difficult when "books, pictures, ball-rooms, theatres and streets offer temptations." [18]

Banning cheap literature, alcohol, and prostitution constituted an extraordinarily negative and censorious strategy for social reform, but Alcott, like other social purists, advocated as well more positive approaches to ameliorating the evils of an urban, industrial America. Like the WCTU and other women's organizations, Alcott gave great weight in her fiction to the value of persuasion, or, as it was then called, moral and cultural uplift. The strategy of uplift, with its fusion of helpfulness and condescension, rested on the assumption that social progress could best be achieved by spreading the influence of a moral and cultural elite. Among the moral elite who people Alcott's fiction are males like the Reverend Power and David Sterling, but most are women who have acquired, either by inheritance or by virtue of experience, a moral and cultural wisdom that sets them apart from most men and a good many other women. Such women spread their influence through voluntary organizations, of course, but more typically one finds them in Alcott's fiction wielding their power through their dominant influence in the home, where they pass along their ideals to their sons and daughters and serve as examples to other women less enlightened than themselves. Although Alcott might suggest privately that for women like Diana destiny lies in a career outside the home, the bulk of her fiction subscribed to the idea that cultured women hold an obligation peculiar to themselves to promote the moral regeneration of society through their influences as wives and mothers, which is to say that Alcott saw a reformed family as the key to a reformed society. This "domestic feminism," as one historian has called it, was a form of Utopianism, but of a kind characteristic of the Gilded Age. Like the sentimental writers of the Jacksonian period, Alcott confined her hopes for a better world to the boundaries of the domestic circle. Even her endorsement of women's organizations had its justification in the protection of the home more than in the alteration of the community. Alcott thus lent the power of her pen to the drift of opinion begun by the sentimental revolution, a drift that can be called the privatization of Utopia. Pinning her hopes on the nuclear family, Alcott ultimately rejected her father's dreams of a "consociate family" broader than the ties of blood and marriage. [19]

Beginning with *Little Women*, most of the families of which Alcott approved were families dominated by women, and they are families that are curiously insulated from the larger world. As Nina Auerbach has pointed out, masculine influence is scarcely visible in the world of *Little Women*. [20] Father March is conveniently sent away to the war, and even after his return, his distant and vague moral influence is no match for day-to-day direction provided by Marmee. Moreover, the March household has little to do with neighboring households, with the exception of the wealthy Lawrence family, and even young Laurie gains access to the closed March circle only with difficulty. The March household consists, in fact, of a "little nunnery," as Laurie's grandfather notes perceptively, and Alcott managed to convey in the detailed description of the household a sense of the coziness with which the closely knit family envelops itself. The crackling fire, the comfortable, plain furniture, the flowers all lend a "pleasant atmosphere of home-peace."[21] Meg and Amy venture outside this cozy nest in an attempt to establish relationships with fashionable families in the community, but their experience provides only cautionary tales of the dangers that fashion presents to the proper development of little women. Following each such dangerous excursion, Marmee's influence reasserts itself, saving the girls from the temptation of folly. Nor do churches or schools provide any serious competition for Marmee's influence over the girls. None attends church, it seems— an omission which affronted some of the more pious readers of the novel—and only Amy is enrolled in school, until such time as the schoolmaster resorts to corporal punishment.

The domestic Utopia of little women is destroyed of course, first by death, which claims Beth, and then by Laurie, who proves to be the insidious if charming serpent in the March Garden of Eden. Through him, Meg meets his tutor, John Brooke, and falls in love, and it is Laurie's importunate proposal that drives Jo from the household to visit New York, where she meets her future husband. The last girl is taken from Marmee when Amy marries Laurie himself. Alcott might have wished to keep the girls together, perpetuating a feminist Utopia in the March family, but her later fiction is largely devoted to exploring ways in which such ideal domestic worlds as the March family represents may spread their influence to other families and ensure the proper upbringing of the next generation. The strategy endorsed depended in large measure on the economic condition of the needy family. Firmly middle-class in her sympathies, it was Alcott's belief that the rich stood as much in need of domestic reform as the poor, and for these affluent families of fashion she recommended persuasion and example. Sometimes the agent of reform is a poor young girl like Polly, who serves in *An Old-Fashioned Girl* as a catalyst to reform the Shaw household. At other times, as in *Work*, the agent is a wealthy young lady who is advised by Christie to convert families of fashion to the "fashion of common sense" by the simple device of transforming her home into a cultural salon where rich but empty-headed men and women may be led to contemplate "high ideals and noble purposes," as Christie puts it.

But what of that vast range of families of the middling sort—those who are neither rich nor poor but yet in need of cultural uplift? Alcott provided an answer of sorts in her juvenile novel, *Jack and Jill*. On the surface this work appears to be simply a tale of friendship between a boy and a girl, each struggling toward maturity—yet another testimony to Alcott's belief in the value of coeducation. At another level, however, *Jack and Jill* concerns the way that Jack's mother, Mrs. Minot, provides an example of ideal family life and spreads her influence through the village community. There is no reference to Mr. Minot, but the reader is left to conclude that he has died, leaving Mrs. Minot a wealthy widow who resembles Marmee in her wisdom, cheerfulness, and firm discipline. She is a devoted mother to her two sons, Jack and Frank, but not so preoccupied with them that she has no time to think of three girls in the village—Jill, Molly, and Merry—each of whom resides in a household in need of help and guidance.

Jill Pecq is still another version of Jo, a "willful little baggage" whose tomboy ways lead her to accept a dare from Jack, with the result that she injures her back in a sledding accident. As the story develops it appears that Jill's faults stem principally from the lack of firm guidance. Her father is dead and her mother, though a good-hearted soul, is too poorly educated and distraught by poverty to provide the discipline Jill requires. The second girl, Molly Bemis, has a somewhat different problem, for she is a sweet-tempered but dishevelled young girl, whose lack of good taste and good breeding bids fare to make her a slovenly woman. Unlike Jill, Molly has a father, but no mother, unless one counts Miss Bat, a middle-aged spinster who lives with the Bemis family but proves to be only an indifferent housekeeper. She "thought she had done her duty if she got three comfortable meals, nursed the children when they were ill, and saw that the house did not burn up."[22] The consequence is that Molly and her little brother Boo are taking on an uncouth appearance and behavior that is making them different from better brought-up children. As for Molly's father, he is too preoccupied with his business affairs to pay much attention to the two youngsters, having, for example, only the vaguest idea of exactly how old his daughter is.

Merry Grant, the third in the trio of culturally deprived young ladies, possesses both a mother and a father and poverty is no threat to the Grant household, but Merry suffers from her family's lack of gentility. Clearly cast in the mold of Amy, Merry has "high flown ideas of elegance" and is painfully embarrassed by her uncultured parents and brothers (pp. 82–83).

In a variety of ways Mrs. Minot begins to work her influence on all three girls and on their families. Her first move is to extend help and sympathy to her poor neighbor, Jill's mother, and before long she is busy redecorating the cheerless room in which the bedridden Jill is confined (p. 34). Next Mrs. Minot decides that the easiest way to reform the Pecq household is to incorporate it into her own by hiring Mrs. Pecq to serve as her housekeeper, bringing Jill with her to reside in the Minot household. Having resolved the Pecq family's financial problems, Mrs. Minot can now also work a more direct influence on Jill herself, teaching her the lessons of obedience.

Mrs. Minot is in fact if not in name a home missionary, and the spirit of home missions is explicitly evoked in a scene involving Mrs. Pecq and the three girls. As they talk in Jill's newly decorated room, the conversation turns to the subject of missions. Says Molly: "I'd like to be a missionary and go where folks throw their babies to the crocodiles. I'd watch and fish them out, and have a school, and bring them up, and convert all the people till they know better" (p. 38). Whereupon Mrs. Pecq reminds the girls that there are missionaries in America also, "and they have their hands full with the poor, the wicked, and the helpless." Warming to the subject, Mrs. Pecq suggests that the girls can organize a home missionary society and begin by working on themselves. Before long the three girls are busy with their "home missions." Upon moving into the household of Mrs. Minot, Jill uses her convalescence as an opportunity to improve her character under the guidance of Mrs. Minot. As the good lady tells Jill sternly: "This painful little back will be a sort of conscience to remind you of what you ought to do and leave undone, and so you can be learning obedience" (p. 81). By the end of the novel, Jill has learned her lesson, and a decidedly antifeminist one it is, for Mrs. Minot takes evident satisfaction in her success at "taming a wild bird till it is nearly as meek as a dove" (p. 301).

Merry has a somewhat more difficult task, for not only must she reform herself by becoming more industrious but, as she sees it, she must "convert her family to a liking for pretty things." It proves a formidable assignment, for her parents and her brothers exhibit a kind of peasant simplicity that has little appreciation for the amenities, sitting about the table "shovelling in pork and beans with their knives, drinking tea from their saucers, and laughing out with a hearty 'Haw, Haw,' when anything amused them" (p. 83). Remembering the room Mrs. Minot had redecorated for Jill, Merry sets to work coaxing her parents to allow her to remodel her room, promising her mother that in return she will do her chores without fussing. Having filled her room with flowers, curtains, and pictures, she next longs to transform the family parlor, "for it was, like most country parlors, a prim and chilly place, with little beauty and no comfort" (p. 197). Meeting resistance from her mother, Merry then fixes her attention on the dining room, filling the bay window with flowers, installing a lamp that struck her fancy, and banishing from the hearth the "black demon of an air-tight stove," proving in this instance, at least, that the usually sensible Alcott was placing beauty above utility (p. 198). Newly decorated and with the fireplace the centerpiece, the room gradually lures the entire family to its cozy comfort, and even the loutish brothers begin to see that "Merry's notions" make some sense.

Molly has the most difficult mission of all. Having no mother, she has full responsibility for the care of her little brother and has to contend with the slovenly Miss Bat. Like Merry, however, Molly has before her the example of Mrs. Minot's lovely household, and she sets to work attempting to bring some cleanliness and order to her home, beginning with her own clothes (pp. 93–94). Next Molly goes to work on improving the appearance of her little brother, and the result unexpectedly brings about the reform of even Miss Bat. Accidentally overhearing two neighbor ladies praising her for the improved appearance of Molly and Boo, Miss Bat is conscience-stricken: "Miss Bat was a worthy soul in main, only, like so many of us, she needed rousing up to her duty. She had got the rousing now, and it did her good, for she could not bear to be praised when she had not deserved it" (p. 213). Chastened, Miss Bat sets to work on spring-housecleaning with a vengeance, much to the surprise and delight of Mr. Bemis.

It would appear to the casual reader that Louisa placed undue weight on interior decoration and physical order as a means of familial reform, and without doubt, Louisa shared the popular belief of the time that cleanliness is next to godliness. She took pains to point out, however, the ways that the rearrangement of the home can work a subtle transformation in the behavior and character of family members. Merry's campaign to redecorate the Grant household exerts, for example, a beneficial effect on her brothers' behavior, for one begins brushing his hair and washing his hands, while another tries to lower his boisterous laughter, and a third even gives up smoking in the dining room. Molly's efforts are rewarded at still a deeper level, for the absentminded Mr. Bemis begins to take notice of his neglected children, and he is pleased to see that Molly is changing from a waif into a "nice little girl." By novel's end, Molly's transformation earns her an invitation to enter the Minot household, where she can receive, together with Jill, further instruction from Mrs. Minot herself in ways of becoming a proper lady. In such subtle ways, Alcott imagined, the ferment of domestic reform is spread.

Persuasion and example might serve to transform the families of the wealthy and even those of more modest circumstances like those portrayed in *Jack and Jill,* but what of the truly destitute? A "rousing up" might be sufficient to bring about the reform of Miss Bat and the Bemis household, but what if the family's attentions were occupied with more basic questions of survival? The traditional Christian response had been direct, voluntary charity, but Alcott remained skeptical of the value of such philanthropy. In her fiction she did frequently portray incidents of charity. Mrs. Wilkins extended help to her neighbors out of the goodness of her heart, and Mrs. Minot saw fit to lend a hand to poor Mrs. Pecq. Nor is any reader of *Little Women* likely to forget the dramatic scene in which the March girls troop off to take their Christmas breakfast to a destitute widow with six starving and freezing children. But while Alcott might depict such episodes, she elsewhere made clear her belief that charity was of little use to the poor and might even be harmful. When advising a wealthy friend to devote her energies to the conversion of her own class, Christy specifically tells her to avoid direct aid to the poor, for, she points out, "so much pity and money are wasted in sentimental charity."[23] In her personal life, Alcott adhered to a similar code, providing only small sums in charity outside the immediate Alcott family.

The only hope that she could hold out to the truly poor was a small one, and one that was well in keeping with her emphasis on the family as the key to social reform. Her response to poverty consisted in suggesting the possibility that proper families might open their homes to the children of the poor, especially if the youngsters are orphans.[24] Vaguely reminiscent of Bronson's Fruitlands experiment, this strategy for dealing with poverty was educational in essence, and grounded in the belief that by making proper families into cultural asylums for deprived youngsters, the next generation could be saved from poverty and ignorance. Given such a view, it was entirely reasonable that Alcott would endorse the work of the Children's Aid Society, an organization which gathered orphans from the streets of New York City and sent them to live with rural—and presumably proper—families in the West.[25]

The notion of expanding proper families to include deprived children found its literary expression in the last two novels of the March trilogy, during which the March family is literally reconstituted as "Plumfield." Although described as a school, it is really, Alcott reminded her readers, a "great family," differing from the earlier March household only in that the domestic circle is widened to include orphan boys, together with boys from wealthy but unenlightened families of fashion: "These were the boys, and they lived together as happily as twelve lads could, studying and playing, working and squabbling, fighting faults and cultivating virtues in the good old-fashioned way. Boys at other schools probably learned more from books, but less of that better wisdom which makes good men."[26] Although expanded beyond blood kin, Plumfield is in all other respects very much a March family affair. Aunt March laid the financial foundation with a bequest, supplemented by aid from Amy and her husband Laurie. As for the governance of the new household, Marmee is in her declining years, but her place is taken by Jo, who becomes Mother Bhaer and rules her kingdom as firmly as Marmee ever did. Professor Bhaer, although more in evidence than the distant Father March had been, nonetheless plays second fiddle to his wife. Plumfield is a matriarchy, whose chief business is the rearing and education of the next generation.[27] It is entirely reasonable for Jo to look about her with the satisfaction of a job well done and to confess that "one of my favorite fancies is to look at my family as a small world, to watch the progress of my little men."[28] It is also reasonable for Jo to look at her family as a "small world," for in its impregnable boundaries Plumfield resembles the March household it replaced. Maintaining a March-like integrity and insularity, Plumfield has only the most casual and tenuous connection with the world outside it, being safely removed from the contamination of an urban, industrial America. Indeed, it was a kind of Utopia, and Jo could dream of "a new and charming state of society in which people lived as happily and innocently as her flock at Plumfield."[29]

The limitations of such an approach to the problems of the poor is evident, for it hinged on the willingness of proper families like the Marches and the Bhaers to open their doors to the children of poverty. However appealing in imagination, it was not a reform likely to catch hold in reality. Even Alcott herself, who certainly possessed the wealth and gentility necessary to turn her household into an asylum for poor children, could not bring herself to do it. Late in life, while responsible for the care of her niece Lulu, Alcott expressed worry about the welfare of four children whose mother had died and whose father was a drunkard. While tempted to imitate Mrs. Jo's example, she nevertheless declined a request to take one of the children into her home, explaining, "Lulu is all we can manage now."[30] Indeed, the very notion of expanding the domestic circle by taking in the unfortunate was itself potentially at odds with the belief, which she also subscribed to, that the nuclear family must carefully protect itself against contamination from the wicked community around it.

One of the reasons that Alcott had difficulty confronting the problems of the destitute was that she had so little acquaintance with them. She drew on her own adolescent experience of poverty to tell the story of Christie, to be sure, but although poverty proved for Alcott a humiliation, it never threatened her physical survival nor had it robbed her of her parents. When, relatively late in life, Alcott encountered poverty on an entirely different scale, she seemed either complacent or bewildered. In 1875, during a visit to New York City, she accepted invitations to visit institutions that attempted to deal with the suffering of orphaned and abandoned children. One such agency was the Newsboys Lodging House, which, for a small fee, provided food and lodging and some education and discipline for orphaned boys who made a living by hawking newspapers out on the streets of the city. Witnessing several hundred boys living in a dormitory, Alcott professed to be pleased with what she saw, describing the boys as a "smart-looking set, larking round in shirts and trousers, barefooted, but the faces were clean, and the heads smooth, and clothes pretty decent." She noted with approval that the boys were encouraged to save their money, and she seemed to like the institution's stern discipline, so unlike that of Plumfield: "After nine (if late in coming in) they are fined five cents; after ten, ten cents; and after eleven they can't come in at all. This makes them steady, keeps them out of harm, and gives them time for study."[31] The remarks seem smug, coming from a woman who, in her fiction, celebrated the importance of tender and intimate relations between parents and children. More disturbing for her was a Christmas Day trip to a foundling hospital on Randall's Island: "So sad it was to see these poor babies, born of want and sin, suffering every sort of deformity, disease and pain. Cripples, half blind, scarred with scrofula, burns and abuse—it was simply awful and indescribable."[32] Such scenes never found their way into Alcott's fiction, and it is evident that when she spoke of poverty in her stories—as she often did—it was of a different order altogether. She liked to tell her readers that poverty strengthens families and ennobles character, a comforting thought that is plausible only if one remembers that for Alcott poor families usually meant those of modest circumstances, not those who were utterly destitute. Although the March girls complain frequently of their poverty, the fact is that the family can afford a housekeeper and they are able to fill their stomachs and dress decently if not fashionably.

That Alcott could overlook the condition of the truly destitute was also a product of her insistence on drawing a line between the "worthy" and the "unworthy" poor. It was a line she adhered to both in her personal life and in her fiction. The meager sums she gave in charity outside the Alcott family were confined to the "needy but respectable," which, given Alcott's standards of respectability, would exclude a larger proportion of the poor people of America.[33] Looking back on her adolescent difficulties, Alcott classified herself among the worthy poor—those of respectable family background who have fallen on hard times but who possess both ambition and integrity and require only fair treatment and a bit of luck to improve their condition. Christie, her fictional alter ego, also fits in the category of the worthy poor, and when describing Christie's efforts to help working women, Alcott took pains to mark the differences between Christie and her beneficiaries. Unlike them, Christie possesses "fine instincts, gracious manners and an unblemished name." Alcott could be short with those poor who did not fall within this pale of respectability. This would include most of the Irish, for she shared in full measure the Alcott hostility against the "ignorant Patricks" and, in *Little Women*, she candidly describes Irish children as the "sworn foes" of girls like Amy March.[34] Sometimes even the poor who are not clearly identified as Irish might fail to prove worthy of a marriage to a member of the March clan, as an incident in *Jo's Boys* reveals. Even though loved by Mother Bhaer, Dan is tainted by the blood of his scapegrace father, making him unworthy of the angelic daughter of Amy and Laurie. As Jo tells the love-stricken young man: "I wish I could give you any hope; but we both know that the dear child is the apple of her father's eye, the pride of her mother's heart, and that the most perfect lover they can find will hardly seem to them worthy of their precious daughter. Let her remain for you the high, bright star that leads you up and makes you believe in heaven."[35]

The tone of condescension expressed toward Dan and others like him is unmistakable, and it provides evidence of the social-class bias in Alcott's writing that is all the more insidious because embedded so deep below the level of awareness. This bias accounts for Alcott's inability to project a picture of family life that bore any connection to the reality most poor Americans experienced in the nineteenth century. Victorian ideals placed extraordinary demands on parents to provide care and education for their young, demands which could be met only by parents who possessed considerable formal education and enough money to put them in comfortable circumstances. What, however, if the man were unable or unwilling to play his role as breadwinner? Victorian America, even as it worshipped at the cults of womanhood and childhood, provided a legion of examples of mothers and children bereft of economic support by men who had died, abandoned their families for some frontier lure, turned to alcoholism, or were simply unable to meet the requirements that Victorian society imposed for success in the marketplace.[36]

Alcott's answers—social purity, moral persuasion, and cultural uplift—were also the answers of most respectable Victorians, but these Victorian crusades scarcely made a dent in the problems of poor families. On the contrary, as Sheila Rothman has pointed out, the decades following the Civil War witnessed a growing economic disparity between the families of the rich and the poor.[37] Alcott did not perceive the limitations of social purity and cultural uplift because she had so little comprehension of the difficulties faced by those who lived outside the circle of Victorian respectability, which included such groups as the Irish and what she called the "unworthy poor." Like most respectable Victorians, she assumed that the problems of poverty could be traced to a failing of character, and that the salvation of the unworthy poor lay in their moral conversion to the ranks of the worthy. After all, she had raised herself from poverty by her own heroic efforts, and she had little patience for those who seemed mired in their misfortune. It never occurred to her, for example, that alcoholism might be more the result of poverty than its cause. The poor, she thought, could lift themselves by adopting higher standards of behavior, which in turn required proper child-rearing. Such a strategy placed, as we have seen, a very large burden on parents, and deflected attention from more promising reforms aimed at enhancing the health, education, and welfare of poor women and children. Although giving fervent support to women's suffrage, social purity, and cultural uplift, Alcott paid little attention to efforts to promote the spread of universal schooling, the beginnings of pediatric health care, the establishment of a separate system of justice for young people who ran afoul of the law, the beginnings of the kindergarten movement, much of it aimed at the care and instruction of poor children, the spread of day nurseries for the children of working mothers, the campaign to eradicate child abuse, the beginnings of the long battle against the employment of children in mines, factories, and textile mills, and, most significant of all, the effort to redress economic inequality by the militant organization of farmers and workers, which led eventually to the formation of the Populist political movement.[38]

Although Alcott successfully bridged in her imagination the gulf which the sentimental revolution had placed between the sexes, she was unable, in the final analysis, to surmount in her sympathies the barrier between the worthy and the unworthy poor. Her inability to cross this particular class barrier was, it should be noted, nothing idiosyncratic but was rather a trait she shared in America's Gilded Age with most respectable men and women, who ignored the plight of the truly poor and who maintained that the path to human progress lay through the moral conversion of individuals. Drawing on a vague blend of nineteenth-century liberalism and Christian charity, these philanthropic men and women pinned their hopes for reform on crusades against the saloon and the brothel.[39] Likewise it seemed reasonable to Victorian Americans like Alcott that a reformed family life, carefully insulated from the world outside it and dedicated to the proper rearing of the next generation, would not only enhance the status of women but would also provide the key to moral, cultural, and economic progress in the society at large.[40] These Victorian assumptions represented, then, the full flowering of the sentimental cult of domesticity. Only when these Victorian assumptions fell away would it become evident to later generations of Americans that the privatization of Utopia offered little hope to those who fell outside the pale of respectability.

Epilogue: The Legacy of
Victorian Domesticity

Immediately following World War II there was a brief period when Victorian ideals of family life enjoyed a resurgence of popularity in America.[1] Indeed, it could be argued that sustained economic prosperity during the years 1945–1963 enabled more Americans than ever before to establish families that appeared ideal by Victorian standards. Labeled the "feminine mystique" by Betty Friedan, popular culture in the 1950s celebrated a Victorian view of woman's place. She belonged, of course, in the home. In deference to the doctrine of the two spheres, men were to concentrate on their roles as breadwinners, but they too were expected to help around the house and to participate enthusiastically in family "togetherness." Several decades of economic deprivation and war had denied Americans the pleasures of domesticity, and they seemed determined in the postwar years to earn money and invest it in the private Utopia of family life, a Utopia probably located in the new suburbs.[2] The postwar home itself was "child-centered" in a double sense: first, couples gave birth to more children than at any time since the 1920s, reversing historical downward trends in the birthrate and creating the "baby boom"; and second, preoccupation with proper child-rearing reached new heights, as evidenced by the astounding popularity of child-rearing manuals like Dr. Benjamin Spock's *Common Sense Book of Baby and Child Care.*[3]

Anyone familiar with American history since 1963 will know, of course, how far Americans have drifted from the familism of the postwar period. Even before the birth of women's liberation, women were entering the labor market in unprecedented numbers, either by

157

choice or by necessity.[4] Most astounding was the rise in the number
of middle-class women, married women, and mothers of young
children entering the labor force, a rise which broke from historical
patterns and defied Victorian notions of woman's proper place.
Friedan's *Feminine Mystique* provided an ideological rationale for this
shift in female behavior by codifying the notion of "woman as person."[5] Unlike some earlier versions of feminism, women's liberation
rejected all claims for the moral superiority of women and couched its
demands for justice in woman's rights as a person, rather than on her
contribution to society. Moreover, it was asserted that the key to a
woman's identity is, or should be, broader than any particular function that she performs within the family. The new ideology held that
she is a person before she is a daughter, wife, or mother. The concern
of most middle-class feminists shifted to affirming that women have a
right to pursue a career outside the home on equal terms with men.
The evidence is that the bulk of American women did not share the
more radical feminist sentiments, but the actions of women also
revealed that they were challenging traditional patterns of American
family life. A signal that women were taking seriously the new
conceptions of female independence could be found not only in increased labor force participation, but also in the rising tendency of
women to postpone marriage, to have fewer children than at any
point in American history, and to boost the rate of divorce to the
highest point in American history.

Less impressive than the changes in notions of woman's place and
identity, but significant nonetheless, were signs that American men
were cooperating in these trends and that they were beginning to
challenge what some called the "masculine mystique," and with it the
neat bifurcation of gender roles that the Victorians bequeathed us.[6]
Increasing numbers of men seemed to find less satisfaction in their
employment and indicated they were ready to take on at least some of
the responsibilities for housework and child care that had been the
province of women. One concrete result of these changes in gender
relationships was that by the early 1980s, only 11 percent of American households conformed to the Victorian ideal—a full-time breadwinner, a full-time homemaker, and children in the home—while
the number of two-breadwinner households and single-parent house-

holds was on the rise.[7] The precipitous decline in the birthrate after 1963, combined with increasing numbers of elderly women living alone, meant also that fewer households contained young children.

Beyond these obvious changes in gender roles and in household size and structure during the postwar years was a transformation in popular attitudes toward love, courtship, and marriage. One aspect of this transformation was the so-called sexual revolution of the 1960s and 1970s, which introduced more Americans to new forms of sexual intimacy, both inside marriage and out, and which seemed to grant license to explore forms of sexual expression that would have shocked earlier generations.[8] More subtle were shifts in the very meaning of adulthood. Some observers detected a decline in the notion that issues of love and work are to be settled, once and for all, at the point of transition from youth to adulthood. Instead, there was emerging a belief that all commitments—to a marriage partner, to a career, to a set of values, even to a personal identity—are tentative and subject to continuous revision throughout the course of the life cycle. The result might be, as some have predicted, the emergence of a "culture of narcissism," or, as others have maintained, a greater opportunity for a fuller and richer development of the self.[9]

Inevitably, changes in the family affected the lives of children. One departure from Victorian norms of childhood was evident already during the immediate postwar period. Middle-class mothers even then were drifting toward more flexible ways of dealing with their offspring.[10] Labeled "permissive," these middle-class mothers found support from Doctor Spock, who advocated a more easygoing regime in matters of feeding, toilet training, and discipline of children than Victorians would have regarded as proper. It should be noted, however, that permissive techniques were not inconsistent with the notion of child-centered family. It could be argued, in fact, that a mother following Doctor Spock's advice would give more, not less, time and attention to her children, for the permissiveness of middle-class families flowed not from an indifference to the welfare of the young but rather from a desire to rear them in an atmosphere relatively free of conflict and toward an adulthood relatively free of guilt.[11]

Even more significant changes in the lives of children lay in the future, however—changes which involved challenges to the entire concept of Victorian childhood. Some have argued that childhood itself suffered a decline during the 1960s and 1970s, at least childhood as Victorians understood it. The unprecedented entrance of mothers into the labor force made increasingly difficult the achievement of a child-centered family life. Moreover, feminist commentators were prepared to argue that Victorian ideas of family life, especially in the forms they assumed during the immediate postwar period, had raised preoccupation with children to a level harmful both to women and to their offspring. [12] One heard less of the dangers of neglecting children and more of the dangers of overprotection. Women, it was argued, should spend more time in self-fulfillment and less time in trying to live their lives through their children. The weakening of the cults of motherhood and childhood was matched also by pressures coming from new forms of the mass media, especially television, which hurried the young along toward a precocious, if vicarious, experience of adult life, and which penetrated that cocoon within which Victorians had sought to envelop childhood and youth. [13] Beyond the challenges to Victorian childhood presented by feminism and the mass media there lay the fact that many children of single-parent families were forced by economic necessity to become wise early in the ways of the world. As a consequence of these fundamental changes, many observers and scholars were beginning to speak in the early 1980s of the "disappearance" of childhood, a phrase suggesting that children were talking like adults, thinking like adults, acting like adults, and even having children themselves. [14] Such a change in the behavior of children would seem to be a logical accompaniment to the observed tendency of adults to act more like the young in their repudiation of commitments. The net result seemed to be a decline in the age segregation which Victorian America had labored to enforce.

Changing conceptions of manhood, womanhood, adulthood, and childhood have been accompanied by criticism of the Victorian tendency to view families as self-sufficient units. For many middle-class young people, this revolt against the cult of domesticity took the form of a faddish movement toward the establishment of communes, featuring a deliberate effort to expand intimacy and caring beyond the

160

boundaries of the nuclear family so as to embrace a community of the like-minded.[15] More significant in the long run, however, was the "discovery" of poverty during the 1960s, followed in due course by the "war" on poverty.[16] Although the war has since settled into a stalemate with no hope of anything like final victory, it did become apparent to many scholars and commentators that poor families could not easily survive without the help of what became known in the jargon of our time as "support systems." The cult of domesticity also came under fire from middle-class feminists who recognized that their demands for equality in the marketplace required community support for child-rearing, particularly in the form of publicly funded day care.[17] Ironically, feminists won support from political conservatives, who saw publicly founded day care as a device to get poor women out of the home and off the welfare roles. This strange political alliance meant that American public policy was drifting away from any pretense of loyalty to Victorian notions of woman's proper place and of the self-sufficiency of the nuclear family. Although easily accessible day care is not yet a reality, it appears evident that powerful forces are at work in changing the attitude of Americans toward the family and its relationship to the state. In sum, although one might agree with scholars who argue that the family itself is "here to stay," it is evident also that it is moving away from its Victorian past.[18] It appears in the 1980s that the legacy of Victorian domesticity has disappeared altogether, except among religious groups of a more conservative persuasion.

As Americans grope toward alternative forms of family life, Louisa May Alcott might give us the benefit of perspective on these wrenching changes if we grant her the final word. Given the complexity of the subject, the word is bound to be ambiguous. On the one hand, there can be little doubt that she would have welcomed transformations in relationships of gender. Indeed, as we have seen, androgynous convictions led her to anticipate in her fiction many of the changes in sex-role relationships that have occurred since 1945. Given the popularity of her books with American girls, it might even be argued that she helped bring about some of these changes. Although she might remain somewhat skeptical about the "lords of creation" being prepared to give up the masculine mystique, still she would certainly welcome any sign that men were prepared to play a larger and more sensitive role in family life. She was certainly aware that any significant change in woman's role would depend upon an accompanying alteration in man's view of himself. Given these changes, perhaps at last Americans might begin to achieve her dream of a companionate family, bringing to an end the war of the sexes.

As for postwar changes in woman's role, it will be recalled that Alcott was a feminist who deeply resented the second-class citizenship to which she had been consigned by Victorian society. Equal access for women to the ballot box and to the workplace were causes to which she had devoted both her life and her fiction, while the effort of twentieth-century feminists to pull women down from the moral pedestal on which they had been placed by nineteenth-century sentiment would also win her approval, for she herself broke with convention on this issue more than a century ago. Once she gave up her vain effort to win the approval of the respectable, she created in her stories girls and young women who could match men in their possession of character defects and moral failings. Alcott had managed to transcend her own father's extravagant notions about the purity of children, notions which had laid such a burden on his second-born and which contributed much to damage her self-esteem. In a move both creative and therapeutic, Alcott possessed the courage to portray angry young women like herself. Before Mark Twain departed from saccharine convention to give us Huck Finn, the good bad boy, she had created in Jo the good bad girl. Her achievement may, in fact, have proved a source of inspiration down through the intervening decades for women who sensed that sentimentality limited and degraded them. Writing on the centennial of the appearance of *Little Women* Elizabeth Janeway could acknowledge the faults of the novel and yet say: "Miss Alcott preached, and the conclusions she came to are frequently too good to be true; but the facts of emotion that she started with were real. She might end by softening the ways to deal with them, but she began by looking them in the eye. Her girls were jealous, mean, silly and lazy; and for 100 years jealous, mean, silly, and lazy girls have been ardently grateful for the chance to read about themselves."[19]

In the above ways, then, Alcott anticipated and would undoubtedly welcome trends in American family life that appeared during the years after World War Two. At the same time, however, she was firmly embedded in the nineteenth century. If she was a feminist, she was a Victorian feminist. On issues of social justice for women she spoke with a voice recognizable to twentieth-century ears, but on the equally profound issues of morals, manners, and mores she would undoubtedly have been shocked and dismayed by the unraveling of Victorian notions of propriety and civility. The sexual revolution of the 1960s and 1970s has undermined the very foundation of Victorian morality to which she subscribed and which, given her child-rearing, she could hardly have escaped. Our tolerance for exotic forms of sexual expression, both within marriage and without, would doubtless arouse in Alcott fears that the liberated libido would destroy the rational restraint and self-control on which Victorians believed character and integrity rested. As we have seen, she believed there was a link between celibacy and autonomy, a link most evident in her own life, but in her fiction too she suggested that sexual restraint, if not abstinence, was an essential condition for nobility of character for both men and women. In this regard she embodied the respectable, conventional wisdom of her day. Likewise, the trend toward a protean concept of personal identity, which rejects lasting commitments in love and work, would challenge her principled—some might say obsessive—devotion to romantic love and the heroic life.

Matters of propriety and civility raise, of course, significant issues of child-rearing. One set of issues has to do with parental governance. Although Alcott would find much to like in Doctor Spock's advice, and although she advocated gentle means of discipline, she would not endorse the relaxed assumption that there is no inevitable conflict between the nature of the child and his destiny. Her unbending sense of right and wrong required also that parents insulate their children from the world of adulthood, shielding them from the workplace and from the adult experience of sex, drugs, and alcohol. Given these requirements for proper child-rearing, she could only be alarmed by the evidence that childhood, as a carefully monitored and regulated stage in the life cycle, is disappearing in our culture. If the

163

demise of childhood is indeed occurring, it would annihilate whatever is left of Victorian domesticity, as well as the very core of Victorian sensibilty.

It is precisely here that Alcott would encounter the sharpest dilemma in her contemplation of modern American family life. The destruction of Victorian notions of proper child-rearing owes much to the increasing influence of the mass media over the young, but equally significant are the claims of women to a new identity outside the family, claims which threaten a precarious balance achieved in the nineteenth century. Over Alcott's own protest, Victorian America had arrived at something like a bargain. Raising child-nurture to a new importance in the life of the family, Victorians wished to place nearly the entire burden of proper child-rearing on the shoulders of women. Now it is becoming evident that the bargain is no longer acceptable to millions of American women as they struggle for equality in the public sphere of life. The resulting dilemma may be stated simply: the value of equality for women, which Alcott celebrated, seems to contradict the value of child nurture, which she also honored.

There may be several ways to escape this dilemma between the interests of women and the interests of children. One is the growing tendency of couples to forego parenthood altogether, creating what is becoming known as the child-free family. Another is to lower the expectations that Victorian domesticity placed on parenthood, without at the same time reverting to the condition of brutality and neglect that was the fate of all too many children before the sentimental revolution of the nineteenth century began to transform attitudes toward the young. Still a third avenue of escape from the dilemma—and the one that Alcott herself would certainly favor—is to persuade men to accept greater responsibility for the nurture of the young, although such an arrangement would require not only a massive reorientation of the male ego, but also a reordering of the priorities of American business and industry so as to allow men to respond more sensitively to the needs of family life.

Taken together, all three developments might serve to ease tensions between the values of sexual equality and the values of child nurture, but they hardly preclude the importance of reexamining one of the central assumptions of Victorian domesticity, an assumption about the relationship between the nuclear family and the world that surrounds it. That world included, in Alcott's day, the sometimes helpful and sometimes meddlesome networks of kin, neighborhood, and local community, all of which were prepared to give assistance to the parents of young children. Indeed, although custodians of Victorian culture may not have given such voluntary aid the full recognition it deserved, it is apparent that poor families in the nineteenth century relied heavily on grandparents, aunts, uncles, neighbors, and local charity to help out when the burdens of child care became heavy. There remain even to this day vestiges of such arrangements, but the decades of the twentieth century have witnessed a steady erosion of such informal support systems, leaving exposed the bare bones of the Victorian argument for the self-sufficiency of the nuclear family. One of the chief casualties of woman's entrance into the labor force has been the spirit of voluntarism itself, which in the past eased the isolation of poor families and softened the blows of adversity. The place of voluntarism and informal family assistance has been filled to some extent by private enterprise and also by the state, but in such a way as to satisfy few. In any event, it has proved difficult to secure a political consensus to support a reformed and expanded role for the state in providing such help as day care, welfare, and family income assistance. Given these difficulties it is tempting for some to call for a return of family life and family policy to the principles of Victorian domesticity. Conservative religious groups who oppose the intervention of the state in family life, even in the form of benign help, have been joined by scholars and commentators who profess to see in all forms of state intervention the potential tyranny of a therapeutic society.[20] Given her assumptions, Alcott might be expected to sympathize in some ways with these fears, and she would doubtless be gratified at these signs that the cult of domesticity is alive, yet her greater concern was always with the equality of women and with the proper nurture of the young. She might tell us, were she here, that we should move beyond the politics of the nineteenth century to encourage a family life that is at odds with neither the aspirations of women nor the welfare of children.

Notes

CHAPTER 1

1. Henry F. May, *The End of American Innocence: A Study of the First Years of Our Own Time, 1912–1917* (New York, 1959), p. vii.

2. Robert Falk, *The Victorian Mode in American Fiction* (East Lansing, Mich., 1965), p. 3.

3. See, for example, Jessie Bernard's *The Future of Motherhood* (New York, 1974), especially pp. 3–16.

4. Trends in nineteenth-century family life are summarized in chap. 1 (pp. 3–25) of Carl Degler's *At Odds: Women and the Family in America from the Revolution to the Present* (New York, 1980). More specialized works include Mary Ryan, *Cradle of the Middle Class: The Family in Oneida County, N.Y., 1790–1865* (New York, 1981); Ann Douglas, *The Feminization of American Culture* (New York, 1977). Reviews of monographs include N. Ray Hiner, "The Child in American Historiography," *The Psychohistory Review* 7 (Summer 1978): 13–23; and Lawrence Stone, "Family History in the 1980's," *Journal of Interdisciplinary History* 12 (Summer 1981): 51–87.

5. Degler, *At Odds*, chap. 1.

6. Ryan, *Cradle of the Middle Class*, pp. 230–41.

7. Studies of black families in the nineteenth century include Eugene Genovese, *Roll, Jordan, Roll: The World the Slaves Made* (New York, 1974); Herbert Gutman, *The Black Family in Slavery and Freedom, 1750–1925* (New York, 1976); John W. Blassingame, *The Slave Community: Plantation Life in the Antebellum South* (New York, 1972); Paul Lammermeier, "The Urban Black Family of the Nineteenth Century: A Study of Black Family Structure in the Ohio Valley, 1850–1880," *Journal of Marriage and the Family* 35 (August 1973): 44–56. Among the studies of immigrant and working-class families are Virginia Yans-McLaughlin,

Family and Community: Italian Immigrants in Buffalo, 1880–1930 (Ithaca, 1977); Lawrence Glasco, "The Life Cycles and Household Structure of American Ethnic Groups: Irish, Germans, and Native-Born Whites in Buffalo, New York, 1855," in Tamara Hareven, ed., *Family and Kin in Urban Communities, 1770–1930* (New York, 1977), pp. 122–33. Studies of rural families include John Modell, "Family and Fertility on the Indiana Frontier," *American Quarterly* 23 (1971): 615–34; and Julie Jeffrey, *Frontier Women: The Trans-Mississippi West, 1840–1880* (New York, 1979).

8. The literary sources of the sentimental revolution are surveyed in E. Douglas Branch, *The Sentimental Years, 1836–1860* (New York, 1934); Herbert Brown, *The Sentimental Novel In America, 1789–1860* (Durham, N.C., 1940); and Helen Waite Papashvily, *All the Happy Endings: A Study of the Domestic Novel in America; the Women Who Wrote It, the Women Who Read It, in the Nineteenth Century* (New York, 1956). See also William F. Bridges, "Family Patterns and Social Values in America, 1825–1875," *American Quarterly* 17 (Spring 1965): 3–11.

9. Douglas, *Feminization*, especially pp. 80–117; Papashvily, *All the Happy Endings*, especially pp. xvi–xvii.

10. Degler, *At Odds*, p. 377; Douglas, *Feminization*, pp. 81–83. Herbert Brown points out that between 1784 and 1860, at least a hundred magazines were published for women, while one-third of American novels before 1820 were written by women (*Sentimental Novel*, pp. 101, 104).

11. Alice Felt Tyler, *Freedom's Ferment: Phases of American Social History from the Colonial Period to the Outbreak of the Civil War* (Minneapolis, 1944); R. W. B. Lewis, *The American Adam: Innocence, Tragedy and Tradition in the Nineteenth Century* (Chicago, 1955).

12. Ralph Waldo Emerson, *Journals and Miscellaneous Notebooks*, ed. William H. Gilman et al. (Cambridge, 1960), 7:403–4.

13. Kathryn Sklar, *Catharine Beecher: A Study in Domesticity* (New Haven, 1973), especially chap. 11 (pp. 151–67). The ambivalence of Jacksonian Americans toward "progress" is discussed in Marvin Meyers, *The Jacksonian Persuasion: Politics and Belief* (Stanford, 1957).

14. Sklar, *Catharine Beecher*, pp. xiii–xiv, 161–64.

15. Brown, *Sentimental Novel*, especially chap. 5 (pp. 100–165).

16. Ibid., pp. 167–72.

17. Leslie Fiedler, *Love and Death in the American Novel*, rev. ed. (New York, 1966), p. 67.

18. Brown, *Sentimental Novel*, p. 175; Papashvily, *All the Happy Endings*, p. 29.

19. Quoted in Brown, *Sentimental Novel*, pp. 35–37.

20. Ibid., pp. 107–57.

21. Bridges, "Family Patterns," pp. 3–11; Kirk Jeffrey, "The Family as Utopian Retreat from the City: The Nineteenth-Century Contribution," in Sallie TeSelle, ed., *The Family, Communes, and Utopian Societies* (New York, 1972), pp. 21–42; Walter E. Houghton, *The Victorian Frame of Mind, 1830–1870* (New Haven, 1957), especially pp. 341–93; Sklar, *Catharine Beecher*, pp. xi–xii; Brown, *Sentimental Novel*, pp. 282, 312.

22. Sarah Hale, introduction, *Ladies Magazine* 1 (1828): 1–2.

23. L. E. of Portsmouth, "Home," *Ladies Magazine* 3 (1830): 217–20; Brown, *Sentimental Novel*, p. 281; David Grimsted, *Melodrama Unveiled: American Theatre and Culture, 1800–1850* (Chicago, 1968), especially pp. 166, 227–29. The Victorian philosopher John Ruskin wrote that "this is the true nature of home—it is the place of Peace: the shelter, not only from injury, but from all terror, doubt, and division" (quoted in Houghton, *Victorian Frame of Mind*, p. 343).

24. Brown, *Sentimental Novel*, p. 312.

25. Jeffrey, "Family as Utopian Retreat," p. 28; Brown, *Sentimental Novel*, pp. 312–14.

26. John Demos, *A Little Commonwealth: Family Life in Plymouth Colony* (New York, 1970), p. 186.

27. Degler, *At Odds*, especially pp. 26–51; Sklar, *Catharine Beecher*, pp. 211–13.

28. Brown, *Sentimental Novel*, pp. 108–10, 291, 315–16.

29. Sarah Hale, for example, urged the importance of women's education, not, however, to "usurp the station or encroach on the prerogative of the man; but that each individual may lend her aid to perfect the moral and intellectual character of those within her sphere" (*Ladies Magazine*, pp. 1–2). Catharine Beecher was equally adamant, arguing that American women enjoyed privileges superior to mere political and economic equality, and that in the public sphere they should take a "subordinate station" (*A Treatise on Domestic Economy for the Use of Young Ladies at Home and at School* [Boston, 1841], p. 4). See also Brown, *Sentimental Novel*, p. 111.

30. Beecher, *Treatise*, p. 9. Ironically, it was a nineteenth-century feminist, Mary Livermore, who coined the phrase "better half," in her book *On the Sphere and Influence of Women*: "Regarding her as I do as the better half of humanity—with a more delicate and sensitive nature than man—with a more refined and spiritual organization—woman should be the conservator of public morals" (quoted in Andrew Sinclair, *The Better Half: The Emancipation of the American Woman* [New York, 1965], p. ix). Daniel Smith sees the increasing emphasis on a woman's role as wife and mother as

a form of "domestic feminism," and suggests that it may be related to the decline in the fertility rate. See "Family Limitation, Sexual Control, and Domestic Feminism in Victorian America," in Mary Hartman and Lois Banner, eds., *Clio's Consciousness Raised: New Perspectives on the History of Women* (New York, 1974), pp. 119–36.

31. Brown, *Sentimental Novel*, pp. 300–308; Robert Sunley, "Early Nineteenth-Century American Literature on Child Rearing," in Margaret Mead and Martha Wolfenstein, eds., *Childhood in Contemporary Cultures* (Chicago, 1955), pp. 150–67; Anne L. Kuhn, *The Mother's Role in Childhood Education: New England Concepts, 1830–1860* (New Haven, 1947); Bernard Wishy, *The Child and the Republic: The Dawn of Modern American Child Nurture* (Philadelphia, 1968). William Bridges has argued that the symbol of the American mother was one of two foci around which the culture of popular poetry in the nineteenth century revolved ("Warm Hearth, Cold World: Social Perspectives on the Household Poets," *American Quarterly* 21 [Winter 1969]: 764–79).

32. Sunley, "Literature on Child Rearing," p. 153; Brown, *Sentimental Novel*, p. 319.

33. Horace Bushnell, *Christian Nurture* (New York, 1860), pp. 249–50.

34. Kuhn, *Mother's Role*, pp. 134–38.

35. Sunley, "Literature on Child Rearing," p. 155.

36. Beecher, *Treatise*, pp. 233–34; Kuhn, *Mother's Role*, p. 108; Bushnell, *Christian Nurture*, p. 121. The full flower of this effort to screen out harmful influences was reached in the post–Civil War period. See David Pivar, *Purity Crusade: Sexual Morality and Social Control, 1868–1900* (Westport, 1973).

37. Nancy Cott has reviewed the relevant literature in "Notes toward an Interpretation of Antebellum Childrearing," *Psychohistory Review* 6 (Spring 1978): 4–20. See also Wishy, *Child and Republic*.

38. Lydia H. Sigourney, *Letters to Mothers* (Hartford, 1838), p. 10.

39. Brown, *Sentimental Novel*, p. 300.

40. Charles Strickland, "American Attitudes toward Children," in *Encyclopedia of Education* (New York, 1970), 2:80–83. See also Judith Plotz, "The Perpetual Messiah: Romanticism, Childhood and the Paradoxes of Human Development," in Barbara Finkelstein, ed., *Regulated Children / Liberated Children: Education in Psychohistorical Perspective* (New York, 1979), pp. 63–95; Albert Stone, *The Innocent Eye: Childhood in Mark Twain's Imagination* (New Haven, 1961), pp. 14–32.

41. T. S. Arthur, *The Angel of the Household* (Boston, 1854), p. 5.

42. T. S. Arthur, *Ten Nights in a Bar Room, and What I Saw There* (Boston, 1854).

43. Edward Foster points out that *The Wide, Wide World* was "with the sole exception of *Uncle Tom's Cabin* the most famous and popular book of the day, and it continued to find enthusiastic readers and reviewers and to sell astonishingly well for more than half a century" (*Susan and Anna Warner* [Boston, 1978], p. 35).

44. Susan Warner, *The Wide, Wide World* (New York, 1850), p. 310.

45. Ibid., p. 12.

46. Fiedler, *Love and Death*, p. 264.

47. Ibid., p. 264.

48. Harriet Beecher Stowe, *Uncle Tom's Cabin; or, Life among the Lowly* (New York, 1958), pp. 82–83. This edition, published by Harper and Row, reprints the text of the first edition, which was issued in 1852 by John P. Jewett and Company of Boston.

49. Stowe, introduction to the 1878 edition, reprinted in the 1958 edition cited above, p. xxv. Further references to this edition are in the text.

CHAPTER 2

1. Discussion of the lives and family activities of Bronson Alcott and Abigail May Alcott is based on the Alcott Family Manuscripts deposited in the Houghton Library, Harvard University, Cambridge, Mass. All citations of manuscripts refer, without further designation, to this collection. The author is also indebted to Odell Shepard's excellent biography *Pedlar's Progress: The Life of Bronson Alcott* (Boston, 1937); Dorothy McCuskey's *Bronson Alcott, Teacher* (New York, 1940); and Sandford Salyer, *Marmee: The Mother of Little Women* (Norman, Okla., 1949). For Louisa May's life I have relied heavily on Madeleine B. Stern's *Louisa May Alcott* (Norman, Okla., 1949), supplemented by the Alcott Family Manuscripts and *Louisa May Alcott: Her Life, Letters, and Journals*, ed. Ednah D. Cheney (Boston, 1889). I have also found insightful and provocative Martha Saxton's *Louisa May: A Modern Biography of Louisa May Alcott* (Boston, 1977), which is written from a psychoanalytic and feminist perspective.

2. Bronson Alcott to his daughters, 1 February 1843, in Bronson Alcott, *The Letters of A. Bronson Alcott*, ed. Richard L. Herrnstadt (Ames, Iowa, 1969), p. 96.

3. Ralph Waldo Emerson, "Ode Inscribed to W. H. Channing" in *The Complete Works of Ralph Waldo Emerson*, ed. Edward Waldo Emerson (Boston, ca. 1903–1921), 9:78.

4. Emerson, "Self Reliance," in ibid., 2:50.

5. Entry for 13 April 1830 in Bronson Alcott, *The Journals of Bronson Alcott*, ed. Odell Shepard, 2 vols. (Port Washington, N.Y., 1938), 1:24.

6. Entry for 1 September 1828, Fragments of Diaries of Abigail Alcott.

7. Abigail Alcott to Samuel May, August 1828; to Lucretia May, 15 June 1830, Family Letters, 1828–1861.

8. Entry for 2 August 1828, Bronson Alcott, *Journals*, 1:12.

9. Entry for 2 September 1828, ibid.

10. Entry for 16 January 1830, Journals of Bronson Alcott in Alcott Family Manuscripts.

11. Entry for 9 April 1830, ibid.

12. Abigail Alcott to Lucretia May, 15 June 1830, Family Letters.

13. Entry for 8 July 1831, Journals of Bronson Alcott.

14. Abigail Alcott to Samuel May, 22 May 1831, Family Letters.

15. Bronson Alcott, "Observations on the Spiritual Nurture of My Children," a manuscript which is bound with another entitled "Researches on Childhood." To Alcott's sorrow, the observations were never published in full, but they provide the basis for a monograph by Charles Strickland, "A Transcendentalist Father: The Child-Rearing Practices of Bronson Alcott," *Perspectives in American History* 3 (1969): 5–73. Alcott's observations, which filled 2,500 pages, mark the beginning of child psychology in America, a full half-century before G. Stanley Hall launched the "child-study" movement. See Charles Strickland and Charles Burgess, *Health, Growth and Heredity: G. Stanley Hall on Natural Education* (New York, 1965), pp. 1–26.

16. Entry for 16 March 1831, Bronson Alcott, *Journals*, 1:27.

17. Abigail Alcott to Samuel May, 27 March 1831, Family Letters.

18. Bronson Alcott, "First Child, First Year," pp. 26, 69–70.

19. Bronson Alcott to Anna Alcott, 29 November 1832, in *Letters*, p. 18.

20. Bronson Alcott, "Researchers," p. 258.

21. Bronson Alcott, "Spiritual Nurture," p. 201. In extracting Alcott's conversations with his daughters, I have occasionally altered punctuation and capitalization for the sake of clarity.

22. Ibid., p. 202.

23. Louisa May Alcott, *Life, Letters*, p. 29.

24. Ibid., p. 27.

25. Entry for 16 March 1846, in Bronson Alcott, *Journals*, 1:173.

26. Bronson Alcott, "Spiritual Nurture," pp. 22–23.

27. Ibid., p. 154.

28. Ibid., p. 20.

29. Ibid., pp. 109–10.

30. Ibid., pp. 111–12.

31. Bronson Alcott, "Psyche," p. 485.

32. Ibid., p. 488.

33. Abigail Alcott to Louisa May Alcott, 29 November 1846, Family Letters.

34. Louisa May Alcott, *Life, Letters*, p. 30.

35. Clara Gowing, *The Alcotts as I Knew Them* (Boston, 1909), p. 6.

36. Louisa May Alcott, Journal entries for 1 September 1843, 24 September 1843, in *Life, Letters*, pp. 35–36.

37. Bronson Alcott to Louisa May Alcott, 29 November 1839, *Letters*, p. 43.

38. Bronson Alcott to Louisa May Alcott, 29 November 1842, ibid., pp. 92–93.

39. Abigail Alcott, Journal entry for 26 July 1842, in Bronson Alcott, *Journals*, 1:145.

40. Abigail Alcott to Louisa May Alcott, 29 November 1846, Family Letters.

41. Louisa May Alcott, Journal entry for March 1846, quoted in *Life, Letters*, p. 48.

42. Louisa May Alcott, Journal entry for 9 October 1845, ibid., p. 45.

43. Louisa May Alcott, "My Kingdom," in ibid., p. 32.

44. Entry for 25 December 1848, Fragments of Diaries of Abigail Alcott.

45. Louisa May Alcott, *A Modern Mephistopheles* (Boston, 1877), p. 241.

46. Bronson Alcott to Anna, Louisa, Elizabeth, and May Alcott, 1 February 1843, *Letters*, pp. 96–97.

47. Abigail Alcott to Samuel and Lucretia May, 20 February 1833, Family Letters.

48. Bronson Alcott, "Observations on the Experience of a Child during the Third Year of Its Existence," p. 28.

49. Entry for 23 April 1834, Journals of Bronson Alcott.

50. Entry for 9 June 1839 in Bronson Alcott, *Journals*, 1:129.

51. Bronson Alcott to Samuel May, 10 August 1840, *Letters*, pp. 52–53.

52. Bronson Alcott to Junius S. Alcott, 28 October 1844, ibid., pp. 114–15.

53. Abigail Alcott to Samuel May, 24 January 1841, Family Letters.

54. Ralph Waldo Emerson, "English Reformers" in *Uncollected Writings: Essays, Addresses, Poems, Reviews, and Letters* (New York, 1912), p. 97.

55. Louisa May Alcott, "Transcendental Wild Oats," first appearing in *The Independent* 25 (18 December 1873), reprinted in her volume *Silver Pitchers* (Boston, 1876), pp. 97–99.

56. Abigail Alcott to Samuel May, December 1843? Family Letters.

57. Bronson Alcott to Junius Alcott, 3 January 1845, *Letters*, p. 117.

58. Journal entry for 20 March 1850, Bronson Alcott, *Journals*, 1:229.

59. Journal entries for 6 April, 27 May, and 30 June 1850 in Bronson Alcott, *Journals*, 1:230–32. Years later, after the death of his wife, Bronson still expressed regret for his failing as a breadwinner, yet remained puzzled as to anything he might have done differently. See entry for 10–14 June 1878, 2:490–91.

60. Abigail Alcott to Samuel May, 15 November 1840, as preserved in Journals of Bronson Alcott, November 1840.

61. Diary of Anna Alcott, entry for 1 November 1839.

62. Ibid., 26 November 1840.

63. Diary of Louisa May Alcott, entry for 10 December 1843, as quoted in Clara Endicott Sears, *Bronson Alcott's Fruitlands* (Boston, 1913), p. 111.

CHAPTER 3

1. Louisa May Alcott, Journal entry for June 1860, in *Life, Letters*, p. 122.

2. Writing in his journal for 1862 Bronson commented on his "deplorable lack of early discipline in expression that leaves me lame at last" (*Journals*, 2:349).

3. Louisa May Alcott, Journal entry for 29 November 1856, in *Life, Letters*, p. 88.

4. Abigail Alcott to Samuel May, 13 February 1848, Family Letters; Diary entry of Abigail Alcott, 28 August 1842.

5. Abigail Alcott to Samuel May, 9 August 1845 and 13 February 1848, Family Letters.

6. Entry for 1–3 September 1848, Fragments of Diaries of Abigail Alcott.

7. Abigail Alcott to Samuel May, 13 February 1848, Family Letters.

8. Abigail Alcott to Samuel May, 8 February 1847, ibid.

9. Abigail Alcott to Samuel May, 19 September 1853, ibid.

10. Anna Alcott to Abigail Alcott, 9 August 1853, ibid.

11. Abigail Alcott to Bronson Alcott, 9 July 1852, ibid.

12. Abigail Alcott to Bronson Alcott, 4 December 1853, ibid.

13. Abigail Alcott to Samuel May, 2 November 1852, ibid.

14. Abigail Alcott to Louisa May Alcott, 12 March 1843, ibid.

15. Louisa May Alcott, *Life, Letters*, p. 48, Journal entry for March 1846.

16. Ibid., p. 57.

17. Ibid., p. 122, Journal entry for May 1860.

18. Ibid., p. 136.

19. Ibid., p. 121, Journal entry for April 1860.

20. Ibid., p. 166, Journal entry for May 1865.

21. Ibid., p. 89, Louisa May Alcott to Bronson Alcott, 29 November 1856.

22. Ibid., p. 85, Journal entry for October 1856.

23. Ibid., p. 62, Journal entry for July 1850.

24. Ibid., Journal entry for August 1850.

25. Abigail Alcott to Samuel May, 28 February 1851, Family Letters.

26. Journal and Account Book of Louisa May Alcott, 1850–1885. Louisa made yearly summary notations of her earnings and their sources.

27. Louisa May Alcott, *Life, Letters*, p. 63, Journal entry for August 1850.

28. Ibid., p. 99, Journal entry for June 1858.

29. Louisa May Alcott, *Work: A Story of Experience* (Boston, 1873), p. 46.

30. Louisa May Alcott, *Life, Letters*, p. 20.

31. Abigail Alcott to Louisa May Alcott, 29 November 1842, Family Letters; Fragments of Diaries of Abigail Alcott, entry for 29 November 1846. See also Louisa May Alcott, *Life, Letters*, pp. 42, 76–77. Upon publishing her first book, Louisa told her mother: "Whatever beauty or poetry is to be found in my little book is owing to your interest in and encouragement of all my efforts from the first to the last" (p. 77).

32. Diary of Anna Alcott for 1845, p. 133.

33. Louisa May Alcott, *Life, Letters*, p. 79, Journal entry for 1 January 1855.

34. Ibid., p. 68, Journal entry, 1852.

35. Ibid., pp. 76–77, Louisa May Alcott to Abigail Alcott, 25 December 1854.

36. Ibid., p. 80, Journal entry for April 1855.

37. Bronson Alcott to Anna, Louisa, and May, 9 September 1857 in Bronson Alcott, *Letters*, p. 253.

38. Ibid., p. 264, Bronson Alcott to Anna Alcott, 21 November 1857.

39. Louisa May Alcott to Bronson Alcott, 28 November 1855, Family Letters.

40. Louisa May Alcott to Bronson Alcott, 29 November 1856, in *Life, Letters*, p. 89.

41. Ibid., p. 99, Journal entry for May 1858.

42. Ibid., pp. 100–101, Journal entry for October 1858.

43. Ibid., pp. 382–83, Louisa May Alcott to Louisa Greenwood Bond, 16 October 1887.

44. Ibid., p. 68, Journal entry for 1853.

45. Ibid., p. 77, Louisa May Alcott to Abigail Alcott, 25 December 1854.

46. Ibid., p. 103, Journal entry, 1858.

47. Ibid.

48. Ibid., pp. 104–5, Journal entry for November 1859.

CHAPTER 4

1. Madeleine B. Stern has provided a thorough bibliography in her biography, *Louisa May Alcott*, pp. 343–60.

2. Madeleine Stern has edited, with appreciative introduction, a re-printing of two volumes of Alcott's sensational stories: *Behind a Mask: The Unknown Thrillers of Louisa May Alcott* (New York, 1975) and *Plots and Counterplots: More Unknown Thrillers of Louisa May Alcott* (New York, 1976).

3. Louisa May Alcott, "Love and Self-Love," *The Atlantic Monthly* 5 (March 1860): 298–310.

4. Ibid., p. 299.

5. Ibid., p. 310.

6. A reference to her "great book" appears in Alcott's journal for 1858, although it was another two years before she plunged into the writing of it. See Louisa May Alcott, *Life, Letters*, p. 103.

7. Louisa May Alcott, Journal entry for August 1860, quoted in *Life, Letters*, p. 122.

8. Louisa May Alcott, Journal entry for November 1864, ibid., p. 162.

9. Louisa May Alcott, *Little Women; or, Meg, Jo, Beth and Amy*, 2 vols. (Boston, 1869), p. 52.

10. Louisa May Alcott, *Moods* (Boston, 1864), p. 115.

11. Ibid., pp. 115–16.

12. Ibid., p. 265.

13. Ibid., p. 199.

14. Ibid., p. 260.

15. Bronson Alcott incorporated the note in *Journals,* 2:367.

16. Ibid., pp. 367–68, Bronson Alcott's journal entry for 26 December 1864. See also his entry for 25 February 1861, in which he recognized, after reading a rough draft of the novel, that it was a "personal and family history, but slightly shaded" (p. 336).

17. Louisa May Alcott, *Life, Letters*, p. 165.

18. Henry James, review in *The North American Review* 101 (July 1865): 279–80.

19. Louisa May Alcott, *Life, Letters*, p. 166.

20. Louisa May Alcott to Moncure Conway, 11 February 1865, as quoted in Saxton's *Louisa May*, p. 281.

21. Louisa May Alcott to Alf Whiteman, 22 June 1862, as quoted in Stern, ed., *Behind a Mask*, p. vii.

22. Louisa May Alcott, *Little Women*, 2:49.

23. Ibid., 2:170–72.

24. Louisa May Alcott, "Pauline's Passion and Punishment," in Stern, ed., *Behind a Mask*, p. 107. Subsequent citations are in the text.

25. From a conversation with Louisa May Alcott quoted in L. C. Pickett, *Across My Path: Memories of People I Have Known* (New York, 1916), pp. 107–8, as cited by Stern in her introduction to *Behind a Mask*, p. xxvi.

26. Louisa May Alcott, Journal entry for May 1868, in *Life, Letters*, pp. 198–99.

27. Ibid., p. 201, Journal entry for 1 November 1868.

28. Ibid., p. 202, Journal entry for April 1869.

29. Ibid., p. 227, to "Dear Folks," 30 May 1870; p. 261, Journal entry for January 1872; p. 266, Journal entry for August 1872.

30. Ibid., pp. 272–73, Journal entry for January 1874.

31. Ibid., p. 296, Journal entry for January and February 1877.

32. Ibid., p. 357, Journal entry for September 1885.

33. Louisa May Alcott, *Jo's Boys, and How They Turned Out* (Boston, 1886), p. 364.

34. Louisa May Alcott, *Little Women*, 2:349.

35. Quoted in a letter from Louisa May Alcott to Bronson Alcott, 14 July 1870, *Life, Letters*, p. 240.

36. Review in *The Ladies Repository* 28 (December 1868): 472; Review in *The Nation* 7 (22 October 1868): 335.
37. Review in *Godey's Ladies Book* 77 (December 1868): 546.
38. *Putnam's Magazine,* n.s. 2 (December 1868): 760.
39. Bronson Alcott, *Journals,* 2:391, entry for 14 October 1868.
40. Ibid., p. 397.
41. Quoted by Sarah Elbert, ed., in her introduction to Louisa May Alcott, *Diana and Persis* (New York, 1978), p. 8.
42. *Putnam's Magazine,* n.s. 2 (December 1868): 760.
43. Louisa May Alcott, *Little Women,* 1:152. Subsequent citations are in the text.

CHAPTER 5

1. Louisa May Alcott, Journal entry for 1 November 1868, in *Life, Letters,* p. 201.
2. Ibid., Journal entries for August 1879 and September 1880, pp. 321, 337.
3. Ibid., p. 324, Louisa May Alcott to Thomas Niles, 19 February 1881.
4. Degler, *At Odds,* p. 160.
5. William O'Neill, *Everyone Was Brave: A History of Feminism in America* (Chicago, 1971), pp. 19–20.
6. Louisa May Alcott, entry for February 14, 1868, in *Life, Letters,* p. 197. "Happy Women" appeared in the *New York Ledger,* 11 April 1868, p. 1.
7. Louisa May Alcott, *Little Women,* 1:146.
8. Ibid., 1:209.
9. Ibid., 2: 282, 356.
10. Louisa May Alcott, *Jo's Boys,* p. 285.
11. Ibid., pp. 11–13, 83.
12. Louisa May Alcott, *Diana and Persis,* p. 64. Subsequent citations are in the text.
13. Louisa May Alcott, Journal entries for March and April 1878 in *Life, Letters,* pp. 315–16.
14. See Degler's *At Odds,* pp. 144–51, which summarizes the recent literature on the nineteenth-century "sentiment of sorority."
15. Carroll Smith-Rosenberg, "The Female World of Love and Ritual: Relations between Women in Nineteenth-Century America," *Signs* 1 (Autumn 1975): 1–29.

16. Degler, *At Odds*, p. 150.

17. See Nina Auerbach's *Communities of Women: An Idea in Fiction* (Cambridge, 1978): "Despite its reputation as a sugary children's classic, *Little Women*'s implicit paradigm is not an escape to childhood innocence, but the formation of a reigning feminist sisterhood whose exemplary unity will heal a fractured society" (p. 37). See also Sarah Elbert's insightful introduction to a recent edition of *Work* (New York, 1977), pp. ix–xliv.

18. Louisa May Alcott, *Little Women*, 1:295.

19. Louisa May Alcott, *Work*, p. 11. This and subsequent citations in the text refer to the 1873 edition.

20. Louisa May Alcott, *An Old-Fashioned Girl* (Boston, 1870), p. 168. Subsequent citations are in the text.

CHAPTER 6

1. Louisa May Alcott, *An Old-Fashioned Girl*, p. 228. Subsequent citations are in the text.

2. Louisa May Alcott, *Moods*, pp. 86–98.

3. Louisa May Alcott, *Work*, p. 164. Subsequent citations are in the text.

4. Louisa May Alcott, "A Whisper in the Dark," in *Plots and Counterplots*.

5. Stern, ed., introduction to *Behind a Mask*, p. xxii.

6. Louisa May Alcott, "Behind a Mask; or, A Woman's Power" in ibid., p. 6. Subsequent citations are in the text.

7. See Daniel Scott Smith's treatment of this issue in "Family Limitation, Sexual Control, and Domestic Feminism in Victorian America," in Mary S. Hartman and Lois Banner, eds., *Clio's Consciousness Raised: New Perspectives on the History of Women* (New York, 1974), pp. 119–36. Carl Degler has recently entered the discussion with *At Odds*, in which he argues that the sentimental cult of domesticity "in the short run could, and probably did improve women's status by increasing their power and enhancing their self-confidence" (p. 49). Similarly, John S. Haller and Robin M. Haller have argued, in *The Physician and Sexuality in Victorian America* (Urbana, Ill., 1974), that "the social norms which prevented the Victorian woman from public display of her sexuality did not prevent her from attempting to challenge her traditional role in the home circle" (p. xiii).

CHAPTER 7

1. Louisa May Alcott, *An Old-Fashioned Girl*, pp. 341–42.

2. Louisa May Alcott, *Little Men: Life at Plumfield with Jo's Boys* (Boston, 1871), p. 327–28.

3. Louisa May Alcott, Journal entry for April 1861, in *Life, Letters*, p. 127.

4. Louisa May Alcott, *Jo's Boys*, p. 109.

5. Louisa May Alcott, *Hospital Sketches*, ed. Bessie Z. Jones (Cambridge, 1960), pp. 30–31.

6. Ibid., pp. 14, 89.

7. Ibid., p. 38.

8. Ibid., pp. 49–58. See also *Life, Letters*, pp. 142–43, for her journal entry of January 1863 from Union Hotel Hospital, Georgetown, D.C.

9. Louisa May Alcott, *Hospital Sketches*, p. 32.

10. Louisa May Alcott, Journal Entry for 16 January 1863, in *Life, Letters*, pp. 146–47.

11. Louisa May Alcott, *Little Women*, 1: 153, 49.

12. Louisa May Alcott, *An Old-Fashioned Girl*, p. 30.

13. Louisa May Alcott, *Little Men*, p. 374.

14. Louisa May Alcott, *Work*, p. 242. Subsequent citations are in the text.

15. Louisa May Alcott, *Life, Letters*, p. 296.

16. Ibid., p. 379.

17. Louisa May Alcott, *A Modern Mephistopheles*, pp. 14–15. Subsequent citations are in the text.

18. Fiedler, *Love and Death in the American Novel*, p. 338.

19. Ibid., p. 349.

20. Joe L. Dubbert, *A Man's Place: Masculinity in Transition* (Englewood Cliffs, 1979), pp. 10–11.

21. Junius Henri Browne, "Are Women Companionable to Men?" *Cosmopolitan* 4 (February 1888): 452–55.

22. Dubbert, *Man's Place*, p. 20.

CHAPTER 8

1. Louisa May Alcott, Journal entries of March 1863 and 18 January 1868, in *Life, Letters*, pp. 148, 195.

2. Journal entry of May and June 1879, in *Life, Letters*, p. 319.

3. Ibid., pp. 343, 344, 352.

4. Louisa May Alcott, *Little Women*, 2:217. Subsequent citations are in the text.

5. Cott, "Notes toward an Interpretation of Antebellum Childrearing," p. 5.

6. Ibid., p. 9.

7. Louisa May Alcott, *Little Men*, p. 62.

8. Louisa May Alcott, *Eight Cousins; or, The Aunt-Hill* (Boston, 1875), p. 39. Subsequent citations are in the text.

9. See Bruce Haley's *The Healthy Body and Victorian Culture* (Cambridge, 1978), which argues that the cult of physical health was more important in Victorian intellectual life than either religion or politics.

10. Louisa May Alcott, *Jo's Boys*, pp. 117–18. Subsequent citations are in the text.

11. See Emily Hahn, *Once upon a Pedestal* (New York, 1974), p. 113; Saxton, *Louisa May*, especially pp. 356–57; and Patricia Meyer Spacks, *The Female Imagination* (New York, 1975), especially pp. 95–101. On the other hand, Auerbach's *Communities of Women*, pp. 35–73, finds in Louisa's fiction a portrayal of more assertive women.

12. Louisa May Alcott, *Jack and Jill: A Village Story* (Boston, 1881), p. 260.

13. R. Gordon Kelly explores this genteel ethic of child-rearing as it is revealed in Victorian literature for children in *Mother Was a Lady: Self and Society in Selected American Children's Periodicals, 1865–1890* (Westport, 1974). See also Daniel Howe's insightful "Victorian Culture in America," which serves as an introduction to the collection of essays entitled *Victorian America* (Philadelphia, 1976), pp. 3–28. Alcott would have agreed perfectly with the values which Howe describes.

14. See Lloyd de Mause's introduction to the collection of essays *The History of Childhood* (New York, 1974), pp. 52–53.

15. Joseph Kett, *Rites of Passage: Adolescence in America, 1790 to the Present* (New York, 1977), pp. 171–72. Also see Oscar Handlin and Mary F. Handlin, *Facing Life: Youth and the Family in American History* (Boston, 1971), especially chap. 4 (pp. 136–210).

16. John Demos, "The American Family in Past Time," *American Scholar* 43 (Summer 1974): 422–46. Similarly bleak views are presented by Stephen Kern in "Explosive Intimacy: Psychodynamics of the Victorian Family," *History of Childhood Quarterly* 1 (Winter 1974): 437–62; and Bryan Strong, in "Toward a History of the Experiential Family: Sex and Incest in the Nineteenth-Century Family," *Journal of Marriage and the Family* 35 (August 1973): 457–66.

17. See, for example, the fascinating study by Alexander L. George and Juliette L. George, *Woodrow Wilson and Colonel House: A Personality Study* (New York, 1956).

18. See Handlin and Handlin, *Facing Life*, especially chap. 4 (pp. 136–210).

CHAPTER 9

1. Louisa May Alcott, "Transcendental Wild Oats," p. 97.

2. Ibid.

3. Louisa May Alcott, Letter to the Editor, *Woman's Journal*, 11 October 1879.

4. Louisa May Alcott, *Work*, p. 442.

5. Louisa May Alcott, Journal entry for August 1879, in *Life, Letters*, p. 321.

6. Louisa May Alcott, *Work*, p. 426.

7. Ibid.

8. Degler, *At Odds*, p. 279. See also Pivar, *Purity Crusade*.

9. Louisa May Alcott, *Eight Cousins*, pp. 197–98, 203. Alcott's comment on *Huckleberry Finn* is quoted in Justin Kaplan, *Mark Twain and His World* (New York: Simon and Schuster, 1974), p. 139.

10. Louisa May Alcott, *Little Women*, 2:26.

11. Louisa May Alcott, *Jack and Jill*, p. 244.

12. Louisa May Alcott, *Jo's Boys*, p. 275.

13. Louisa May Alcott, Journal entry for 17 June 1870, in *Life, Letters*, p. 230.

14. See David Musto, *The American Disease: Origins of Narcotic Control* (New Haven, 1973); H. Wayne Morgan, *Yesterday's Addicts: American Society and Drug Abuse, 1865–1920* (Norman, Okla., 1974); and Harvey Green's *The Light of the Home: An Intimate View of the Lives of Women in Victorian America* (New York, 1983), with the assistance of Mary-Ellen Perry. Green points out (p. 140) that women were the primary users of opium. He also reports that patent medicines widely used by women were heavily laced with alcohol, a fact which sheds more ironic light on the temperance crusade.

15. Louisa May Alcott, *Little Women*, 1:144.

16. Louisa May Alcott, *Jo's Boys*, pp. 181–82.

17. Ibid., p. 277.

18. Ibid., p. 278–79.

19. Carl Degler, borrowing from the research of Janet Giele, makes a

distinction between the "social purity" movement, which emphasized helping the weak and consolidating woman's position in the home, and more "structural" reforms, which stressed labor organization, education, and reform of municipal government (*At Odds*, p. 348). Moreover, the "social purity" movement was consistent with the emergence of what Daniel Smith calls "domestic feminism" in his article "Family Limitation," pp. 119–36.

20. Auerbach, *Communities of Women*, p. 36.

21. Louisa May Alcott, *Little Women*, 1:11.

22. Louisa May Alcott, *Jack and Jill*, p. 88. Subsequent citations are in the text.

23. Louisa May Alcott, *Work*, p. 435.

24. The idea received also the endorsement of the influential domestic reformer Catharine Beecher. See Sklar, *Catharine Beecher*, p. 167.

25. Louisa May Alcott to her nephews, 4 December 1875, *Life, Letters*, p. 283. See also Miriam Langsam, *Children West: A History of the Placing-Out System of the New York Children's Aid Society, 1853–1890* (Madison, 1964).

26. Louisa May Alcott, *Little Men*, p. 28.

27. For the theme of matriarchy in the Plumfield novels, see Auerbach, *Communities of Women*, p. 69.

28. Louisa May Alcott, *Little Men*, p. 373.

29. Ibid., p. 374.

30. Louisa May Alcott to Mrs. Bond, 1886, in *Life, Letters*, p. 276.

31. Louisa May Alcott to her nephews, 4 December 1875, in ibid., pp. 281–83.

32. Louisa May Alcott to her family, 25 December 1875, in ibid., p. 285.

33. See Louisa May Alcott, Journal entry for January 1873, in ibid., p. 270: "Roberts Brothers paid me $2,022 for books. S.E.S. invested most of it, with the $1,000 F. sent. Gave C.M. $100—a thank-offering for my success. I like to help the class of 'silent poor' to which we belonged for so many years,—needy, but respectable, and forgotten because too proud to beg."

34. Louisa May Alcott, *Little Women*, 1:102–3.

35. Louisa May Alcott, *Jo's Boys*, p. 353.

36. Some idea of the difficulties faced by poor families in post–Civil War America is suggested by Robert Bremner in *From the Depths: The Discovery of Poverty in the United States* (New York, 1956), and in his massive collection of documents entitled *Children and Youth in America: A Documentary History*, 3 vols. (Cambridge, Mass., 1970–1974), especially

vol. 2. See also Jacob Riis, *The Children of the Poor* (1892; rpt. ed., New York, 1970); John Spargo, *The Bitter Cry of the Children* (1906; rpt. ed., Chicago, 1968); and autobiographies of those who grew up in poverty during the period, such as Booker T. Washington's *Up from Slavery: An Autobiography* (1901; rpt. ed., New York, 1956) and Theodore Dreiser's *Dawn* (New York, 1931). Focus on the difficulties of poor women is provided by Sheila M. Rothman, *Woman's Proper Place: A History of Changing Ideals and Practices, 1870 to the Present* (New York, 1978), especially chap. 2, and Mary Ryan's *Womanhood in America* (New York, 1975), pp. 195–249.

37. Rothman, *Woman's Proper Place*, p. 13.

38. Lawrence Cremin, *The Transformation of the School: Progressivism in American Education, 1876–1957* (New York, 1961); Joseph Hawes, *Children in Urban Society: Juvenile Delinquency in Nineteenth Century America* (New York, 1971); Elizabeth Ross, *The Kindergarten Crusade: The Establishment of Preschool Education in the United States* (Athens, Ohio, 1976); Margaret Steinfels, *Who's Minding the Children? The History and Politics of Day Care in America* (New York, 1973); Walter Trattner, *Crusade for the Children: A History of the National Child Labor Committee and Child Labor Reform in America* (Chicago, 1970); and Harold Faulkner, *Politics, Reform and Expansion, 1890–1900* (New York, 1959).

39. See David Pivar's thoughtful conclusion in chap. 6 of *Purity Crusade*, pp. 255–80.

40. Sheila Rothman has commented, in *Women's Proper Place*, that the Victorian ideal of "virtuous womanhood bred an outlook that was more comfortable with voluntary than with state action. Since social problems were finally moral ones, solutions demanded the sensitive intervention of the philanthropic individual, not the heavy-handed involvement of the state" (p. 64).

EPILOGUE

1. Landon Y. Jones, *Great Expectations: America and the Baby Boom Generation* (New York, 1980); Godfrey Hodgson, *America in Our Time* (New York, 1976), chap. 3; Douglas T. Miller and Marion Nowak, *The Fifties: The Way We Really Were* (New York, 1977).

2. William Dobriner, ed., *The Suburban Community* (New York, 1958); Bennett Berger, *Working-Class Suburb: A Study of Auto Workers in Suburbia* (Berkeley, 1960); Herbert Gans, *The Levittowners: Ways of Life and Politics in a New Suburban Community* (New York, 1967).

3. Michael Zuckerman, "Dr. Spock: The Confidence Man," in *The Family in History*, ed. Charles Rosenberg (Philadelphia, 1975), pp. 179–208; A. Michael Sulman, "The Humanization of the American Child: Benjamin Spock as a Popularizer of Psychoanalytic Thought," *The Journal of the History of the Behavioral Sciences* 9 (1973): 258–65; Lynn Bloom, *Doctor Spock: Biography of a Conservative Radical* (Indianapolis, 1972).

4. William Henry Chafe, *The American Woman: Her Changing Social, Economic and Political Roles, 1920–1970* (New York, 1972), chap. 9.

5. Betty Friedan, *The Feminine Mystique* (New York, 1963). See also Rothman, *Woman's Proper Place*, chap. 6.

6. Dubbert, *A Man's Place*, chap. 8.

7. Betty Friedan, *The Second Stage* (New York, 1981), p. 100.

8. Gay Talese, *Thy Neighbor's Wife* (New York, 1980), is a popular survey of this subject.

9. Christopher Lasch, *The Culture of Narcissism* (New York, 1978).

10. Robert Sears, et al., *Patterns of Child Rearing* (Stanford, 1957); Daniel Miller and Guy Swanson, *The Changing American Parent: A Study in the Detroit Area* (New York, 1958); Urie Bronfenbrenner, "Socialization and Social Class through Time and Space," in *Readings in Social Psychology*, ed. Eleanor Maccoby, Theodore Newcomer, and Eugene Hartley (New York, 1958), pp. 400–425.

11. Nancy Weiss, "Mother, the Invention of Necessity: Dr. Benjamin Spock's *Baby and Child Care*," *American Quarterly* 29 (Winter 1977): 519–46. See also Zuckerman, "Dr. Spock," esp. pp. 202–3.

12. Friedan, *Feminine Mystique*, esp. chap. 12. See also Miller and Nowak, *The Fifties*, esp. chap. 6; Ellen Peck and Judith Senderowitz, eds., *Pronatalism: The Myth of Mom and Apple Pie* (New York, 1974); Bernard, *Future of Motherhood*.

13. Neil Postman, *The Disappearance of Childhood* (New York, 1982), esp. chap. 8.

14. Ibid. See also John Sommerville, *The Rise and Fall of Childhood* (Beverly Hills, 1982), esp. chap. 19; Marie Winn, *Children Without Childhood* (New York, 1983); and David Elkind, *The Hurried Child: Growing Up Too Fast Too Soon* (Reading, Mass., 1981).

15. Robert Houriet, *Getting Back Together* (New York, 1971).

16. Michael Harrington, *The Other America: Poverty in the United States*, rev. ed. (Baltimore, 1971).

17. Gilbert Steiner, *The State of Welfare* (Washington, 1971), pp. 5–56; Rothman, *Woman's Proper Place*, pp. 272–73; Bernard, *Future of Motherhood*, p. 282.

18. Mary Jo Bane, *Here to Stay: American Families in the Twentieth Century* (New York, 1976).

19. Elizabeth Janeway, *Between Myth and Morning: Women Awakening* (New York, 1974), p. 235.

20. See, for example, Christopher Lasch, *Haven in a Heartless World: The Family Besieged* (New York, 1977). Still another provocative comment on the relation between the family and the state is Charles Burgess, "Growing Up Blighted: Reflections on the 'Secret Power' in the American Experience," in Robert B. Everhart, ed., *The Public School Monopoly: A Critical Analysis of Education and the State in American Society* (San Francisco, 1982), pp. 31–76.

Works Cited

I. Manuscripts

Alcott Family Manuscripts deposited in the Houghton Library, Harvard University, Cambridge, Massachusetts. The manuscripts include letters, diaries, and journals by Abigail Alcott, A. Bronson Alcott, Anna Alcott, Elizabeth Alcott, Louisa May Alcott, and May Alcott.

II. Primary Works

Alcott, A. Bronson. *The Journals of Bronson Alcott*. Edited by Odell Shepard. 2 vols. Port Washington, N.Y.: Little, Brown, 1938.

——. *The Letters of A. Bronson Alcott*. Edited by Richard Herrnstadt. Ames: Iowa State University Press, 1969.

Alcott, Louisa May. *Behind a Mask: The Unknown Thrillers of Louisa May Alcott*. Edited by Madeleine Stern. New York: Morrow, 1975.

——. *Diana and Persis*. Edited by Sarah Elbert. New York: Arno Press, 1978.

——. *Eight Cousins; or, The Aunt-Hill*. Boston: Roberts Brothers, 1875.

——. "Happy Women." *New York Ledger,* 11 April 1868.

——. *Hospital Sketches*. Edited by Bessie Z. Jones. Cambridge: Harvard University Press, 1960.

——. *Jack and Jill: A Village Story*. Boston: Roberts Brothers, 1881.

——. *Jo's Boys, and How They Turned Out*. Boston: Roberts Brothers, 1886.

——. Letter to the Editor. *Women's Journal,* 11 October 1879.

——. *Little Men: Life at Plumfield with Jo's Boys*. Boston: Roberts Brothers, 1871.

——. *Little Women, or; Meg, Jo, Beth and Amy*. 2 vols. Boston: Roberts Brothers, 1869.

————. *Louisa May Alcott: Her Life, Letters and Journals*. Edited by Ednah D. Cheney. Boston: Roberts Brothers, 1889.

————. "Love and Self-Love." *The Atlantic Monthly* 5 (March 1860): 298–310.

————. *A Modern Mephistopheles*. Boston: Roberts Brothers, 1877.

————. *Moods*. Boston: Loring, 1864.

————. *An Old-Fashioned Girl*. Boston: Roberts Brothers, 1870.

————. *Plots and Counterplots: More Unknown Thrillers of Louisa May Alcott*. Edited by Madeleine B. Stern. New York: Morrow, 1976.

————. *Silver Pitchers*. Boston: Roberts Brothers, 1876.

————. "Transcendental Wild Oats." *The Independent* 25 (18 December 1873).

————. *Work: A Story of Experience*. Boston: Roberts Brothers, 1873.

Arthur, T. S. *The Angel of the Household*. Boston: L. P. Crown and Co., 1854.

————. *Ten Nights in a Bar Room, and What I Saw There*. Boston: L. P. Crown and Co., 1854.

Beecher, Catharine. *A Treatise on Domestic Economy for the Use of Young Ladies at Home and at School*. Boston: T. H. Webb and Co., 1841.

Browne, Junius Henri. "Are Women Companionable to Men?" *Cosmopolitan* 4 (February 1888): 452–55.

Bushnell, Horace. *Christian Nurture*. New York: C. Scribner, 1860.

Dreiser, Theodore. *Dawn*. New York: Horace Liveright, 1931.

Emerson, Ralph Waldo. *The Complete Works of Ralph Waldo Emerson*. Edited by Edward Waldo Emerson. Boston: Houghton Mifflin, ca. 1903–1921.

————. *Journals and Miscellaneous Notebooks*. Edited by William H. Gilman et al. Cambridge: Harvard University Press, Belknap Press, 1960.

————. *Uncollected Writings: Essays, Addresses, Poems, Reviews, and Letters*. New York: Lamb Publishing Co., 1912.

Gowing, Clara. *The Alcotts as I Knew Them*. Boston: C. M. Clark Publishing Co., 1909.

Hale, Sarah. Introduction. *Ladies Magazine* 1 (1828): 1–2.

James, Henry. Review of *Moods*. *The North American Review* 101 (July 1865): 279–80.

L. E. of Portsmouth. "Home." *Ladies Magazine* 3 (1830): 217–20.

Pickett, L. C. *Across My Path: Memories of People I Have Known*. New York: Bretano's, 1916.

Review of *Little Women*. *Godey's Ladies Book* 77 (December 1868): 546.

Review of *Little Women*. *The Ladies Repository* 28 (December 1868): 472.

Review of *Little Women*. *The Nation* 7 (22 October 1868): 335.

Review of *Little Women*. *Putnam's Magazine*, n.s. 2 (December 1868): 760.

Riis, Jacob. *The Children of the Poor*. New York: Charles Scribner's Sons, 1892; reprint ed., New York: Garrett Press, 1970.

Sears, Clara Endicott. *Bronson Alcott's Fruitlands*. Boston: Houghton Mifflin Co., 1913.

Sigourney, Lydia H. *Letters to Mothers*. Hartford: Hudson and Skinner, 1838.

Spargo, John. *The Bitter Cry of the Children*. New York: MacMillan, 1906; reprint ed., Chicago: Quadrangle Books, 1968.

Stowe, Harriet Beecher. *Uncle Tom's Cabin; or, Life among the Lowly*. Boston: John P. Jewett, 1852; reprint ed., New York: Harper and Row, 1958.

Warner, Susan. *The Wide, Wide World*. New York: Putnam, 1850.

Washington, Booker T. *Up from Slavery: An Autobiography*. New York: Doubleday & Co., 1901; reprint ed., New York: Dell Publishing Co., 1956.

III. SECONDARY WORKS

Auerbach, Nina. *Communities of Women: An Idea in Fiction*. Cambridge: Harvard University Press, 1978.

Bane, Mary Jo. *Here to Stay: American Families in the Twentieth Century*. New York: Basic Books, 1976.

Berger, Bennett. *Working-Class Suburb: A Story of Auto Workers in Suburbia*. Berkeley and Los Angeles: University of California Press, 1960.

Bernard, Jessie. *The Future of Motherhood*. New York: Dial Press, 1974.

Blassingame, John W. *The Slave Community: Plantation Life in the Antebellum South*. New York: Oxford University Press, 1972.

Bloom, Lynn. *Doctor Spock: Biography of a Conservative Radical*. Indianapolis: Bobbs-Merrill, 1972.

Branch, E. Douglas. *The Sentimental Years, 1836–1860*. New York: Appleton Century Co., 1934.

Bremner, Robert. *From the Depths: The Discovery of Poverty in the United States*. New York: New York University Press, 1956.

———, et al. *Children and Youth in America: A Documentary History*. 3 vols. Cambridge: Harvard University Press, 1970–1974.

Bridges, William E. "Family Patterns and Social Values in America, 1825–1875." *American Quarterly* 17 (Spring 1965): 3–11.

Works Cited

————. "Warm Hearth, Cold World: Social Perspective on the Household Poets." *American Quarterly* 21 (Winter 1969): 764–79.

Bronfenbrenner, Urie. "Socialization and Social Class through Time and Space." In *Readings in Social Psychology*. Edited by Eleanor Maccoby, Theodore Newcomer, and Eugene Hartley. New York: Holt, 1958.

Brown, Herbert. *The Sentimental Novel in America, 1789–1860*. Durham, N.C.: Duke University Publication, 1940.

Chafe, William Henry. *The American Woman: Her Changing Social, Economic and Political Roles, 1920–1970*. New York: Oxford University Press, 1972.

Cott, Nancy F. "Notes toward an Interpretation of Antebellum Childrearing." *Psychohistory Review* 6 (Spring 1978): 4–20.

Cremin, Lawrence. *The Transformation of the School: Progressivism in American Education, 1876–1957*. New York: Knopf, 1961.

de Mause, Lloyd, ed. *The History of Childhood*. New York: Harper and Row, 1974.

Degler, Carl. *At Odds: Women and the Family in America from the Revolution to the Present*. New York: Oxford University Press, 1980.

Demos, John. "The American Family in Past Time." *American Scholar* 43 (Summer 1974): 422–46.

————. *A Little Commonwealth: Family Life in Plymouth Colony*. New York: Oxford University Press, 1970.

Dobriner, William, ed. *The Suburban Community*. New York: Putnam, 1958.

Douglas, Ann. *The Feminization of American Culture*. New York: Knopf, 1977.

Dubbert, Joe. *A Man's Place: Masculinity in Transition*. Englewood Cliffs, N.J.: Prentice-Hall, 1979.

Ehrenreich, Barbara. *The Hearts of Men: American Dreams and the Flight from Commitment*. New York: Anchor, 1983.

Elkind, David. *The Hurried Child: Growing Up Too Fast Too Soon*. Reading, Mass.: Addison-Wesley, 1981.

Everhart, Robert B., ed. *The Public School Monopoly: A Critical Analysis of Education and the State in American Society*. San Francisco: Pacific Institute for Public Policy Research, 1982.

Falk, Robert. *The Victorian Mode in American Fiction*. East Lansing: Michigan State University Press, 1965.

Faulkner, Harold. *Politics, Reform and Expansion, 1890–1900*. New York: Harper, 1959.

Fiedler, Leslie. *Love and Death in the American Novel*. New York: Dell Publishing Co., 1966.

Works Cited

Finkelstein, Barbara, ed. *Regulated Children / Liberated Children: Education in Psychohistorical Perspective.* New York: Psychohistory Press, 1979.

Foster, Edward. *Susan and Anna Warner.* Boston: Twayne Publishers, 1978.

Friedan, Betty. *The Feminine Mystique.* New York: Norton, 1963.

——. *The Second Stage.* New York: Summit Books, 1981.

Gans, Herbert. *The Levittowners: Ways of Life and Politics in a New Suburban Community.* New York: Vintage Books, 1967.

Genovese, Eugene. *Roll, Jordan, Roll: The World the Slaves Made.* New York: Pantheon Books, 1974.

George, Alexander L., and Juliette L. George. *Woodrow Wilson and Colonel House: A Personality Study.* New York: John Day Co., 1956.

Green, Harvey. *The Light of the Home: An Intimate View of the Lives of Women in Victorian America.* New York: Pantheon Books, 1983.

Grimsted, David. *Melodrama Unveiled: American Theatre and Culture, 1800–1850.* Chicago: University of Chicago Press, 1968.

Gutman, Herbert. *The Black Family in Slavery and Freedom, 1750–1925.* New York: Pantheon Books, 1976.

Hahn, Emily. *Once upon a Pedestal.* New York: Crowell, 1974.

Haley, Bruce. *The Healthy Body and Victorian Culture.* Cambridge: Harvard University Press, 1978.

Haller, John S., and Robin M. Haller. *The Physician and Sexuality in Victorian America.* Urbana: University of Illinois Press, 1974.

Handlin, Oscar, and Mary Handlin. *Facing Life: Youth and the Family in American History.* Boston: Little, Brown, 1971.

Hareven, Tamara, ed. *Family Kin in Urban Communities, 1770–1930.* New York: New Viewpoints, 1977.

Harrington, Michael. *The Other America: Poverty in the United States.* Rev. ed. Baltimore: Penguin, 1971.

Hartman, Mary, and Lois Banner, eds. *Clio's Consciousness Raised: New Perspectives on the History of Women.* New York: Harper Colophon Books, 1974.

Hawes, Joseph. *Children in Urban Society: Juvenile Delinquency in Nineteenth Century America.* New York: Oxford University Press, 1971.

Hiner, N. Ray. "The Child in American Historiography." *The Psychohistory Review* 7 (Summer 1978): 13–23.

Hodgson, Godfrey. *America in Our Time.* New York: Doubleday, 1976.

Houghton, Walter E. *The Victorian Frame of Mind, 1830–1870.* New Haven: Yale University Press, 1957.

Houriet, Robert. *Getting Back Together*. New York: Coward, McCann and Geoghegan, 1971.

Howe, Daniel, ed. *Victorian America*. Philadelphia: University of Pennsylvania Press, 1976.

Janeway, Elizabeth. *Between Myth and Morning: Women Awakening*. New York: Morrow, 1974.

Jeffrey, Julie. *Frontier Women: The Trans-Mississippi West, 1840–1880*. New York: Hill and Wang, 1979.

Jeffrey, Kirk. "The Family as Utopian Retreat from the City: The Nineteenth-Century Contribution." In Sallie TeSelle, ed., *The Family, Communes, and Utopian Societies*. New York: Harper and Row, 1972.

Jones, Landon Y. *Great Expectations: America and the Baby Boom Generation*. New York: Coward, McCann and Geoghegan, 1980.

Kelly, R. Gordon. *Mother Was a Lady: Self and Society in Selected American Children's Periodicals, 1865–1890*. Westport: Greenwood Press, 1974.

Kern, Stephen. "Explosive Intimacy: Psychodynamics of the Victorian Family." *History of Childhood Quarterly* 1 (Winter 1974): 437–62.

Kett, Joseph. *Rites of Passage: Adolescence in America, 1790 to the Present*. New York: Basic Books, 1977.

Kuhn, Anne L. *The Mother's Role in Childhood Education: New England Concepts, 1830–1860*. New Haven: Yale University Press, 1947.

Lammermeier, Paul. "The Urban Black Family of the Nineteenth Century: A Study of Black Family Structure in the Ohio Valley, 1850–1880." *Journal of Marriage and the Family* 35 (August 1973): 44–56.

Langsam, Miriam. *Children West: A History of the Placing-Out System of the New York Children's Aid Society, 1853–1890*. Madison: University of Wisconsin Press, 1964.

Lasch, Christopher. *The Culture of Narcissism: American Life in an Age of Diminishing Expectations*. New York: Norton, 1978.

————. *Haven in a Heartless World: The Family Besieged*. New York: Basic Books, 1977.

Lewis, R. W. B. *The American Adam: Innocence, Tragedy and Tradition in the Nineteenth Century*. Chicago: University of Chicago Press, 1955.

McCuskey, Dorothy. *Bronson Alcott, Teacher*. New York: MacMillan Company, 1940.

May, Henry F. *The End of American Innocence: A Study of the First Years of Our Own Time, 1912–1917*. New York: Knopf, 1959.

Mead, Margaret, and Martha Wolfenstein, eds. *Childhood in Contemporary Cultures*. Chicago: University of Chicago Press, 1955.

Meyers, Marvin. *The Jacksonian Persuasion: Politics and Belief.* Stanford: Stanford University Press, 1957.

Miller, Daniel, and Guy Swanson. *The Changing American Parent: A Study in the Detroit Area.* New York: Wiley, 1958.

Miller, Douglas T., and Marion Nowak. *The Fifties: The Way We Really Were.* New York: Doubleday, 1977.

Modell, John. "Family and Fertility on the Indiana Frontier." *American Quarterly* 23 (1971): 615–34.

Morgan, Wayne H. *Yesterday's Addicts: American Society and Drug Abuse, 1865–1920.* Norman: University of Oklahoma Press, 1974.

Musto, David. *The American Disease: Origins of Narcotic Control.* New Haven: Yale University Press, 1973.

O'Neill, William. *Everyone Was Brave: A History of Feminism in America.* Chicago: Quadrangle Books, 1971.

Papashvily, Helen W. *All the Happy Endings: A Study of the Domestic Novel in America; the Women Who Wrote It, the Women Who Read It, in the Nineteenth Century.* New York: Harper, 1956.

Peck, Ellen, and Judith Senderowitz, eds. *Pronatalism: The Myth of Mom and Apple Pie.* New York: Crowell, 1974.

Pivar, David J. *Purity Crusade: Sexual Morality and Social Control, 1868–1900.* Westport: Greenwood Press, 1973.

Postman, Neil. *The Disappearance of Childhood.* New York: Delacorte Press, 1982.

Ross, Elizabeth. *The Kindergarten Crusade: The Establishment of Preschool Education in the United States.* Athens: University of Ohio Press, 1976.

Rothman, Sheila M. *Woman's Proper Place: A History of Changing Ideals and Practices, 1870 to the Present.* New York: Basic Books, 1978.

Ryan, Mary. *Cradle of the Middle Class: The Family in Oneida County, N.Y., 1790–1865.* New York: Cambridge University Press, 1981.

———. *Womanhood in America.* New York: New Viewpoints, 1975.

Salyer, Sandford. *Marmee: The Mother of Little Women.* Norman: University of Oklahoma Press, 1949.

Saxton, Martha. *Louisa May: A Modern Biography of Louisa May Alcott.* Boston: Houghton Mifflin, 1977.

Sears, Robert. *Patterns of Child Rearing.* Stanford: Stanford University Press, 1957.

Shepard, Odell. *Pedlar's Progress: The Life of Bronson Alcott.* Boston: Little, Brown and Co., 1937.

Sinclair, Andrew. *The Better Half: The Emancipation of the American Woman.* New York: Harper and Row, 1965.

Works Cited

Sklar, Kathryn. *Catharine Beecher: A Study in Domesticity*. New Haven: Yale University Press, 1973.

Smith, Daniel. "Family Limitation, Sexual Control, and Domestic Feminism in Victorian America." In Mary Hartman and Lois Banner, eds., *Clio's Consciousness Raised: New Perspectives on the History of Women*. New York: Harper Colophon Books, 1974.

Smith-Rosenberg, Carroll. "The Female World of Love and Ritual: Relations between Women in Nineteenth-Century America." *Signs* 1 (Autumn 1975): 1–29.

Sommerville, John. *The Rise and Fall of Childhood*. Beverly Hills: Sage Publications, 1982.

Spacks, Patricia Meyer. *The Female Imagination*. New York: Knopf, 1975.

Steiner, Gilbert. *The State of Welfare*. Washington: Brookings Institution, 1971.

Steinfels, Margaret. *Who's Minding the Children? The History and Politics of Day Care in America*. New York: Simon and Schuster, 1973.

Stern, Madeleine B. *Louisa May Alcott*. Norman: University of Oklahoma Press, 1949.

Stone, Albert. *The Innocent Eye: Childhood in Mark Twain's Imagination*. New Haven: Yale University Press, 1961.

Stone, Lawrence. "Family History in the 1980's." *Journal of Interdisciplinary History* 12 (Summer 1981): 51–87.

Strickland, Charles. "American Attitudes toward Children." In *Encyclopedia of Education*. New York: MacMillan, 1970.

———. "A Transcendentalist Father: The Child-Rearing Practices of Bronson Alcott." *Perspectives in American History* 3 (1969): 5–73.

———, and Charles Burgess, eds. *Health, Growth and Heredity: G. Stanley Hall on Natural Education*. New York: Teachers College Press, 1965.

Strong, Bryan. "Toward a History of the Experiential Family: Sex and Incest in the Nineteenth-Century Family." *Journal of Marriage and the Family* 35 (August 1973): 457–66.

Sulman, A. Michael. "The Humanization of the American Child: Benjamin Spock as a Popularizer of Psychoanalytic Thought." *The Journal of the History of the Behavioral Sciences* 9 (1973): 258–65.

Talese, Gay. *Thy Neighbor's Wife*. New York: Doubleday, 1980.

TeSelle, Sallie, ed. *The Family Communes, and Utopian Societies*. New York: Harper and Row, 1972.

Trattner, Walter. *Crusade for the Children: A History of the National Child*

Works Cited

Labor Committee and Child Labor Reform in America. Chicago: Quadrangle Books, 1970.

Tyler, Alice Felt. *Freedom's Ferment: Phases of American Social History from the Colonial Period to the Outbreak of the Civil War*. Minneapolis: University of Minnesota Press, 1944.

Weiss, Nancy. "Mother, the Invention of Necessity: Dr. Benjamin Spock's *Baby and Child Care*." *American Quarterly* 29 (Winter 1977): 519–46.

Winn, Marie. *Children without Childhood*. New York: Pantheon Books, 1983.

Wishy, Bernard. *The Child and the Republic: The Dawn of Modern American Child Nurture*. Philadelphia: University of Pennsylvania Press, 1968.

Yans-McLaughlin, Virginia. *Family and Community: Italian Immigrants in Buffalo, 1880–1930*. Ithaca: Cornell University Press, 1977.

Zuckerman, Michael. "Dr. Spock: The Confidence Man." In *The Family in History*, edited by Charles Rosenberg. Philadelphia: University of Pennsylvania Press, 1975.

Index

Index

About the Author

Charles Strickland teaches history at Emory University. He received his bachelor's degree at Southwest Missouri State College and his master's degree and doctorate at the University of Wisconsin. He was a Fulbright Scholar at the University of Copenhagen and a Charles Warren Fellow at Harvard University. He is coeditor of *Health, Growth and Heredity: G. Stanley Hall on Natural Education*.